Company Man

Man

THIRTY YEARS OF CONTROVERSY
AND CRISIS IN THE CIA

John Rizzo

SCRIBNER
New York   London   Toronto   Sydney   New Delhi

SCRIBNER
A Division of Simon & Schuster, Inc.
1230 Avenue of the Americas
New York, NY 10020

For my family

Contents

Acronyms

DCI: Director of Central Intelligence

DNI: Director of National Intelligence. A position created by Congress in 2004 to serve as the head of the U. S. intelligence community.

DOD: U. S. Department of Defense

DOJ: U. S. Department of Justice

NSA: National Security Agency

NSC: National Security Council

OLC: Office of Legal Counsel, U. S. Department of Justice

CENTRAL INTELLIGENCE AGENCY

CTC: Counterterrorist Center, DO/NCS.

DO: Directorate of Operations, CIA. The CIA's clandestine service, responsible for all covert activities.

EUR: Europe Division of the DO/NCS.

LA: Latin America Division of the DO/NCS.

Langley: A shorthand reference to the location of the CIA headquarters compound in Virginia.

NCS: National Clandestine Service, CIA. The DO's new name as of 2005.

NE: Near East Division of the DO/NCS.

NHB: New CIA headquarters building, constructed as an adjunct to the OHB in the 1980s.

OCA: Office of Congressional Affairs, CIA.

OGC: Office of General Counsel, CIA.

ACRONYMS

OHB: Original CIA headquarters building, constructed in the 1950s.

OIG: Office of Inspector General, CIA.

OPA: Office of Public Affairs, CIA.

OSS: Office of Strategic Services, the World War II U. S. intelligence organization. Predecessor entity to the CIA.

SAD: Special Activities Division of the DO/NCS. The CIA's paramilitary component.

CONGRESS

HPSCI: House of Representatives' Permanent Select Committee on Intelligence.

SASC: Senate Armed Services Committee.

SSCI: Senate Select Committee on Intelligence.

MISCELLANEOUS ACRONYMS AND TERMS

EITs: Enhanced Interrogation Techniques.

Finding: A document signed by the president of the United States authorizing the CIA to conduct a covert action program.

Gitmo: Guantanamo Bay terrorist detention facility.

HVDs: High Value terrorist Detainees.

HVTs: High Value terrorist Targets.

KSM: Khalid Shaeikh Mohammad, the CIA's highest-level post-9/11 detainee.

MON: Memorandum of Notification, a document signed by the president amending or expanding a previous Finding.

Company Man

The Tale of
the "Torture" Tapes

In early November 2010, the Justice Department announced its decision not to bring obstruction-of-justice charges against the CIA officials who had been involved in the decision, five years earlier, to destroy videotapes depicting the Agency's 2002 interrogation of an Al Qaeda operative named Abu Zubaydah. He was not just any terrorist thug. Zubaydah was a senior figure in the Al Qaeda hierarchy at the time of the 9/11 terrorist attacks, and he had been the CIA's first significant "catch" in the post-9/11 era. As such, he was also the first high-level Osama bin Laden lieutenant to be spirited off to one of the Agency's newly constructed covert detention facilities—what would come to be infamously known around the world as "the CIA's secret prisons." Zubaydah had another dubious distinction: He was the first CIA detainee ever to be waterboarded. The CIA had captured it all on videotape. Three years later, the Agency burned the tapes.

The Justice Department criminal investigation into the tapes' destruction, which lasted almost three years, was led by John Durham, a career federal prosecutor from Connecticut brought in specifically for the task. He was appointed in December 2007, shortly after the *New York Times* broke the story in a series of page 1 articles by Mark Mazzetti and Scott Shane. The series ignited an immediate firestorm in the media and Congress. As the *Times* accurately reported, no one in the CIA had ever told anyone in Congress that it had destroyed the tapes.

It was a hell of a story about a hell of a mess. And I knew it better than anyone, since I was the only member of the CIA's top leadership to have been part of the episode from the beginning to just about its end. I was the Agency's chief legal advisor for most of the eight years encompassing the story. The tale of the tapes' destruction and its aftermath bedeviled me right up to the time of my retirement from the CIA in December 2009, after more than thirty years of service. The saga ended for me only when Justice announced there would be no indictments.

For the first three years, I fended off repeated entreaties from my Agency colleagues that I approve destroying the tapes, only to have them go behind my back and destroy them anyway in 2005. Then, after the story exploded in the media, I was the only CIA official to be hauled before Congress and grilled—alone—by two dozen angry lawmakers. Two years later, in September 2009, I had to testify for seven hours before a grand jury convened by the prosecutor, Durham.

The case was still hanging over me when I left the Agency for good two months later. In a long career fraught with dealing with controversies, it was the final one, and it was unfinished business. And so I could not drift gently, at long last, into a peaceful retirement. Would I be called back to testify before Congress? Before the grand jury? Would I be prosecuted for something I said, or something I did, somewhere along the way?

The November 2010 Justice Department announcement that there would be no indictments brought me a mixed range of emotions. First, of course, I felt a huge sense of belated relief. At the same time, it seemed oddly anticlimactic—by November 2010, the tapes' destruction was old news, a distant if unpleasant memory.

Finally, it all struck me as very ironic. The entire affair, long and tortuous as it turned out to be, had begun for me way back at a time when I thought I was getting out of the line of fire at the CIA.

In October 2002, my nearly one-year tour of duty as acting general counsel was coming to a close. The Senate had just confirmed Scott Muller as the new CIA general counsel.

By this time, twenty-five years into my CIA career, I had "broken in" a number of incoming general counsels, so I had the drill down pat: The Office of the General Counsel (OGC) staff prepared briefing books containing summaries of key classified policy and legal documents as well as ongoing programs (per standard procedure, no incoming GC had access to classified information before reporting for duty), and I put together a list of the "hot" items that the new guy would have to confront the day he arrived on the job.

The Tale of the "Torture" Tapes

I felt a profound sense of relief about passing the Agency's legal baton. Barely a year after 9/11, I could have put fifty items on the "hot" list. It seemed like every day we were facing a new, imminent Al Qaeda threat. And we had been operating in an entirely new and perilous legal terrain, capturing, brutally interrogating, and conducting lethal operations against senior Al Qaeda figures. I didn't want Scott totally overwhelmed on his first day of work, so I was determined to keep the list short.

A couple of weeks before he arrived in November 2002, however, I learned about something I had no choice but to add to the list. Three months earlier, CIA officers, in a secret Agency detention facility overseas, began videotaping the first top Al Qaeda operative in our custody. He was also the first terrorist subjected to the Agency's Enhanced Interrogation Techniques (EITs). The sessions were captured on the tapes, apparently in graphic detail. Jose Rodriguez, the chief of our Counterterrorist Center (CTC), came to me seeking permission to destroy the tapes. Immediately.

The story began in March 2002, when the CIA and its Pakistani counterparts, with a combination of meticulous intelligence work and good luck, captured a senior Al Qaeda operative named Abu Zubaydah in Pakistan's third-largest city, Faisalabad. It didn't come off quietly—there was a furious gun battle, and Zubaydah was shot three times. The Agency rushed a team of doctors from Johns Hopkins to Pakistan to save his life. It was hardly a humanitarian gesture; our intelligence indicated that Zubaydah was Al Qaeda's main logistics planner for attacks against the United States. The CIA was desperate to keep him alive in order to find out what he knew about any upcoming attacks. This was barely six months after 9/11, and the government was still seized with dread about another horrific strike coming any day.

Zubaydah pulled through, and as soon as the doctors determined he was well enough to travel, he was whisked from Pakistan to the first of a succession of overseas detention facilities that would eventually enter into the public lexicon as "black sites" or "secret prisons." Zubaydah, a young, smart, cold-blooded, unrepentant psychopath, was the first really "big fish" the Agency had caught post-9/11. Soon after the questioning began, CIA inquisitors became convinced, based on his smug and arrogant responses, that he knew a lot more than he was telling about Al Qaeda's terrorist plans. By early April 2002, the Agency, lacking other options and desperate to stop another cataclysmic attack, made the fateful decision to explore tougher methods to try to get Zubaydah to talk. This was how the "enhanced interrogation program" came to be, along with yet another word soon to enter the public lexicon: *waterboarding*.

Later in the book I will provide an eyewitness narrative of the period from April through July 2002, when the Agency conceived the EIT program, which I shepherded through policy review at the White House and legal review at the Justice Department. This process culminated on August 1, when the Justice Department issued to me the first of what would come to be known infamously as the "torture memos," which legally approved waterboarding and other brutal interrogation tactics against Zubaydah. After I received the Justice memo, the waterboarding of Zubaydah began, with my knowledge and concurrence.

What I didn't know then and wouldn't know until two months later was the decision—I could never determine whether someone at CIA Headquarters or in the field with Zubaydah came up with the idea—to videotape Zubaydah around the clock while he was in custody, including periods of interrogation. When he first told me about the videotaping in October 2002, Jose offered two reasons. First, our people at the interrogation site wanted to make sure everything Zubaydah said was recorded and preserved. They were taking careful and copious contemporaneous notes, which were duly transcribed in cables sent back to CIA Headquarters every day, but they were terrified they might miss something. It's important to note here that, prior to 9/11, the CIA had never in my quarter-century experience held and questioned anyone incommunicado. In a popular culture steeped with films, TV shows, and potboiler spy novels portraying the CIA as a no-holds-barred instrument of mayhem, this may be hard for an outsider to believe. But it's true. The videotaping was seen not just as a reference tool but as a security blanket.

The other reason Jose gave me for the decision to videotape Zubaydah was more basic: His people didn't want the SOB to die on them. CIA medical personnel at the detention facility monitored Zubaydah round the clock, but he was about to face some very tough interrogation in the most solitary of confinements. If Zubaydah were to die in captivity, who would believe—either inside or outside the CIA—that they weren't to blame? Videotaping Zubaydah in captivity would cover their asses.

After several days of taping, however, everyone who had bought into the idea looked at the videotapes, compared them with the notes transcribed and forwarded to headquarters, and concluded that the notes captured everything Zubaydah was saying. In fact, the notes were better; Zubaydah's voice was occasionally inaudible on the recordings, but the interrogators had been able to get down most everything he was saying. Besides that, Zubaydah had recovered from his wounds and was exhibiting no desire to journey to the afterlife—even with the seventy-two virgins presumably awaiting his arrival—anytime soon. The hundred or so hours of videotapes were packed up and stored at the detention facility.

But Jose's sudden desire that October to destroy the tapes was not spurred by an urgent need to eliminate unnecessary clutter. It was based on what the tapes showed.

The round-the-clock videotaping had lasted only a few days in August 2002 before it was stopped, and the bulk of it recorded Zubaydah alone in his cell, either saying prayers, sleeping, reading, or otherwise—um—entertaining himself. The rest of the tapes showed the interrogation sessions, and Jose assured me that the scenes of Zubaydah being waterboarded, comprising only a small portion of the tapes, were uncensored, and everything had followed the guidelines formulated by CIA Headquarters and approved by the Justice Department in its August 1 top-secret memorandum to me (the so-called torture memo). That was his good news. His bad news was that the scenes were "tough to watch" and, more to the point, clearly showed the faces of the CIA employees and contractors on the scene.

Jose was convinced that someday, somewhere, somehow, the tapes would become public and the identities of the interrogators inevitably "outed." "*Sixty Minutes* will do slow-mo, stop-action pictures of their faces," Jose emotionally put it to me, "and they and their families will become targets for some Al Qaeda crazy wherever they are."

I had known Jose for over a decade, and I had no reason to doubt his sincerity or his word. A short, dark man in his late forties whose voice carried the lilt of his upbringing in Puerto Rico, Jose (who had a law degree) could be fiery and over the top rhetorically at times, but I always found him to be honest, straightforward, and utterly without guile—traits I suspect the public would not normally ascribe to a long-time CIA operative. He was an honorable, decent guy, and I considered him a friend. I still do.

I also didn't think at the time that Jose and his colleagues were being paranoid in fearing that the tapes would someday be made public. If all my years and experience at the CIA taught me anything, it's that virtually every secret doesn't stay secret forever, and that the shelf life of new secrets is getting shorter all the time. As I write this today, consider all that happened in the eight years since I first learned about the tapes: the steady stream of media leaks about "secret prisons" and "waterboarding"; the ensuing drumbeat of outrage from elements of Congress, pundits, and the academic community as the shock and horror of 9/11 receded into history; and finally, a new president and his attorney general who publicly repudiated and voluntarily declassified virtually every detail of the CIA's interrogation program. If those tapes were still in existence, what do you suppose are the chances they would now be in the public domain? Somewhere between probably and slam-dunk.

But that is now, and this was then. Although I sympathized with Jose's motivations, I thought destroying the tapes was fraught with enormous risk for the Agency. Any minimally competent attorney would instinctively react the same way if his client were to come to him seeking the go-ahead to destroy sensitive materials in his possession, even if the client was not under any cloud of suspicion or investigation. Someone does something like that when he has something to hide.

And the tapes, obviously, were not ordinary material. Given who Zubaydah was, and given why it was considered so critical to get him to talk, a Congress and a nation still shell-shocked by 9/11 might have understood and even supported such tactics. Indeed, only a month earlier, in September 2002, the bipartisan leadership of Congress (the so-called Gang of 8) had been briefed by the CIA on the newly approved techniques, including waterboarding, and expressed no concern whatsoever. But to have this disturbing stuff captured on videotape, and then to destroy it without telling anyone . . . I mean, Jesus. I trusted Jose and believed his assurances that everything on the tapes was within the approved guidelines, but once they were gone, and once someone on the outside inevitably found out about the tapes and what had happened to them, who was going to accept those assurances at face value?

So that was the big turd dumped on my desk shortly before the arrival of the new general counsel. "Who else in senior management knows about the tapes and what you want to do with them?" I asked Jose. "What about Pavitt?," referring to his superior, Jim Pavitt, the head of CIA covert operations.

"Pavitt knows, and he's ready to authorize the destruction, but he said I needed to get your okay," Jose responded.

"Where is George Tenet on this?" I then asked as calmly as I could, referring to the CIA director.

"I don't know. I haven't spoken to him about it."

I informed Jose that he was not to do anything with those tapes. Not then, and not until further notice. I needed to talk about this with the new general counsel.

Poor Scott Muller, I thought. Here he was coming in from private life, with a totally blank slate, and now I had to firehose him not only on a counterterrorist program of an unprecedented scope and nature, but also, by the way, on an urgent request to destroy hair-raising evidence about the program. I was hoping he wouldn't quickly conclude he was joining an organization, and inheriting a deputy, who were completely crazy.

Thankfully, Scott proved to be a quick study and not easily rattled. He agreed that precipitously destroying the tapes was a terrible idea. At the same time, after hearing out Jose and Jim Pavitt, he came to the same conclusion I had: These were honorable men whose deep concerns about the security risks the tapes posed to the interrogators were genuine. Absent some legal requirement that the tapes had to be preserved forever, Scott and I were not prepared to simply rule out ever destroying them. As we put it to Director Tenet in late December 2002 (Scott insisted that we deliver the message together), "the question is not whether to destroy the tapes, but when."

First, we decided, a CIA lawyer had to review every minute of the tapes, but it had to be someone with no connection to the interrogation program who could look at them with no preconceived notions or stake about what was on them. We settled on John McPherson, one of our most experienced lawyers, and the chief of the CIA's Litigation Division. He was someone I knew to be disciplined, thorough, and unflappable. John had had no prior role, or even any knowledge of, the interrogation program, but we thought it made sense to bring him into the loop, given the certainty that the program would be implicated in prosecutions of captured Al Qaeda terrorists in the years to come.

In the days after Christmas 2002, John traveled to the country where Zubaydah had been held and where the sole set of tapes in existence was under zealous guard in the local CIA office. By this time, Zubaydah had been moved to a new detention facility in another part of the world. But the last thing we needed was to have the damn things get somehow lost or damaged in transit.

John methodically plowed through the roughly hundred hours of videotape, each tape recording a day's work of interrogation. Ninety-six of the videotapes were recordings of the Zubaydah sessions. (There were also recordings of the interrogation of Abd al-Rahim al-Nashiri, a key perpetrator of the October 2000 bombing of the USS *Cole*. He was captured in October 2002 and taped only briefly before the CTC halted all videotaping.) Much of the ninety-six tapes depicted Zubaydah simply being questioned or sitting alone in his cell, so John skimmed those parts. But he painstakingly watched the segments where EITs were being applied. He compared everything that the interrogators said and did, and everything Zubaydah said and did, with the daily reports the interrogators sent back to CIA Headquarters. He particularly focused on the waterboarding sessions.

After three days, John was done. His conclusions, contained in a written report, boiled down to this: The reports were accurate and complete, and the interrogators had done nothing to Zubaydah that was outside the guidelines or not described in the reports. But when he returned home I made sure to ask him about two things he hadn't covered in his written findings. Were the faces of the interrogators visible? "Clear as day, and over and over again," he replied in his usual just-the-facts way. And what about Zubaydah, when he was being waterboarded? "Up close and personal. Some crying. Some gagging. Just very unpleasant to look at."

No wonder Jose wants them to be destroyed, I thought.

By comparison, the next item on our to-do list was easy: telling Congress about the existence of the tapes and why the Agency intended to destroy them as soon as feasible. Scott was part of the team dispatched in late January 2003 to brief Senators Pat Roberts and Jay Rockefeller, the leaders of the Senate Intelligence Committee, and their House counterparts, Porter Goss and Jane Harman. Their reactions, as Scott later reported to me, were typical of those of congressional leaders in any dicey, sensitive briefing I had ever participated in or heard about in my years at the CIA. They sat there, clearly uncomfortable, said little if any-thing in response to what they were being force-fed, with a "Why are you telling me this?" look frozen on their faces, and gave every impression of wanting desperately to get the hell out of the room.

In fairness, I should note that shortly thereafter Jane Harman did send a letter to the CIA expressing concern about the wisdom of destroying the tapes. Otherwise, none of the leaders ever followed up about the issue until the story leaked to the media almost five years later.

Still, even with our lawyer's report in hand and the congressional notification box checked, Scott and I weren't prepared to green-light the destruction. Far from it. In 2003, several internal and external investiga-tions were under way in which the tapes were potentially relevant, and we had to see how each would play out.

Early that year, CIA inspector general John Helgerson began a review of the still-unfolding interrogation program. We told Helgerson about the tapes, and he wanted his people to look at them. Helgerson's office was already in the midst of a major investigation into the CIA's failure to uncover and prevent the 9/11 attacks, and the CTC was the focus of the investigation. The tension between the two offices within the CIA was palpable. What's more, Helgerson, an Agency veteran of more than three decades, had expressed to me misgivings about the wisdom and moral-ity of the interrogation program. But I had developed great respect for him over the years as professional and fair-minded. I don't recall any-one expressing any objection to giving the IG access to the tapes, and a couple of Helgerson's investigators reviewed all of them sometime in 2003. In its report on the interrogation program issued in May 2004, the Office of the Inspector General (OIG) made a number of references to the tapes. It noted that it had looked at the tapes and, apart from ques-tioning the CTC's numbers on how many waterboarding sessions were conducted, did not find that any unauthorized techniques were used on Zubaydah.

The IG report was sent to the two intelligence committees shortly after its completion in May 2004 for review by the committees' leader-ship. None of the four leaders would ever ask to look at the tapes. None of them ever inquired about their status, even though the CIA had put them on notice more than a year earlier that the Agency intended to destroy the tapes at some point. None of them ever asked anything about the tapes. Not, that is, until the shit hit the fan years later, courtesy of the *New York Times*.

Concurrently with the OIG review, the presidentially mandated 9/11 Commission got under way. Its charter was markedly different from the OIG review: It was conducting a comprehensive postmortem on the events, and the U.S. Government's actions, in the years leading up to the 9/11 attacks. It was not the 9/11 Commission's mandate to look into the measures the government took, such as the interrogation program, in response to the attacks.

The 565-page final report the commission issued in late 2004 relied heavily on the CIA-prepared accounts of Abu Zubaydah and several other key Al Qaeda figures (including the self-proclaimed 9/11 mastermind, Khalid Sheikh Mohammed [KSM]) the CIA had in its custody by 2003. The commission staff, led by a very aggressive former federal prosecutor named Dieter Snell, pressed the Agency hard for access to the detainees so they could pose their own questions to them. I could understand why; after all, our interrogators were most focused on Al Qaeda plans and actions post-9/11, not before.

Nonetheless, the Agency strongly opposed the idea, and we didn't budge. First, the foreign location of the "black site" was a zealously guarded secret; outside the Agency, fewer than a dozen people in the entire government knew where it was (indeed, to this day it is one of the very few details about the interrogation program that remains classified). The foreign government hosts, in allowing the CIA to build its detention facility, insisted that only CIA personnel could have access to it; they themselves stayed away. Second, our psychologists and analysts studying the detainees argued against introducing any new interlocutors on the scene beyond the handful already there. They feared that diabolical but cagey manipulators like Zubaydah and KSM would seize the opportunity to posture, prevaricate, and rupture the flow of the ongoing interrogations.

Finally, the 9/11 Commission leadership grudgingly agreed to a compromise: Their staffers could submit their questions in writing and the CIA interrogators would sprinkle them into their regular sessions with the detainees as unobtrusively as possible.

For months, the commission also bombarded the Agency with a relentless volley of requests for thousands of documents, and the CIA provided mostly all of them. We scoured all of the requests, provided in writing and in specific detail by the commission staff. They knew exactly what they wanted, and they took pains to spell it out. They never asked us if we had any videotapes of the detainees. If they had, we would have told them the truth.

Instead of parsing literally every word in each of the commission's requests, should we have taken the initiative to tell the commission about the existence of the videotapes? In hindsight, I think the answer is clearly "Yes."

Volunteering their existence would have prompted the commission to ask to look at them. But then we could have just said "No." Just as we did when they wanted access to the detainees, and just as we did when the commission wanted a briefing on the EIT program. Both times the commission backed down.

The commission's co-chairs, Lee Hamilton and Tom Kean, were serious, substantial men. They were consistently fair and trustworthy in their dealings with the Agency. We could have told them, and them alone, about the tapes and why we couldn't give the commission access to them. We didn't. Big mistake, as things turned out.

The third matter to come along in 2003 that argued against destroying the tapes was the criminal prosecution of Zacarias Moussaoui, a malignant but spectacularly inept Al Qaeda operative who had been arrested in Minneapolis about a month before 9/11. Moussaoui, who proved to be as unhinged as Zubaydah but nowhere near as capable, had managed to draw attention to himself by seeking lessons in Texas and Minnesota flight training schools and by loudly insisting on instructions on how to fly a 747, but not how to take off or land one. The 9/11 Commission would ultimately conclude that he had been dispatched to the United States by Al Qaeda as part of the original roster of hijackers. For two years, he had been sitting in jail awaiting trial for his role in the conspiracy, and the case was now beginning in federal district court in Alexandria, Virginia. Although Zubaydah's interrogation did not appear to yield anything that would bear on Moussaoui's case, there was no way of knowing which way the frequently chaotic proceedings would go. We weren't going to do anything that might sabotage the only 9/11 criminal case the government had going.

And so, with all these investigative balls in the air, as 2003 turned to

2004, it fell to me to tell Jose and his people that any decision to destroy the tapes would have to wait.

"How much longer?" they would periodically ask, politely but persistently.

"I don't know," I would respond each time, "but don't hold your breath." I had spent my entire career hand-holding anxious CIA operatives who were upset or frustrated by one thing or another, and I thought I had gotten pretty good at the art of assuaging. Looking back at that period now, however, I clearly misjudged the depth of angst and impatience.

And it was only going to get worse in the months to follow.

By mid-2004, the OIG had completed its report, and Helgerson told me that as far as he was concerned, the fate of the tapes was now a "policy call" for senior CIA management. The 9/11 Commission had also wrapped up its investigation, and we still hadn't seen, in their many requests for materials, anything that implicated the tapes. The Moussaoui prosecution was still careering along, however, with the defendant shouting daily epithets in court at the judge and the prosecutors when he wasn't trying to fire his capable but besieged court-appointed lawyers.

But that was no longer the only roadblock to destroying the tapes. During that summer, George Tenet resigned as CIA director. George had known about the existence of the tapes—and Jose's strong desire to destroy them—for about as long as I did. My sense had always been that he would have been happy to see the issue somehow go away, but that he didn't want his fingerprints on any decision to destroy them. Jim Pavitt and Scott Muller also left the Agency about the same time. None of the departures had anything directly to do with the simmering internal controversy over the tapes: Tenet was leaving after seven grueling years as director, the second-longest tenure ever; Pavitt was retiring after a long and successful career in our clandestine service; and Muller was simply exhausted and burned out after eighteen months in a job that, post-9/11, was way more politically pressurized than he, or anyone else, for that matter, could have imagined.

Still, I couldn't help suspecting that none of them was unhappy about not being in the chain of command when the legal impediments were gone and a decision had to be made whether or not to destroy the tapes. Tenet, Pavitt, and Muller were no longer at the CIA, but the tapes were.

The Tale of the "Torture" Tapes

About a month before he left, Scott got the White House into the act. The catalyst was the Iraq/Abu Ghraib scandal, which had exploded into the nation's consciousness several weeks earlier with the release of repulsive photographs of U.S. military prison guards tormenting Iraqis in their custody. The photographs sparked a national outrage, and the White House was in major political damage-control mode.

Early in the Bush administration, a process was established whereby Scott Muller or I, or both of us, would travel to the White House every month to meet with the president's counsel, Alberto Gonzales; the vice president's counsel, David Addington; and the national security advisor's counsel, John Bellinger. The meetings were held in Gonzales's West Wing office, and they were intended as a way for us to discreetly alert and update the White House about CIA legal matters that weren't already being covered in the larger interagency lawyers' group meetings the White House was frequently convening post-9/11. When the scheduled June 2004 meeting took place, I had a scheduling conflict, so Scott took with him Bob Eatinger, our senior lawyer for counterterrorism matters.

As far as I know, no one in the White House at that time had been told about the existence of the tapes. It was not a matter of hiding them. Instead, our thinking at the CIA was that the time was not yet ripe: The tapes were being safeguarded thousands of miles away, their destruction was on indefinite hold, and there was nothing we were asking the White House to do. In short, up to that point we didn't think the White House had a "need to know," the classic litmus test in the intelligence business.

Abu Ghraib changed that calculation, even though that debacle had little to do with the CIA. As Scott later explained it, John Bellinger, in the context of a discussion of the Abu Ghraib photos, asked him an open-ended question in the meeting, along the lines of "the Agency doesn't take any pictures of its detainees, does it?" I suspect he was assuming/hoping that the question was rhetorical, but Scott decided on the spot, correctly in my view, that the time had come to tell Gonzales, Addington, and Bellinger not only that the tapes existed, but also that the CIA planned to destroy them at some point. Their reaction was immediate and unanimous: "You plan to do *what*?"

The fact was that we CIA lawyers would never have taken the ultimate step to destroy the tapes without first clearing it with the White House.

Not as long as I had anything to say about it. Here, the White House lawyers weighed in sooner than they really needed to, but their reaction wasn't exactly surprising. "Don't do anything with those tapes without coming back to us first," they admonished Scott.

"No problems there, fella," I told Scott when he relayed that message back to me. Then, a few weeks later, he resigned. I was acting general counsel. Again.

Porter Goss was confirmed as the new CIA director in the fall of 2004. A longtime congressman from Florida, he gave up a seat in a safe district to take the DCI job. Porter had been a young CIA officer for a number of years in the '60s before resigning to get into local politics. He was always interested in intelligence issues, and during his final years in Congress he chaired the House Permanent Select Committee on Intelligence (HPSCI).

In our first meeting I went through a list of matters that I thought he would need to focus on soon. It wasn't a long list, but the status of the tapes was on it. Porter, unlike his predecessor, is not a very demonstrative man, but when I mentioned the tapes he clearly seemed taken aback. "The tapes are still around?" he asked with quiet incredulity. "I thought you guys told us you were going to destroy them."

It was then my turn to be taken aback, until I quickly realized that Porter was referring to the briefings the Agency gave him and the other congressional intelligence leaders in early 2003 about the existence of the tapes and our intent to destroy them at some point. "Uh, no, sir, they are still around," I responded as matter-of-factly as I could. Porter seemed mildly disconcerted at hearing this. Understandably. The hot potato was now on his plate.

Several weeks later, Porter promoted Jose Rodriguez to the position of deputy CIA director for operations, Jim Pavitt's former job. What's more, Jose installed as his chief of staff an officer from the Counterterrorist Center who had previously run the interrogation program. Between them, they were the staunchest advocates inside the building for destroying the tapes.

They were now in a position to lobby the director directly. Yet I never had any indication they did so. Instead, they continued to come to me, persistently pressing their case. In June 2004, Jose had been upset to learn of the White House objections, and I could tell he was becoming more frustrated as the months went by.

As 2004 turned to 2005, it was increasingly apparent that the "right" time to destroy the tapes was nowhere in sight. The Moussaoui prosecution seemed to be dragging on forever; and in the meantime, another court case was presenting another potential complication. The American Civil Liberties Union (ACLU) had filed a Freedom of Information Act lawsuit seeking disclosure of all Bush administration materials relating to terrorist detainee policies and practices. As in the Moussaoui case, the tapes had not yet been implicated in the court proceedings, but the possibility remained that they could be. Until both cases sorted themselves out, destroying the tapes was out of the question.

But even if the court cases somehow went away, I knew that there were powerful voices inside the administration weighing in against destruction. John Negroponte, the highly respected career diplomat appointed the first director of national intelligence (DNI) in late 2004, was briefed on the tapes by Director Goss in mid-2005. Shortly after the briefing, Negroponte sent word back to the Agency (and as DNI, he basically was the CIA's boss) that he was strongly opposed to destruction under any circumstances. This was on top of the White House lawyers' objections from the year before.

Nonetheless, Jose and his chief of staff kept coming to me. On the edges of meetings on other subjects, in the hallways, they would raise the subject almost every week. And then, when Al Gonzales left his White House counsel position in March 2005 to become attorney general, they began lobbying me to revisit the issue with the new White House counsel, Harriet Miers, in the hope that she might not have the same deep reservations about destruction that Gonzales and the other White House lawyers expressed to Scott Muller in June 2004. At first, I put off Jose and his chief of staff by saying that we shouldn't be hitting Miers, who had no previous experience in CIA matters, with a thing like this so early in her tenure. I promised them that I would talk to her about it at some point; at the same time, I told them that I didn't think she would like the idea of destruction any more than Gonzales did. In any case, I figured she ought to be apprised of the tapes and assumed (accurately, as it turned out) that her predecessor hadn't told her anything about them.

In May 2005, I told Porter Goss about Jose's relentless queries and said I thought it was time to bring Miers into the loop. By this time, I had attended two meetings with Porter where CTC representatives, as a part of their regular updates on the interrogation program, made a pitch about their strong desire to destroy the tapes because of the security risks to the officers depicted in them. Porter would express sympathy about their concerns, which he thought were genuine, but he never took the issue up with me. So when I raised the idea of briefing Miers, Porter's response was pretty much what I expected. "Go ahead," he replied laconically, "but just so you know, I am not comfortable about the tapes being destroyed on my watch."

"Me, neither," I replied.

I arranged to meet with Harriet Miers a week or so later in her White House office. David Addington, who had been present when Scott Muller told Gonzales about the tapes the year before, was in attendance again. Dan Levin, who had replaced John Bellinger as the legal counsel to the national security advisor, also sat in. I brought along John McPherson. Besides having reviewed the tapes at the end of 2002, John was the CIA lawyer who was responsible for tracking the ongoing court cases where the tapes could be potentially implicated. He gave a brief update on the cases, and I then told the group that our senior operational personnel were continuing to push hard for destruction of the tapes. I tried to convey fully and fairly the reasons why they felt so strongly about the issue, because I thought our people deserved that. Finally, I noted the strong opposition to destruction expressed by DNI Negroponte.

The reaction I got was predictable. Addington, a longtime friend who had worked for me at the CIA years earlier, vigorously asserted (he was not a man to mince words) that he had told Scott Muller a year before that destroying the tapes was a terrible idea and, by God, he still strongly thought so. Levin, a low-key but first-rate lawyer with prior White House and Justice Department experience, said little if anything; he was entirely new to the issue and the expression on his face was somewhere between incredulous and appalled. Harriet Miers was typically calm and meticulous, taking notes and asking a few follow-up questions. Still, she echoed Addington's sentiments, albeit a good deal more quietly. She stopped short of saying that the tapes should never be destroyed, but the message from the White House remained clear: Do not do anything to the tapes before coming back here first.

• • •

I reported back to Porter as soon as I returned to Langley. He was neither surprised nor upset by the White House's reaction. I then told Jose and his chief of staff (I can't recall if I talked to them separately or together). They were crestfallen, because they were now on notice that the DNI, two successive White House counsels, and the vice president's top lawyer had weighed in strongly against destroying the tapes. To top it off, I confided to them that Porter Goss seemed distinctly unenthusiastic about the idea, too. I offered Jose the following advice: Cool it for a while because the powers that be are simply not on board.

My advice seemed to have an effect. Jose never again approached me on the subject.

I don't remember hearing anything more about the tapes for months afterward. But then, around the beginning of November 2005, the top two lawyers from my office responsible for covert operations told me that Jose and his senior staff had come to them wanting to revisit the issue. I am still not entirely certain what, other than the passage of time, prompted his renewed effort. The two lawyers did tell me that the chief of our overseas office, who had been safeguarding the tapes for years, was preparing to retire shortly and was pressing headquarters for final resolution before he left.

It had been six months since my meeting with Harriet Miers. I had no reason to believe she and the others who had strongly opposed destroying the tapes had moderated their views in the interim. But I still clung to the conviction that the advocates for destruction were sincere in their belief and deserved a hearing. In retrospect, I was being naïve. In the years since, I have often wondered whether I should have gone to Jose at that point and told him, in no uncertain terms, "Forget it, Jose. No one is ever going to agree to destruction." I came to conclude that telling him that wouldn't have made any difference.

With my agreement, my two lawyers began to work with Jose and his staff to draft language that would be included in a classified cable that would come from the chief of our overseas office, formally requesting permission to destroy the tapes. This would serve to officially "tee up" the issue for headquarters. Once the request was in hand, we lawyers tentatively agreed that I would go back to the director and propose that

I revisit the issue with the White House lawyers. At about the same time, DNI Negroponte would be alerted and consulted about the renewed request. Then, in the extremely unlikely event that all of these officials withdrew their previous strongly expressed objections, we would "scrub" all of the ongoing and pending court cases, congressional investigations, and so on, to ensure that destruction could not conceivably impact any of them. Finally, if all of these hurdles were cleared, the Agency would return to the leadership of the intelligence committees to inform them of the Agency's intention to go ahead and destroy the tapes.

That was the game plan. In truth, I never thought that destruction was a realistic possibility. There were too many people adamantly opposed to the idea. Too many potential risks and complications. And it had now been over four years since the 9/11 attacks, and questions and concerns were beginning to surface in the media and Congress about the CIA's still top-secret detention and interrogation program. The tapes were not going to be destroyed, I confidently concluded, not soon and probably not ever.

A few days later I received an e-mail from one of the two lawyers working with Jose's people on the language that would be included in the cable "teeing up" the request for approval to destroy the tapes. I had thought they were still at this first step of the process. But what I got in the e-mail was a cable, forwarded without comment, that headquarters had just received from the field installation holding the tapes. The cable was terse but its message was unmistakable: Pursuant to headquarters authorization, the tapes had just been destroyed.

Within seconds of reading it, I e-mailed my own one-word comment back to him: "WHAT?!?!"

In those first dizzying moments, I wasn't sure from whom to demand an explanation first. Jose Rodriguez or my own lawyers? Since Jose's office was right down the hall and my lawyers were in an adjacent building on the CIA's Langley Campus, I opted for Jose. As I raced out of my office I told my assistant to get the two lawyers up to my office. Now.

I knew Jose was around, but I couldn't find him in his office. I ran into his deputy and blurted out what I had just learned. He seemed to know all about it. "I understand your lawyers chopped on it," he replied calmly, meaning they were aware of and approved the destruction order. He only seemed surprised that I was surprised.

Now my head was spinning.

I ran back to my office, where my lawyers were waiting, holding a copy of the cable from headquarters that authorized the destruction a day or two earlier. Each was normally unflappable in demeanor, but on this occasion they looked shaken. Did they see this thing before it went out? I asked as evenly as I could. Absolutely not, they both assured me. In fact, they said, there was language in it that bore no resemblance to what they had been working on with Jose's staff. I had worked with these two guys for two decades, and I trusted their word completely. What sealed it for me, though, was the "coordination" line at the bottom of the cable, which appears on all outgoing CIA operational cables in order to record who in headquarters has seen and agreed to the contents. In my career, my name was probably on thousands of such cables; the whole point is to document that a CIA lawyer has concurred in the message. It was an axiom passed down through three generations of CIA operatives: To cover your ass, get a lawyer's name on your cable.

No names of CIA lawyers were on the coordination line of the cable Jose signed authorizing the tapes' destruction. Case closed. My guys never saw it before it went out.

I began grilling my two lawyers about their conversations with Jose and his people in the hours before the cable was sent. Did he tell either lawyer what he was about to do? No, they responded. So what did he say to them? Well, they said, they remember him asking two questions: If there were any "legal impediments" to destroying the tapes, and if he had the "legal" authority to order destruction. They told him they were not aware of any legal impediments, meaning there were no court cases or pending investigations that required preservation of the tapes. They also said they had told Jose he had the legal authority to destroy them.

Both of their answers were technically accurate, as best I could tell. But that was beside the point, and Jose had to have known it. He had been on notice by me for three years that the fate of the tapes was not his call. It had nothing to do with his "legal authority." He had chosen to ignore and defy the White House, the director of national intelligence, and the director of the CIA. And, of course, me.

In my thirty-four-year career at CIA, I never felt as upset and betrayed as I did that morning.

Somewhere in the maelstrom of running between offices, trying to piece together what had happened, I barged into the director's office—about thirty yards down the hall and around the corner from mine—to tell him what I had learned. At the time, I thought I was the one who broke the news of the destruction to him, but in reviewing the internal Agency e-mails later, it appears that either Porter's chief of staff, Pat Murray, or someone on Jose's staff had told Porter earlier that morning. In any event, when I saw him he seemed as nonplussed about the developments as I was. I had gotten to know Porter well in the year since he arrived at the CIA, and despite his background as a politician, I had come to judge him as utterly without artifice. In the years since, there has been occasional speculation that Porter had to have known in advance what Jose was up to. I didn't believe that then, and I don't believe that now.

"What's done is done," I told him, doing my best to regain composure by grasping at a cliché. We agreed that we needed to inform the outside "stakeholders," and we divided up this exceedingly unpleasant duty. Goss would tell DNI Negroponte, and I would tell Harriet Miers. As for the leadership of the intelligence committees, Porter had some definite ideas. He would inform them—Pat Roberts and Jay Rockefeller on the Senate side, Pete Hoekstra and Jane Harman from the House—in one of his regular, off-the-record meetings with them. But not with any of their staffers present. Just a year removed from being a member of Congress himself, he told me he didn't trust the staffers not to leak the information. He would tell the members when he could get them alone.

There was one final loose end, which was what to do about Jose. "I'll deal with him separately," Porter said. Which was fine with me. I was too pissed off and hurt at that point to talk to him. Besides, I was not Jose's boss. Goss was. It was his responsibility to deal with his act of gross insubordination.

I called Harriet Miers a short time later. I don't remember the details of that talk, which is odd because I like to think I have a pretty good memory and would vividly recall something like that. I later saw a contemporaneous e-mail from another senior CIA official whom I apparently told about the call. He said I described Harriet as "livid." Sounds about right to me.

Because Jose's office was yards away from mine in the Agency's seventh-floor executive wing, in the days and weeks that followed I inevitably ran into him in the halls or at meetings that we both attended. It was awkward at first, but he was still in place and I still had to work with him. Besides, in spite of everything, I still liked and respected the guy. Eventually, he briefly broached the subject of the destruction with me. "It was my decision, and I take responsibility for it," he simply said. I never asked him why he had gone around me to order the destruction. I am convinced he did it because he realized, after three years of relentless pleas, that he was never going to get the go-ahead to destroy the tapes. Not from me, certainly. Maybe, in his own way, he was trying to protect me. I'd like to think that, at least.

It would be two years before the tapes' destruction episode would reenter my life. With a vengeance.

Those next two years were a time of tumult for the Agency, and for me. Details about the detention and interrogation program, still shrouded in the highest secrecy and officially known to only a relative handful of officials in the Bush administration and the Hill, nonetheless kept leaking, drip by drip, into the media. *Secret prisons* and *waterboarding* were becoming national buzzwords, and the CIA found itself enmeshed in an increasingly toxic political controversy. The White House abruptly removed Porter Goss as CIA director in the summer of 2006, with General Mike Hayden of the air force named as his replacement.

Meanwhile, in March 2006, President Bush formally nominated me for CIA general counsel, a position I had been holding on an "acting" basis since Scott Muller's unexpected departure almost two years earlier. Sent to Congress, my nomination languished for months and then blossomed into a full-blown piece of political theater. My June 2007 Senate confirmation hearing, televised on C-SPAN, turned into a free-for-all over the detention and interrogation program, with me playing the role of public punching bag for half a dozen Democrats. In late September, recognizing that confirmation was hopeless (the Democrats having regained control of the Senate in the '06 midterm elections), I asked the White House to withdraw my nomination. I reverted to my role as acting general counsel, heading the office again in everything but title. The Democrats, presumably satisfied they had publicly exacted their pound of flesh with the maximum number of sound bites, left me alone to continue as the CIA's chief legal officer.

• • •

At the beginning of December 2007, a former colleague, Jennifer Miller-wise, called me about a phone call she had just fielded from Mark Mazzetti, a national security correspondent for the *New York Times*. Shortly after Porter Goss had become CIA director in 2004, he had brought in Jennifer to be the Agency's director of public affairs. We became friends and stayed in touch after she left the CIA following Porter's departure in the summer of 2006.

Now she told me Mazzetti had cryptically said he was working on a story about the "CIA destroying some interrogation videotapes depicting waterboarding." He said that the destruction apparently occurred during Porter's tenure, and Mazzetti asked her to convey this information to him to see if he had any reaction or comment. Mazzetti was very low-key about it, but Jennifer was puzzled and alarmed by the call. Puzzled because she had never been brought into the tapes debate while she was at the CIA, so she had no idea what Mazzetti was talking about. Alarmed because a reporter from the most influential newspaper in the country was tossing around the words *CIA*, *videotapes*, *waterboarding*, and *destruction*. She didn't need to know much more to recognize that a story like that in the *Times* would be dynamite. So she decided to call me to let me know.

I nearly dropped the phone.

My first priority was to alert Mark Mansfield, Jennifer's successor as head of Public Affairs, and Director Hayden. I felt bad about dropping this bomb on Hayden, a brilliant career military officer and intelligence professional who inherited the vexing CIA interrogation program when he took over as director in the summer of 2006. As Negroponte's deputy DNI, he had been aware of the tapes and the fact that they had been destroyed. But he had been an innocent bystander to the whole thing.

By now Jose was gone, having recently entered the CIA's retirement transition program. I never had any indication that he suffered any repercussions from his unilateral decision to destroy the tapes. Meanwhile, the intervening period had been a very busy and often stressful time for me (what with my long confirmation battle, among other things), and the tape-destruction debacle had largely receded in my memory. I was aware that lawyers in our litigation division were monitoring the ongoing court cases to determine if the tapes potentially might be implicated, and I would be periodically informed they were not. As best I could tell, everyone who needed to know about the destruction had been informed.

But I thought I needed to call Goss, then in retirement for over a year, to compare our recollections. He was affable and direct as always, and everything was going smoothly until near the end of our conversation. "So please tell me," I asked, "that you briefed the intelligence committee leaders about the destruction and that there's a record somewhere of that briefing."

There was a pause, and then Porter said, "Gee, I don't remember ever telling them. I don't think there was ever the right opportunity to do it."

My heart sank. It was the ultimate nightmare scenario. The *New York Times* was about to break a huge, holy-shit sensational story about the CIA, and our congressional overseers would be finding out about it for the first time. For three decades, I had been an eyewitness to the Agency's complex relationship with Congress, and I immediately knew what the reaction would be: Congress would go berserk. Just as it did twenty years before, when Iran-contra first leaked to the media after Congress had been kept in the dark about it.

This was going to be a giant scandal, and I was in the middle of it.

The *Times*'s first article appeared on Friday, December 7, 2007 (rather fittingly, the anniversary of Pearl Harbor). It was the lead story on page 1, above the fold. Follow-up stories by the *Times* appeared in the days thereafter, each of them given page 1 treatment. Columns of copy, graphic timelines, photos of Porter and me. The *Times* was playing it to the hilt, and why not? It was a hell of a story, and most of it was true. The rest of the media, as it usually does, chased the *Times*'s lead and piled on.

In mid-December, poor Hayden was summoned to two closed hearings before the House and Senate intelligence committees (known by their respective initialisms, HPSCI and SSCI) for a ritual pummeling, especially by the House committee. Hayden kept his dignity and calm in the face of the onslaught, but he was in an impossible position, having to try to explain someone else's mess. The HPSCI members demanded more witnesses. Most of all, they wanted two people: Jose Rodriguez and me.

Jose's lawyer, Bob Bennett, informed the HPSCI that Jose would testify only under a grant of immunity. Current Agency employees are essentially obligated to testify before intelligence committees. Being a CIA employee does not mean you have to relinquish your constitutional rights; still, stonewalling an intelligence committee by taking the Fifth

Amendment is a career-ender for a current CIA employee. Former or retired employees, however, are under no such constraints. Within days, Attorney General Michael Mukasey announced the appointment of John Durham as special prosecutor to launch a criminal investigation into the whole fiasco. There was no way Jose was going to testify without immunity, and there was no way the HPSCI was going to get crosswise with the just-beginning Durham probe by granting him immunity. Stalemate. The HPSCI set its sights on me.

So while I would like to say I agonized over what to do, I really didn't. I was the CIA's chief legal officer. I had to testify under oath, and without any delay or preconditions. It was my duty. Simple as that.

I went to Mike Hayden's office to tell him I was prepared to show up whenever the HPSCI wanted me. He never ordered or even encouraged me to do it; he didn't have to. He called the HPSCI chairman, Representative Silvestre Reyes, to give him the news. After Mike hung up, he turned and looked at me. "Thank you," he said simply.

With Congress about to leave town for Christmas recess, it was agreed that my closed-session testimony before the HPSCI would take place on January 16, 2008.

I spent the holidays reviewing my personal files and searching my memory in an effort to reconstruct my role in the five-year-long tape-destruction saga. I was the only remaining member of senior CIA management who had been in it from start to finish, so I had a lot of ground to cover. Melody Rosenberry, my chief of staff, helped me immensely in preparing for the hearing, but otherwise I worked pretty much alone, talking to no one else. I thought it best not to interact with any of the current or former CIA officers involved in the matter, especially with Durham's criminal probe just getting under way. I seriously considered retaining private legal counsel. After all, I was going to be testifying under oath.

Yet I couldn't bring myself to do it. The perception would have been all wrong: the CIA's top lawyer decides to "lawyer up," so he must have something to worry about or hide. Thinking more from my gut than from my head, I decided to go it alone.

January 16, the day of the hearing, was sunny and not too cold. The hearing was scheduled for the afternoon, and I was driven in a CIA van from

Agency headquarters to the Capitol, accompanied by Melody Rosenberry, my special assistant Donna Fischel, a couple of representatives from our Office of Congressional Affairs (OCA), and Paul Gimigliano from the CIA's Public Affairs Office. The OCA folks assured me on the ride down that they had worked out arrangements with the HPSCI for us to drive to a nonpublic entrance to the Capitol where we would be met and hustled up a private elevator to the HPSCI's secure hearing room, which was located literally in the dome of the rotunda. That way, it was explained to me, I could avoid the expected scrum of cameras and reporters waiting outside the elevator on the floor of the Capitol rotunda. Not to mention all the tourists.

It was a seamless plan that unraveled as soon as we got to the Capitol. No one from the HPSCI was in sight, and the Capitol policeman guarding the perimeter of the grounds insisted that our van go no farther. So we all piled out, trudged up to the main public entrance, waited in line to go through the security screening, and struggled through a gauntlet of our fellow American citizens, of all ages and sizes, staring at the statuary and display cases. Finally, mercifully, the elevator to the HPSCI was in sight. And then I saw the cameras, the microphones, the TV lights, and the reporters holding notepads.

I had a few seconds to decide what to do. What I really wanted to do was turn tail, retreat to the van, and have the OCA folks call and scream bloody murder to the HPSCI staff. I fought off that instinct and kept walking toward the lights. One thing I was not going to do was stop and talk, but I sure as hell wasn't going to skulk, either. And then I was there, abreast with the cameras, lights, and microphones. All I could think to do was . . . smile and wave. A quick, chopping wave that I had never done before, ever. I have no idea where it came from, although months later, watching the classic film *Giant* for the umpteenth time on cable, I noticed that it was a rather abbreviated and arthritic version of a gesture James Dean made several times in the movie. Whatever the subconscious motivation, a photo of me midwave appeared in *USA Today* the next day. Looking far more confident and jaunty than I actually was, I thought the photo more than anything perfectly captured the sense of false bravado I felt at the time.

Finally, I was able to reach the elevator to the HPSCI's secure hearing room, where more surprises would await me.

• • •

Given the lavish media play of the roiling controversy, I expected a large turnout of HPSCI members for the hearing. And indeed there were at least twenty of them sitting in the three-tier dais when I was ushered into the hearing by Chairman Silvestre Reyes. A like number of staffers were perched behind their bosses. They were all staring down at me as I sat at the witness table. Melody Rosenberry and three or four other CIA and DNI congressional liaison officers settled into the chairs behind me. Melody was there to pass me relevant documents as needed during the course of my testimony—documents we had provided two weeks earlier to the HPSCI. She and the others were also there to take notes on what I would say in my sworn testimony; the official HPSCI transcript would not be available for review for weeks, and it was important for the Agency and for me to have an immediate record of what I was testifying to under oath. Even more important, Melody would listen carefully to my answers for any inadvertent errors or omissions and promptly let me know so I could correct the record on the spot. I was going to be under oath, after all. The presence of such backbenchers has been standard operating protocol with the intelligence committees for as long as I can remember.

As I settled in and studied my opening statement one last time before being sworn in, I half-heard some sort of procedural discussion a few members were having. At first, being preoccupied and with a slight case of stage jitters, I paid little attention. But suddenly I looked up to see the members voting to eject from the hearing everyone sitting behind me. I couldn't believe what was happening; not only was the committee's move totally out of the blue, but unprecedented in my long experience at the CIA. I was too flabbergasted to react, and before I knew it, Melody and the others were gone. I was entirely by myself, about to give sworn testimony without any sort of backbench support. Over twenty thoroughly pissed-off congressional inquisitors on one side (not counting staffers), me on the other.

It almost got worse. On the heels of voting to throw out my staff, the HPSCI member John Tierney, a Democrat from my home state of Massachusetts, had an even better idea: to "open" the hearing to the media. In other words, letting in the reporters and cameras that had ambushed me downstairs minutes earlier, presumably to publicly document my flogging by the committee. His motion was voted down—barely.

At last, after all of those unexpected dramatics, Chairman Reyes was ready to swear me in. If the members' intent was to mess with my head, they had succeeded splendidly. Before I cleared my throat to begin, I had one final, fleeting thought: Maybe I should have "lawyered up" after all.

Aside from a couple of brief breaks for votes on the House floor, the members took turns grilling me for four hours. Early on, it was the perfect storm of bipartisan ire. The CIA had never told anyone on the Hill that the tapes had been destroyed. There was no getting around that, and there was no way I could explain that, other than saying it "fell through the cracks," which, although true, is no explanation at all. I shouldered my share of the blame for that failure. Not to serve as the fall guy, but because I deserved it. After Porter Goss told me on that frantic day following the destruction in 2005 that he would handle informing the Hill, I had left it to him and didn't ask him about it until it was far too late. It had been an honest but grievous mistake on my part. I remain convinced that he never intended to hide the information from Congress or otherwise cover up the destruction; I had never heard anyone in the CIA advocate that course of action. But we had been obligated to tell Congress, and collectively we failed in that obligation. That was the essence of my mea culpa, and that's what I told the HPSCI. Repeatedly.

Otherwise, I testified about all the events in the long tapes saga that I have described in these pages. With various members coming and going, the questions, and the criticisms, began to become inevitably duplicative, but I did my best to stay consistent and focused. Round after round, members took their shots at me.

Somewhere around the three-hour mark of the hearing, I sensed the atmosphere in the room changing. Even the most initially hostile HPSCI members—Democrats such as Tierney, Jan Schakowsky, and Rush Holt—seemed to be easing up on me. I like to think it was because they and others on the committee began to think: Hey, this guy readily agreed to come up here, we threw out his support structure, and he's here alone, testifying under oath, answering all of our questions as best he can.

Or maybe they were just tired after throwing so many punches.

In any case, the hearing petered out an hour later. The final question was from Chairman Reyes, and it was pro forma: Would I be willing to return at some later date for additional questioning? "Certainly," I responded, mustering as much sincerity as I could fake.

On the way out, the HPSCI security staff offered to escort me in a way that would shield me from the cameras and reporters still staked out in the Rotunda. I declined because this time I had something I did want to say publicly. Pausing under the TV lights and in front of the microphones, I made a four-word statement: "I told the truth." Then I turned and waded my way back through the crush of tourists to the Agency van, waiting outside where I had left it four hours before.

My appearance garnered some favorable reviews. The HPSCI leaders, Reyes and Pete Hoekstra, told reporters afterward that I had been a "cooperative" witness, with Reyes adding that I had "provided highly detailed" responses and "walked the committee through the entire matter, dating back to 2002." *Legal Times*, a nationwide periodical for the legal community, ran a front-page story (including a large photo of me giving that wave) headlined "The Company's Man," recounting my HPSCI appearance and Agency career in largely positive terms. Another legal publication I had never heard of, *Corporate Counsel*, even did a piece on my appearance. The title: "Not Spooked: CIA Lawyer John Rizzo Keeps His Cool in Contentious Congressional Hearings."

For myself, I was just relieved that I had emerged from the hearing in one piece. With John Durham's criminal investigation in full stream, the HPSCI never bothered calling another witness. The long-running tape-destruction saga was finally behind me. Almost.

Nearly two years later, in the late summer of 2009, I was summoned to testify before the federal grand jury impaneled to determine if any crimes had been committed in the destruction of the tapes. By this time I did have legal counsel, a longtime friend named Larry Barcella, a former federal prosecutor and one of Washington's best criminal defense lawyers. My sworn four-hour testimony before the HPSCI had occurred almost two years earlier, and I had not had access to the hearing transcript in close to that long (the intelligence committees have never allowed the CIA to keep copies of their transcripts). And now I would have to give sworn testimony to the grand jury, with Durham's prosecutors painstakingly marching me through the whole complicated story again. I am far from a maven on criminal law, but I knew that the easiest way to get myself in big-time legal trouble would be to tell Durham's investigators anything under oath that, even inadvertently, was at variance with what I had said under oath at the HPSCI all that time ago. Which is why I retained Larry, whom I trusted like a brother.

My grand jury testimony, conducted over two sessions, stretched to seven hours. I had to recount the whole story in detail one last time. Days before my final grand jury appearance in September 2009, I submitted my retirement papers to the CIA. After thirty-four years at the Agency, and seven years after the fateful decision was made to create the videotapes of the interrogation of Abu Zubaydah.

It was time.

CHAPTER 1

Entering the Secret Club
(1975–1976)

The Agency I left at the end of 2009 was very different from the Agency I had joined in the beginning of 1976—except that both times the CIA was in turmoil. I hardly grasped it at the time, but my arrival at the CIA coincided with a number of seismic legal and institutional changes in the U.S. intelligence community.

Right before Christmas 1974, just a few months after Richard Nixon had resigned in disgrace following the Watergate scandal, the CIA for the first time in its history had been thrust into a harsh public spotlight. An explosive series of page 1 stories in the *New York Times* by Seymour Hersh had detailed a stunning array of questionable and in some cases illegal covert operations stretching back over twenty-five years—operations that included bizarre assassination plots against Fidel Castro and other foreign leaders, drug experiments on unsuspecting U.S. citizens, domestic surveillance of anti–Vietnam War groups on college campuses and elsewhere, and a massive program to monitor the mail of Americans thought to be opposed to the policies of the Johnson and Nixon administrations. This led in 1975 to a sensational series of congressional hearings led by Senator Frank Church, a theatrical politician with presidential aspirations. A passel of current and former senior CIA operatives were paraded before millions of TV viewers, and Church and his colleagues obligingly posed for the cameras with guns and other weapons used in the assassination plots.

I found myself intensely drawn to the proceedings. I had never—save for my brief exposure to a professor in college named Lyman Kirkpatrick, which I will talk about later in the book—given any thought to the

CIA during my life up to that point. I had read a couple of Ian Fleming's James Bond novels and seen a few of the Sean Connery movie adaptations in high school, and I thought they were entertaining in a fantastical, mindless sort of way. I knew very little about the CIA's history—that it was founded at the end of World War II, for instance, as the country's first and preeminent intelligence service—or any of its current or past leaders. I guess I was vaguely aware that it was headquartered in suburban Virginia and that its mission was all sorts of highly secret derring-do, but that was about it.

In that respect, I was probably typical of most Americans at that period in the nation's history. In the decades before the Hersh articles and Church hearings blew the lid off in the mid-'70s, the CIA operated in a largely black vacuum, mostly ignored by the mainstream media and coddled by the very few senior members of Congress who were ever told anything the Agency was doing (and, by all accounts, CIA directors never told them very much). The CIA even stiffed the Warren Commission in its landmark 1964 investigation into the death of President Kennedy—and got away with it.

At the time of the Church hearings, I was working at the U.S. Customs Service, part of the Treasury Department. It had a small office of about fifteen lawyers, and its portfolio included everything from narcotics enforcement to international trade issues. For a rookie lawyer, the job at Customs was fine. The work was reasonably interesting, I got to travel some, I liked the people I worked with, and the hours certainly weren't backbreaking—everybody was in the office by 8:30 a.m., and everybody left at precisely 5:00 p.m. By 1975, however, I was quietly yearning for something different and more challenging. While playing hooky from work, I was glued to my TV, watching the Church Committee proceedings with a mixture of fascination and revulsion. Was this what the CIA was really like?

That was my first reaction. My second reaction was to wonder whether the CIA had any lawyers in its organization. I had no idea, but with Congress and the media demanding top-to-bottom reforms, I figured that if the CIA didn't already have lawyers, it was going to need them. A lot of them.

There was nothing in my background or previous life experience to suggest that I would ever work for the CIA. I was born on October 6, 1947, in the central Massachusetts city of Worcester, the product of a classic melting-pot marriage—an Irish American mother and an Italian American father. My dad's immigrant father, a stonemason by trade, died when my father, Arthur, was sixteen, and that was when he became a man, taking on the role of a surrogate father to his two kid brothers. (He also had five older brothers.) My dad took on all sorts of part-time jobs to support the family, and at the same time attended classes at night at Bentley College in Boston, earning a business degree in 1932. Starting at the bottom, he then began what would be a very successful fifty-year career in the retail department-store business. Throughout his life, my dad was a quiet, somewhat shy, hardworking, thoroughly honest and decent man. Above all, he loved and cared for his family—his mother, his brothers, his wife, and his children.

My mother, Frances, was the daughter of a pharmacist. She was the middle child of five, two of whom died of tuberculosis in their twenties. Despite these early tragedies, my mom lived her entire life with her inherited Irish sense of wit, indomitability, and fierce loyalty to her family. More outgoing and socially active than my dad (she joined a bowling league and exercise club in her fifties), she adored and supported him unstintingly for the more than half century they were married, up to the day my dad died in 1996. She passed away two years later.

I can summarize my childhood and adolescence in five words: very happy and very uneventful. I was the youngest of three children, and the only boy. In a close-knit Italian-Irish American family, that meant I was pampered and indulged from the day I was born. My two older sisters, Maria and Nancy, accepted this with remarkable equanimity. In fact, they were unwaveringly protective of their kid brother as we were growing up (and continue to be to this day). When I was twelve, my dad got a big new job in Boston, so our family moved from Worcester to Wayland, a small town about twenty miles outside the Hub.

I spent my junior high and high school years in the excellent Wayland public schools. I was a pretty good student and active in things like the yearbook and newspaper, but I had no career ideas, save for a vague notion about becoming a Boston sports reporter. My logic was airtight: I could not only go free to Red Sox, Patriots, Celtics, and Bruins games, but get paid to do so, to boot.

Entering my senior year of high school in the fall of 1964, I was facing my first major life decision, which was where to go to college. With the help of Mr. Lewis Oxford, my kindly if somewhat bemused high school guidance counselor, I considered the Ivy League schools. Although my grades had been fairly good, and I had done well on the SATs, I knew my credentials were not exactly eye-popping. So I immediately ruled out Harvard, Yale, and Princeton. Dartmouth or Cornell? Too rural. Columbia or Penn? Too smack dab in the middle of big cities.

That left Brown University, in sleepier Providence, Rhode Island. In the years to come, Brown would become among the most chic and selective of the Ivy schools, but in the mid-'60s it was widely viewed as a safe fallback school for an aspiring Ivy Leaguer. For me, it was my first and only realistic choice. And lo and behold, I got in, much to the evident relief and surprise of the patient Mr. Oxford.

My parents were thrilled. Although my sisters had gone to Tufts, I was the first member of the extended Rizzo family to go to an Ivy League college.

I arrived at Brown in September 1965 and graduated with a bachelor's degree in political science in June 1969. They were the most formative years of my life, and I loved every minute I spent there. Little of it had to do with academics, however. What Brown really taught me was how to go from being a naïve, immature kid to being a grown man. I joined a fraternity, Beta Theta Pi, where I met a group of guys that would become lifelong friends, and which gave me a lifelong taste for fine clothes and good cigars. Being at Brown, and especially being at Beta, also gave me a badly needed set of social skills. I like to think that, on balance, it was a worthwhile return on investment for my proud parents, who happily paid every cent of my tuition plus a generous allowance, which I spent with gusto.

Looking back, the way I arrived at the decision to apply to Brown was markedly similar to the way I arrived at the decision, a decade later, to apply to the CIA. Essentially, both decisions were made on the basis of a leap-of-faith hunch. They were two of the best decisions I made in my life.

There was one other thing that Brown gave me, the significance of which didn't hit me until years later. Brown gave me my first contact—albeit fleeting—with a bona fide CIA legend.

• • •

One course in the political-science department was far more popular than any of the others. It was a twice-weekly lecture taught by a professor named Lyman Kirkpatrick.

He was the most impressive, and most intimidating, physical presence I had ever encountered.

Kirkpatrick had recently arrived at Brown after a two-decade career at the CIA, in which he had held positions of increasing importance, according to his faculty bio, though it was notably sketchy on details. It would be years before I fully understood that Kirkpatrick had been among an elite group that later would be chronicled in Evan Thomas's book *The Very Best Men*, and still later in the movie *The Good Shepherd*: the WASPy, idealistic, Ivy League–bred recruits who famously shaped and led the first generation of the Agency's leadership in the post–World War II years and at the dawn of the Cold War.

Kirkpatrick fit that image perfectly, beginning with his Princeton background and magisterial-sounding name. But it was his physical presence that was the most striking. It was only in doing the research for this book that I realized he was only fifty years old at the time I first saw him. In the eyes of a twenty-year-old kid, Kirkpatrick had an aura of someone older, wiser, immortal, even. He had thick, iron-gray hair, slicked back and crisply parted. He was a strikingly handsome man, with clear blue eyes and a smooth, preternaturally rosy complexion. His voice never wavered from its richly mellifluous, baritone purr. He always appeared in class impeccably groomed.

Besides all that, there was one last thing about Kirkpatrick that added a unique, vaguely mysterious element to his unforgettable image: He was confined to a wheelchair. The word was that in the 1950s polio had left him paralyzed from the waist down. I don't remember him ever acknowledging it or the wheelchair.

Kirkpatrick's lecture was such a hot ticket on campus that it had to be held in a cavernous, amphitheater-style classroom that would be packed with what must have been close to two hundred mesmerized students. I don't recall much in the way of give-and-take between Kirkpatrick and the rest of us—he would just wheel himself behind a desk at the front of the room, glance briefly at everybody arrayed above and around him, and start talking in that unmistakable voice. I don't remember anything he ever said in the lectures that was really memorable, yet none of us seemed to mind. It was not until years later, after I was inside the CIA, that I learned he had been a central figure in some of the most sensitive and controversial Agency programs in the '50s and early '60s.

I was always too cowed to approach him—until I screwed up my courage and approached him at the end of one of his last lectures. I have no idea what I was going to ask him. There was just something inside me that compelled me to interact, just once, with this imposing figure from a world of international intrigue about which I knew nothing.

I sidled up near his wheelchair, anxiously waiting my turn as other students surrounded him. When the moment finally came, and he looked at me with a surprisingly benign gaze, I opened my mouth . . . and nothing came out. I was frozen in fear. After an agonizing moment, I managed to croak, in a quavering voice, something about enjoying his lectures. Kirkpatrick responded briefly and politely, but by then I was too mortified to hear him. I slunk away in embarrassment, and that was the last time I ever saw him. I tried my best to forget the entire painful incident.

Yet when the notion of applying to the CIA first entered my mind almost a decade later, the first person I thought about was Lyman Kirkpatrick. Perhaps he had stayed somewhere in my subconscious all along. If so, I wasn't the only Brown student of that era whom Kirkpatrick affected. Many years later, in the mid-'90s, I stepped into an elevator at CIA headquarters and saw a guy standing there who looked vaguely familiar. I was a relatively well-known figure inside the Agency by that time, and the guy introduced himself. Turned out he had been a year or two ahead of me at Brown, and right after graduation he began a long career as an undercover CIA operative, serving mostly overseas. Intrigued, I asked him what caused him to join up at such an early age. "Two words," he replied. "Lyman Kirkpatrick."

At the beginning of 1969, the year I was to graduate, I had to start—grudgingly—thinking about what to do after Brown. I settled on law school, but first, like every other twenty-one-year-old guy at that time—the height of the Vietnam War—I faced the possibility of being drafted into the military.

Like most everyone else at Brown, I was opposed to our government's involvement in Vietnam, but I was never a part of any of the protest groups or demonstrations. My fraternity brothers and I were far more focused, if that is the word for it, in putting together parties at the house and organizing road trips to all the women's colleges scattered all over New England. All I knew for sure was that I didn't want to go into the military, at least while the war was ongoing.

A few months before graduation, I dutifully reported for my physical at the South Boston naval station. To my utter amazement, I flunked the physical. The summer before, I had suffered a kidney stone attack (doubtless due to the sun and the copious amounts of beer I had consumed in college), the first of what would be a series of attacks stretching over several years. My family's urologist put me on a strict low-calcium regime, which I blithely ignored when my parents were not around, and wrote a letter outlining my medical condition—not so much to get me a deferment (which he said it would not) but to give the doctors a complete picture of my physical health. Letter in hand, I arrived at the naval station and passed all the physical tests with flying colors. However, when one of the military physicians finally scanned the letter, which was only a couple of paragraphs long, he said, with a trace of annoyance, "Why didn't you show us this when you first got here? You can't serve in the military when you have to be on a diet like this." I was then summarily dismissed, having gone from 1A to 4F status in a matter of thirty seconds.

I take no pride in saying this, but that was probably the happiest day of my life up to that time.

Of course, it wasn't right that I felt so happy about escaping service. The entire selective-service process in the Vietnam era was so capricious and unjust. Almost all of my friends from college—and later from law school—managed to avoid military service, and the handful that did serve were never sent to Vietnam. At the same time, tens of thousands of young guys from less privileged backgrounds had no choice but to go, fight, and die there.

Free of the draft, I decided to visit Washington, D.C., for the first time in my life that spring, to check out the law schools of Georgetown and George Washington University. GW became my first choice. I was accepted there, and in the fall of 1969 I was off to the capital.

The summer between leaving Brown and entering GW, I had an epiphany of sorts. After my narrow escape from the draft, it dawned on me that I needed to stop casually coasting through life and start taking my future seriously. I wanted to become a grown-up. I began to apply myself to my academics, getting up early every day, attending all my classes in a coat and tie as if I were going to work in an office, and studying in the library before, between, and after classes. I was selected for the law review at the end of my first year and graduated with honors in June 1972. Arriving to attend my graduation, my parents and sisters had an inadvertent brush with history—they stayed at the Watergate Hotel just a couple of days before the infamous break-in by the Cuban henchmen dispatched by Gordon Liddy and Howard Hunt (another distinguished Brown alum, by the way).

Two summer clerkships in law firms, one in D.C. and one in Massachusetts, convinced me that I had neither the taste nor the temperament for private practice. Instead, I was drawn to government service. I cast the net broadly over a variety of federal agencies, getting some rejections and some bites. Eventually, in August 1972, I started working in Customs as an entry-level attorney, at the princely annual salary of $13,309. It seemed like a fortune.

After nearly three years on the job, the bureaucracy at Customs, and at Treasury, had become increasingly stultifying. It was manifested in any number of small things, like not being permitted to sign any letters or memos I wrote that would go outside of Customs. I was in my midtwenties, restless and frustrated. One day I simply looked in the Martindale-Hubbell legal directory and discovered that, yes, the CIA did in fact have an Office of General Counsel, and that its address was "Washington, D.C., 20505." That was all the listing said. I thought, what the hell, I'll send off my résumé and see what happens.

It was a total shot in the dark. Weeks went by—it was now the summer of 1975—and I heard nothing. No acknowledgment of the letter, no rejection of my interest, no nothing. Well, I assumed, that was that—this was the CIA after all, and it didn't have to acknowledge or explain anything to anybody. And then the phone call came.

It was a quiet, friendly female voice, inviting me out to CIA Headquarters for an interview. The call lasted for less than a minute. A day or two later, a thin letter containing a single page of directions arrived in the mail.

Several days later, on a raw, rainy afternoon in the fall of 1975, for the first of what would be thousands of times, I drove from my apartment in

Georgetown over the Chain Bridge into Virginia, and then up Route 123 for a couple of miles until I took an unmarked exit to a road that led, about a couple of hundred yards down, to a gate, where I showed my ID to a security guard, who waved me through. The CIA's "campus" (as its inhabitants called it, I came to learn) looked then much like it does today—a cross between a bucolic, tree-lined state wildlife refuge and a suburban industrial park. I later was to learn that construction on the sprawling complex, inside a barbed-wire-protected expanse of 250 wooded acres, began in 1959. The first employees, who had been scattered in various facilities in downtown Washington, moved in in 1961 (shortly after the Bay of Pigs invasion) and the rest arrived when the complex was completed in 1963 (shortly before President Kennedy's assassination). The new Langley headquarters was the brainchild of, and a monument to, the storied CIA director Allen Dulles, still the longest-tenured CIA chief in history (1953–1961). Legend has it that Dulles had not only handpicked the site, but trudged around the grounds himself, tying ribbons around the trees that were to be spared from the construction bulldozers.

The security guard had directed me to a small parking lot nestled in front and to the left of the main entrance to a looming, antiseptic-looking seven-story concrete building. I walked slowly through the rain and entered through the heavy glass doors into the large marble lobby. It was quiet and empty, save for a security guard sitting at a desk. I saw nowhere to sit, so I just stood there, nervously.

As I waited for my escort from the general counsel's office, I took in the scene around me. Looking down at the lobby floor, I discovered I was standing on the top end of a large, circular, gray-and-black CIA logo. Instinctively, I edged away from it.

Turning to my right, I saw in the distance, carved into the wall, what looked to be about three dozen stars, each about four inches in size, laid out in rows of seven or eight. The stars were flanked by two flags, one the U.S. flag and the other a dark blue one. Above the stars, also carved into the wall, was an inscription: "In Honor of Those Members of the Central Intelligence Agency Who Gave Their Lives in the Service of Their Country."

It was very quiet. I felt like I had just wandered into a huge museum, or maybe a modernistic, mysterious church—which, in a way, I had.

I was led to a small suite of offices tucked into a corner of the top floor of the headquarters building, not knowing at the time that this was where the CIA director and the rest of the Agency's top leadership were located. My escort was the general counsel's secretary, a petite, cheerful young woman named Sue Nolen. It had been her voice on the phone inviting me out for the interview.

I met separately with the general counsel, John Warner (no relation to the future U.S. senator), and his two top deputies. They all looked to be in their late fifties and were polite and avuncular. I have no recollection of anything they said to me, or anything I said to them. An hour later, the interview was over, and Sue Nolen reappeared to escort me back down to the lobby and out the thick glass front doors. It seemed to be raining harder.

As soon as I was outside, I noticed two things that had escaped my attention on the way in. One of them, about fifty yards to my left, was a squat structure that looked like a large flying saucer with a rounded, circular roof. I would later learn that it was called "the Bubble," and that it was a five-hundred-seat auditorium used primarily for promotion ceremonies and speeches to the workforce by the CIA director and other visiting dignitaries.

The second object was much smaller and was situated about halfway between the Bubble and the headquarters front doors. It appeared to be a life-size statue of a man placed on a square concrete pedestal.

I had no idea if I would ever be coming back to the Agency again. It occurred to me that this could be my only opportunity to see what the statue was. After quickly looking around to make sure no one was watching, I trudged through the rain to get a closer look. It was a statue of the Revolutionary War hero Nathan Hale, the first U.S. spy in the nation's history, who was uncovered, captured, and hanged by the British. And there he was, in bronze, staring directly at the CIA front entrance, depicted with his feet bound and his wrists tied behind him. Wrapped around the base of the statue was a carved inscription of what observers at his hanging said were his immortal last words: "I regret that I have but one life to lose for my country."

The heavy rain made the statue glisten, and I noticed that the trickling streams of water from its head gave the eerie impression that ol' Nathan was crying. It was a strangely poignant, moving moment. Together with the carved stars on the lobby wall, the statue quietly conveyed an unmistakable message to anyone entering the building: People who work here must be prepared to die for their country, and sometimes they do.

And then I snapped out of my reverie. Whoa, I told myself, don't get so carried away. If I were ever to join the CIA, after all, it would be as a paper-pushing lawyer, not a spy. How perilous could that be?

I stood there for a full minute, staring at the statue. Then, thoroughly wet, I walked across the front quadrangle to the small parking lot, got in my car, and drove out through the main headquarters gates, not knowing when, or if, I would ever return.

The next phone call came more quickly than the first. A couple of weeks after the interview, one of John Warner's deputies called and came right to the point. Would I like to come on board as a member of the CIA legal team? After mulling it over for about five seconds, I said yes. It was the call I was waiting for.

The easiest part about getting a job at the CIA is getting the offer itself. Far more arduous is the elongated period an applicant faces once he or she accepts the offer, because it is only then that the security and medical processing begins. Anywhere along the way the applicant can be told that he or she has been disapproved on medical or security grounds, with no further explanation. Over time, and particularly with the advent of the computer age, the CIA's processes have been streamlined and refined considerably. But in 1975, when I had to run the gauntlet, it was far more plodding.

The first step was slogging through what the CIA calls a Personal History Statement (PHS), which was basically a government employment application on steroids. The thing I was given to complete was as thick as a novella. Even a current federal employee like me, already possessing fairly high security clearances, had to start from scratch. I had to list all manner of dimly remembered details from my past, like every place I had lived, every foreign trip I had taken, every non-U.S. citizen I had met, every friend I remained in contact with from high school onward, and so on.

The PHS was primarily used as a reference point from which the CIA Office of Security launched its background investigation. It always takes weeks, if not months, during which time the applicant is kept in the dark about its progress. Somewhere in this interregnum I remember being summoned to the Agency for a two-day-long physical and psychological examination by the medical staff. This all went smoothly—the CIA gives wonderfully thorough medical examinations, and the staff, unlike my draft board five years earlier, largely shrugged off my history of kidney stone attacks.

Then, near the end of the security process, I was called in for the requisite polygraph examination. It is impossible to convey a truly accurate description of the polygraph experience. During my CIA career, I took a half-dozen or more of them. I never looked forward to them, and I never got used to them. I didn't know it at the time, but I would come to learn over the years that lawyers are generally lousy at taking polygraph exams. There are no empirical data on why, but my hunch is that it has something to do with the way law schools train students to analyze questions in class or in written examinations. Typically, the questions are deceptively subtle and nuanced, even when they seem simple and direct on the surface. So a law student is taught to methodically process each question to spot the subtlety, the nuance, in order to arrive at the correct answer.

Questions asked in CIA polygraph examinations are simple and blunt. There is nothing subtle or nuanced about being asked, for instance, if you are in contact with a hostile foreign government or if you are currently using drugs illegally. It's either yes or no. But lawyers instinctively pause to ponder and mentally parse the most basic, black-and-white questions before answering, and when that happens during the polygraph exam, the needle on the polygraph machine tends to jump.

Later, when I hired new lawyers for the office, I would see this phenomenon occur time and again. I vividly recall an instance in the '90s when I got word that a very promising young attorney we had recruited was having a terrible time passing ("clearing out," in CIA parlance) his entrance polygraph exam. I asked our Office of Security for an explanation of the problem, and a polygraph officer dutifully came to see me.

"He's nervous as a cat, reacting to even the most basic questions," the officer patiently explained to me. "He can't even confirm his place of birth."

"How could that be?" I asked, bewildered.

"He says he can't be sure because he doesn't remember being there at the time."

The young lawyer eventually did pass the exam. The CIA Office of Security has always shown understanding in navigating the unique psyches of attorneys.

Anyway, I remember my first polygraph in 1975 as being very long and very uncomfortable. I was asked a long string of detailed questions about my personal habits and predilections going back to my high school years. But I finally got through it, and that was the final hurdle.

On January 18, 1976, I drove through the headquarters gates, reporting for duty. It was my first day of employment at the CIA. I was twenty-eight years old.

The first rite of passage for me, like any brand-new Agency employee, was to attend a basic orientation course ("CIA 101," as it is informally known). When I arrived in January 1976, the course was one week long, and in the years since has periodically varied from three days anywhere up to two weeks. Its purpose has remained unchanged: introducing fledgling personnel to the CIA's history, its organizational structure, its various assigned missions, and both the benefits (insurance, retirement, other bread-and-butter topics) and responsibilities (protection of classified information, security awareness) accorded to every employee upon first walking through the door.

Today, the CIA website provides at least some of this basic background data to aspiring candidates. In 1976, publicly available information about the Agency's inner workings was nonexistent, so all of us new arrivals had one thing in common: We had joined an organization, and a culture, about which we knew virtually nothing. My class was about twenty people, a polyglot of newcomers: analysts, scientists, secretaries, even fledgling spooks. The majority of us were twentysomethings, but there were those in their forties and fifties as well. For five days, we sat together around a large oval table in a paneled conference room at headquarters, listening to a parade of CIA officials—some stern, some jocular, some professorial—offering a collective primer on the organization. On and on they came, immersing us in seemingly everything imaginable about the Agency. And all of it—the papers we were given, the slides we were shown, the lectures we listened to—had a big red SECRET stamp affixed to it.

If the intent of the orientation was to simultaneously educate, thrill, and indoctrinate a neophyte, that SECRET stamp was the coup de grâce.

There was at the time one piece of breaking news that the orientation course didn't cover: President Ford had just fired the CIA director, the iconic Agency figure William Colby. He was a casualty of the recently concluded Church Committee investigation, but not because any abuses had been uncovered. Ironically, he was sacked because Ford, egged on by his secretary of state, Henry Kissinger, was furious at Colby's perceived overwillingness to share too many of the gory details of the past with the committee. Colby, a member of the initial "Good Shepherd" generation after World War II service, had joined the Agency after serving as a derring-do OSS operative in Europe. His Agency career had also been marked with controversy—while heading up operations in Vietnam in the '60s, he oversaw the infamous Phoenix program of organized assassination of Vietcong leaders.

Colby was a complex, shadowy character in CIA lore. In many ways, he was a transitional figure in the Agency's history, and I remember being oddly disappointed when I learned about his abrupt departure. I wanted to see him, at least once. So less than two weeks after I joined the Agency, I got into a long line of employees snaking into the Rendezvous Room (its official name), a large, open room adjacent to the CIA cafeteria used for official receptions. In the distance, at the front of the line, there was Colby, on hand to accept personal goodbyes by the workforce. As the line inched forward, I was feeling a bit out of place—I had arrived at the Agency just days before, after all. What could I possibly say to this legendary figure?

When we finally came to face, all I could think to do was to blurt out the truth. Having read that he had a law degree, I stuck out my hand and said that I was a lawyer, too, who had just joined OGC, and that I was sorry that I wouldn't have an opportunity to serve under him. It was at once an awkward and presumptuous thing for a twenty-eight-year-old rookie to say. And for a couple of seconds he just impassively stared at me through his clear-framed eyeglasses. Then, with a tight, enigmatic smile that I would never forget, he tapped me lightly on the arm and quietly replied, "You're a lawyer and you just got here? Well, you are going to have an interesting time." He then turned his eyes to the next person in line.

In those first couple of weeks, I realized that I was not the only rookie there. The OGC had doubled in size during the previous six months, going from nine to eighteen (with me being the eighteenth). The Church Committee, which had just completed its work, had recommended that the small, insular office—made up of mostly middle-aged men who had spent their entire adult lives at Langley—needed to grow, with younger blood and a fresher perspective. The idea was that an influx of lawyers without any CIA "baggage" would bring more objectivity and rigor, with an ability and willingness to spot and deter any future abuses. It was the first of many attorney-hiring binges I would witness at the CIA during my career, most of them coinciding with the inevitable postmortem of some flap or controversy that the Agency reliably, if unfortunately, managed to embroil itself in every few years. Whenever that happened, the cry would ring out, from Congress and/or the CIA leadership: By God, the Agency needs more lawyers! Inside the CIA, it would become a truism: A scandal would be awful for the Agency institutionally, but it would be great for the OGC's growth potential. I was part of the first wave. We called ourselves the "Church babies."

Coming from the lumbering and impersonal bureaucracy of the Treasury Department, I was startled and delighted by the working environment I found myself in. I noticed from the very beginning how everyone was energized and enthusiastic about what they were working on, and that, provided no outsiders were within earshot, they would talk shop everywhere inside the large cone of silence that was CIA Headquarters—not just in their offices but on the elevators, in the gym, walking out to the parking lot, in the employee cafeteria, and so on. The institutional camaraderie, the feeling of we're-all-in-this-together, was palpable.

Everyone I encountered in those first few weeks—the security guards, the secretaries, the analysts, the operatives, and yes, even the lawyers— radiated a sense of pride and esprit de corps. For someone just arriving from another part of the government, it was a revelation. I would come to understand that a lot of this camaraderie and sense of shared mission derived from the fact that everyone in the CIA, no matter where one is in the pecking order, had to endure a long and exhaustive security clearance process (especially that great equalizer, the polygraph exam) in order to enter this new secret world, and we were all pledged not to discuss any of our classified work to anyone on the outside. The knowledge that we were all part of an exclusive, selective, secret club—that no one on the outside could ever really fully know or understand—created an unspoken but unique and unbreakable bond.

It gradually dawned on me that working in a secret intelligence organization inevitably affects an employee's personal interactions outside the office. In my case, it was never as stark as it is for someone who is "undercover," that is, a CIA employee who is posing as an employee of another U.S. government agency. They are required to "live their cover," sometimes even with their relatives and friends. For them, routine, day-to-day private business transactions—like getting a commercial bank loan or buying life insurance—can become awkward and complicated.

CIA attorneys, on the other hand, are allowed to freely acknowledge our Agency affiliation to family, friends, and the outside world (except when traveling abroad). Still, I decided early on to be somewhat circumspect in whom I told about working for the CIA. My family knew, of course, as did my close friends from college and law school. But I was careful around strangers—people I would run into at bars, on airplanes, and so on. For one thing, you can never be sure who you are talking to. Besides, dropping the CIA name to people you don't know frequently prompts questions like "No kidding! So what kinds of things do you work on?" Which, obviously, you can't talk about. On top of that, you then have to endure a lot of dumb James Bond or Maxwell Smart jokes.

As my years at the CIA wore on, I became more comfortable about maintaining this pose in public, but during my first months at the Agency I found it rather frustrating. The place and the work were so fascinating that the natural human instinct was to want to talk about it. I thought being at the CIA was extremely cool, and I will admit to a youthful temptation to flaunt it. Holding it all in, especially when I was still under thirty, was tough.

What's more, I was struck by how much scope and impact CIA lawyers, even one as wet behind the ears as I was, had on the day-to-day mission of the Agency. The OGC had about the same number of lawyers in it as my former office at Customs, but the OGC—and the rest of the Agency—was much less hierarchal, and we lawyers were given wide sway and discretion in the way we did our jobs. From the first day, I was not only allowed but encouraged to write and sign my own memos and letters going outside the office, which sounds like a small thing but was something I had never experienced before in my brief legal career. And whatever any of us said or wrote seemed to be accepted and followed—albeit on some occasions with some grousing—by our clients in the Agency. (I always considered everyone in the CIA as a "client," from the director on down. I viewed myself as an attorney for all Agency personnel, and that my job was to advise them on the law and protect them from jeopardy for doing their jobs.) It belied the perception that many outsiders had of the CIA being an untrammeled, anything-goes monolith that did whatever it wanted, wherever it wanted, regardless of the law. If that had been true in the '50s and '60s—and it apparently was, to a large extent—that was not the CIA I found when I arrived.

To me the atmosphere at the CIA seemed so bracing, so alive in my early days there. I was too new, too starry-eyed to realize that the Church investigation, and the opprobrium from Congress and the media it had spawned, had left the organization dispirited and on the defensive. It was a state of affairs that I would come to understand all too often in the years to come.

In the aftermath of the Church investigation, Congress and the Ford administration had rapidly put into place a series of reforms that established the legal and political framework under which the CIA has operated ever since. Committees were created in the House and Senate to monitor and scrutinize the activities of the CIA and other intelligence agencies; laws were passed that for the first time mandated prior presidential authorization of covert operations; President Ford issued a detailed executive order (which has been reaffirmed by subsequent presidents and remains virtually intact to this day) setting out the criteria under which the intelligence community can collect information on U.S. citizens while also prohibiting the assassination of foreign leaders and covert actions inside the United States; and, for its part, the CIA began to establish a wide range of internal regulations governing how it would henceforth interact and establish relationships with sensitive sectors of American society, including the media, the clergy, and the academic and corporate communities. Although I didn't know it at the time, these would be the areas that would occupy me for most of my career at the CIA.

At the end of January 1976, George H. W. Bush succeeded Colby as DCI. I remember hearing some of the Agency's old-timers grouse. This guy had no intelligence experience, they would mutter as I nodded sympathetically. He was a longtime political partisan, had even served in Congress, and was obviously a henchman for the president, coming here to dismantle the place.

Bush did make some organizational changes, and one in particular affected me directly. He sacked the general counsel, John Warner, who had been a CIA lawyer since it had come into existence. He was also, of course, the man who had just hired me. Bush brought in an outsider named Tony Lapham, a former federal prosecutor and a partner in a prestigious D.C. law firm. He was not yet forty years old, and all anyone knew about him was that he and Bush seemed to share similar roots—namely, both had a Yale background and were the scions of aristocratic, old-money families.

Barely one month into the job, I had a new immediate boss and a new big boss. I suppose I should have found the situation disconcerting, but I didn't. All I knew was that I was part of an organization with which I was already unabashedly in love.

I was assigned a secretary that I shared with another newly arrived lawyer and a small private office on the seventh floor, just yards away from the CIA director's office suite down the hall. It was prime head-quarters real estate; the Office of General Counsel was still small enough that we all snugly fit in a single, strategically located corridor. (A quarter-century later, with the OGC six times larger and scattered all over the building, I moved into the general counsel's spacious front office for good. It was in the exact same spot where my first office had been all those years before. I had come full circle, literally.)

Even with the size of the staff doubled, we were still fewer than twenty lawyers to oversee the activities of a workforce approaching many thousands of people all over the world. All of us had to be immediately thrown into the fray, dealing with issues from a murky world of intrigue that I, at least, had never remotely contemplated, much less prepared for in my law school studies. Inevitably, during my first few months of gingerly groping around in this strange new world, I made a few memorable blunders, and I learned a few lasting lessons.

I vividly recall the first time I was allowed to attend a meeting chaired by the director in his conference room a few steps from his office on the seventh floor. Then and now, it looks much like any conference room of any corporate CEO, with dark-wood-paneled walls (albeit with no windows) and an oblong polished wood table big enough to accommodate the thirty or so sofa-style chairs encircling it. On the wall was not the string of clocks recording the time of world capitals such as Moscow, Beijing, and so on that you see in countless CIA-themed movies; rather, it was an unremarkable series of circular logos of all the fifteen or so agencies in the intelligence community.

It was sometime in the spring of 1976, and I was there because Tony Lapham asked me to tag along with him. The subject of the meeting was the continuation of benefits for the survivors of CIA sources ("assets," in Agency vernacular) killed in the abortive 1961 Bay of Pigs invasion of Cuba. The legal issues were actually quite dry, but it was thrilling nonetheless. My God, I thought to myself, I am being allowed into the inner sanctum, the director's conference room, to attend a meeting having to do (however tangentially) with the Bay of Pigs.

When we got there, about twenty people were already sitting around the table. Tony casually plopped into one of the empty chairs, and almost clinging to his coattails, I dutifully sat in the chair next to him, doing my best to act like I belonged. Director Bush was running late, so while Tony chatted with the guy on his other side, I scanned the faces around the table, almost all of which were unfamiliar. I did recognize by sight a man who looked to be about fifty, sitting directly across me. His name was Ted Shackley, the number two man in the clandestine service, and he was a fabled character inside the Agency. A wunderkind in the spy world, Shackley was in his early thirties when he headed up the CIA's massive and aggressive anti-Castro operations run out of a base in Miami in the '60s. Later in that decade he was station chief in Laos and Vietnam, where the Agency's activities were also massive and aggressive.

Shackley's name was quietly bandied about inside the CIA with a combination of awe and fear, and it wasn't just because of his meteoric rise and his history of dangerous exploits in world hot spots. People referred to him as "the Ghost," in large part because of his physical appearance. In many ways he looked like the perfect spy, which is to say he was literally colorless. His hair wasn't dark, but it wasn't exactly gray or white, either; it was just sallow. His complexion was similarly pallid, and it was said that it had always been that way, even when he was working those years in the sun of Southeast Asia and southern Florida. It was also said his wardrobe had never varied, no matter where he was—a nondescript dark suit and tie and white shirt. Finally, people would talk about how his demeanor eerily complemented his appearance—clinical, detached, cold.

And there he was, perfectly matching the description, sitting across from me. I cast a couple of furtive glances his way, and damn, if he wasn't coldly staring through his black horn-rimmed eyeglasses directly back at me. And then Shackley leaned across slightly and spoke to me, in a quiet voice that had a hint of icy disdain: "I don't know who you are, but you are sitting in the director's chair."

The room suddenly erupted into laughter. Even Lapham, a man I was learning had a disarming, puckish sense of humor, was softly chuckling. Now I can see the humor. Then I was only mortified. It did teach me a lasting lesson, however. I learned where the director sits in his conference room.

Truly learning about the Agency's culture and atmospherics required actually plunging into the job. No orientation program could convey the kinds of people who worked there—where they came from and what their back stories were. I would come to discover that they represent an astonishing cross section of American society. This reality first hit me on my first overseas trip for the CIA, in mid-1976.

I was dispatched by the OGC to visit several of our stations in South America on what were called "parish visits," a program started shortly after I arrived and geared to give all of us wide-eyed neophytes some exposure to what life is like in the field. Typically, it involves hitting a few stations of varying size in the region, meeting our people in the CIA office, and fielding any informal legal questions they might have (and maybe pass on the latest hallway gossip from headquarters). Since I was still so new and unformed, I didn't have much to offer in the way of advice or gossip. As it happened, however, my traveling companion from Washington was a senior officer from the Office of Logistics, the entity responsible for maintaining the CIA's worldwide network of office and supply facilities. He was a crusty, garrulous Agency veteran who loved to hold forth on anything, so I left most of the talking to him.

At one of our last stops, we went through the usual drill, with all station personnel summoned to an all-hands meeting in a secured conference room. Sitting almost directly across from me was the number two guy in the station, and he was definitely giving off a vibe of not really wanting to be there. Not hostile, but rather bored with the whole thing and eager to get the hell out of there to go back to do real work. The more I looked at him, though, the more I had the feeling that I had seen him somewhere before. He looked to be in his late forties, so he wasn't a guy I could have met in high school or college. And he didn't give his name, so that was no help. Yet I couldn't shake the gnawing feeling that I had seen his face before. As soon as the meeting broke up, he bolted as quickly as he could.

I then left to do some sightseeing, but all through the day, and back at my hotel room later, I found myself still trying to place him. Lying in my lumpy bed in the middle of the night, I bolted upright. I suddenly pictured him, except that he was twenty years younger. It was a photo, actually, and it was on a . . . baseball card. As a young boy in the '50s, I obsessively bought them (at a nickel a pack) and voraciously studied all the pictures on the front and stats on the back. And somehow one card came back into my head that night, all those years later. That same impassive face, staring out from beneath a baseball cap. An obscure utility player on one of those teams of the mid-'50s that routinely pummeled my beloved, downtrodden Red Sox.

I had to be sure, because otherwise I knew it would stick in my craw indefinitely. We had to leave for our next stop the following day, but I made it a point to go to the station one last time, where, summoning what little nerve I had at the time, I marched into his office and just blurted it out: "Are you the guy on my baseball card?" He looked up from his desk, slightly surprised. After a pause, he gave me a small smile and replied, "Yup, and you're the first guy from work in years who's asked me about it." Suddenly, improbably, that broke the ice, and he invited me for coffee in the cafeteria, where for an hour he regaled me with stories about the off-the-field exploits of his legendary carousing teammates. He also gave me my first, candid glimpse of what it was like to live the life of a CIA case officer abroad, as he had done for virtually all of his two-decades-long career. (He would continue to serve, mostly overseas, until his retirement in the mid-'80s.)

I sat there, mesmerized. Partly because he was the first, battle-hardened "street spook" ever to open up to me. But mostly because there I was, in this little cafeteria in this faraway place, talking to a guy on a baseball card magically reincarnated. It was on the plane that night that it really hit me for the first time about the CIA: This is an amazing place, with amazing people.

Late that year, I made the acquaintance of a storied figure in the CIA's history, a man who would offer me a valuable lesson about life in the Agency. It came in the form of informal, but prescient, career advice.

His name was Cord Meyer. In his 2001 obituary, the *Washington Post* observed that his "life was characterized by great privilege and considerable personal tragedy." The product of a wealthy and well-connected family, Meyer graduated early from Yale to join the marines shortly after the start of World War II. He was grievously wounded in combat in the Pacific, and while recovering wrote dispatches for U.S. magazines and later a prizewinning book. His politics were decidedly liberal (the FBI suspected him of Communist sympathies), and by all accounts he had stunned his liberal friends by deciding to join the CIA. He would spend the next quarter-century there, gaining increasing stature, and occasionally enduring media controversy, for his groundbreaking but highly covert anti-Communist initiatives. Over the years, Meyer fully earned his reputation inside the CIA, and inside the salons of Georgetown society, as a patrician, dashing, enigmatic swashbuckler.

At the end of 1976, when I first met him, he was largely a burned-out case. By the time Stansfield Turner arrived as Jimmy Carter's DCI in March 1977, Meyer had been shunted aside, given a do-nothing job with the amorphous title of "special assistant" to Turner, a man he grew to despise. (He contemptuously referred to Turner as "His Eminence.") Our paths crossed when I was assigned to help draft a new internal regulation governing CIA relationships with the U.S. media; with nothing else to do, and with his background in journalism, Meyer passed the word to Lapham that he would be happy to help.

From the beginning, Meyer was a mysterious, compelling figure to me. It was very similar to my initial reaction to Lyman Kirkpatrick at Brown a decade before. Like Kirkpatrick, he conveyed an aura born of privilege and a life in the shadows. They had the same refined features, including the carefully coiffed, thick gray hair (these guys from the "Good Shepherd" generation all seemed to have great hair) and the tweedy, expensive clothes. Both had a serious and visible physical disability, yet somehow it made them look even more intimidating and glamorous: For Kirkpatrick it was a wheelchair, for Meyer it was a black eye patch, one he had worn since losing an eye in World War II combat.

I don't know exactly why, but Meyer seemed to take a paternal shine to me. He invited me to lunch a few times at one of his favorite local haunts, a dark and quiet Turkish restaurant in nearby McLean. I particularly remember one lunch in the fall of 1976 because it took place not long after the public revelation of one more truth-is-stranger-than-fiction piece of Meyer's past. That July, the magazine *New Times*, a long-since-defunct countercultural periodical similar in style to *Rolling Stone*, published a long article entitled "The Curious Aftermath of JFK's Best and Brightest Affair." It chronicled the story of Meyer's former wife, Mary, who had been murdered in 1964 on the Potomac River towpath near her Georgetown home. The murder was never solved, but the article mostly focused on the Meyers' troubled marriage (they had divorced in 1958), his shadowy CIA career, and—most sensationally—the fact that Mary Meyer carried on an affair with President Kennedy in the early '60s. It hinted at a possible furtive Agency role in the murder or, at a minimum, in an effort to cover up evidence of the affair in the days after the murder occurred.

It was a mysterious, lurid, utterly irresistible tale that was still resonating in the media the day we had lunch, and God, I was bursting to ask Meyer about it. But I knew I just couldn't do so—it would have been unbelievably tasteless, and besides, Meyer still intimidated me a bit.

But then, out of nowhere, Meyer began talking about Kennedy, about how the president used to summon him to the Oval Office to discuss Agency operations. He talked about Kennedy in an admiring way, which I found exceedingly odd under the circumstances. Indeed, the fact that he brought up Kennedy's name at all was strange. Meyer soon dropped the subject of Kennedy and went on, in an offhand sort of way, to offer me some career advice, perhaps because he was about to retire.

Meyer's own career had largely foundered in the early '70s after his name was publicly linked to the CIA's clandestine role in reviewing the galleys of a book critical of the CIA, as well as the Agency's secret subsidy of the National Student Association. The activities took place years before, yet they still clearly weighed heavily on him. And there was a lesson from what had happened to him that he wanted to impart. "To succeed at the Agency," Meyer counseled, "you can't ever get your name into the newspapers."

I was grateful and flattered that he cared enough to offer me advice, but I couldn't imagine how it would ever apply in my CIA career. And, sure enough, I did stay safely under the media radar for the next twenty-five years. Until, that is, the months and years after the 9/11 attacks.

CHAPTER 2

Not Your Everyday Legal Issues (1977–1980)

Jimmy Carter had taken office in January 1977 after vowing during his campaign to curb the "rogue elephant"—the phrase coined by Senator Church for the CIA. His first nominee for director, Ted Sorensen, had to drop out because of his perceived anti-CIA animus in the past. (In his memoirs three decades later, Sorensen suggested that his failed nomination was in part due to some sort of covert cabal against him by CIA insiders. What nonsense.) Carter then appointed a navy admiral, Stansfield Turner, a starchy, self-righteous man with no previous intelligence experience, who quickly proceeded to alienate the workforce by slashing the ranks of CIA operational personnel. The Agency, still trying to recover from the impact of the Church Committee revelations, was a largely ignored, shrunken, demoralized shell of its fabled image in those first couple of years of the Carter administration.

However, for my part, I was still enthralled with my job, particularly with the breathtaking diversity of matters that the OGC handled. With only eighteen lawyers, the legal office didn't have the luxury of assigning us specific areas of practice, say, litigation or administrative law. So we were all deemed "generalists," meaning the legal assignments from all over the building were parceled out across the office as they came in.

I was beginning to realize that practicing law at the CIA was unlike any other attorney job in the government. Few federal statutes were meant to apply to the Agency's activities, and those that did traced back to the late '40s and were, by congressional design, cryptic and ambiguously worded. Judicial precedents (basic "case law," as it's called) were virtually nonexistent. It was as if lawmakers and judges implicitly recognized that the existence and work of the CIA were by definition secret, and they were content to keep it that way. So trying to do legal research was a largely fruitless exercise.

And the assignments were about things that law schools could never prepare you for.

Defectors, for example. Beginning with the CIA Act of 1949, Congress gave the Agency unique authority to identify foreign government officials and other individuals of interest and recruit them to the U.S. side by offering one of the Agency's ultimate "carrots": resettlement in the United States, with new identities and new lives. Up through the end of the Cold War, the vast majority of these defectors were from the Soviet Union. Some had been recruited by the CIA to operate "in place" until they had lost their operational value or, more frequently, were in danger of being uncovered. Others, however, were so-called walk-ins, meaning they simply decided to jump ship from their countries and seek refuge in a new life of freedom and plenty in the United States.

By the very nature of who they are, defectors have always been at once among the Agency's most valuable and most vexing accounts. They are, after all, essentially traitors to their country or cause, and they come weighed down with all sorts of psychological baggage—senses of guilt, entitlement, grandiosity, and so on. Often, they are simply not very nice people, demanding enormous tax-free bankrolling and constant pampering and indulgence. And the CIA is responsible for their care and well-being for the rest of their lives, long after they have lost any value as sources of intelligence. I should note that some defectors over the years have shown the character, pride, and wherewithal to become self-supporting, productive citizens in their new American surroundings. But from three decades of dealing with these guys, I have to say that more of them than not have proved to be morally bankrupt basket cases and enormous pains in the ass.

Still, the Agency has always thrown a huge amount of resources and effort into its defector program, because every once in a while a defector can be an intelligence gold mine. And during the Cold War, probably the most highly sought-after prize was an active-duty officer from the Soviet KGB.

All of which brings me to Yuri Nosenko, a complex, controversial, and irresistibly fascinating character I encountered in early 1977. A decade earlier, the CIA had given him a new name, a new "life history," and a new life in a bucolic, Mayberry-like little town in the southeast United States—a seemingly unlikely, fish-out-of-water landing spot for a hulking KGB apparatchik with the gap-toothed mug of Ernest Borgnine and the gravelly Russian-soaked drawl of Akim Tamiroff.

But this was not just any erstwhile KGB thug. In 1964, just months after the assassination of President Kennedy, Nosenko, a hard-drinking carouser already on the radar of CIA's Moscow Station, came running in panic, claiming he was in hot water with his KGB bosses for gambling away some official funds. So this guy was clearly no saint. Still, Nosenko appeared to be a plugged-in KGB official, which would've been tantalizing enough at the height of the Cold War, but his sales pitch was even more explosive: He had firsthand knowledge of everything the KGB knew about Lee Harvey Oswald. Of course, the Agency instantly bit, and Nosenko was soon in the CIA's care and custody in the States. Right away, he gave his handlers his take on the KGB-Oswald relationship: There was none. He was so seemingly confident and authoritative in what he said that many of Nosenko's interlocutors concluded he was telling the truth. But James Angleton didn't, and that made all the difference.

Angleton was the longtime, legendary, paranoid, and in retrospect quite likely deranged head of the CIA's counterintelligence office, and he was absolutely, irrevocably convinced (by another recent Soviet defector, ironically enough) that Nosenko was a plant—a double agent diabolically dispatched by the Soviets to throw the United States off track, to cover up the fact that the Soviets knew far more about Oswald—and the plan to kill Kennedy—than they could ever let ever come to light. The all-powerful Angleton decided that Nosenko had to be not only disbelieved, but broken.

So for three years, Nosenko was imprisoned in a tiny room in one of the Agency's facilities in downstate Virginia. Deprived of sleep, cut off from any outside contact, subjected to relentless and brutal interrogation. And yes, he recanted some of the things he claimed originally about his background and rank at KGB. But he never wavered about Oswald. Finally, mercifully, the CIA leadership called off the confinement in 1967. Nosenko was cleared of suspicion (although Angleton never would concede) and by 1977 was quietly resettled in the small southern hamlet where I was sent to meet with him.

My legal mission was mundane—I was to meet privately with the local probate judge (a courtly old gentleman; picture Wilford Brimley in judicial robes) to explain to him why, for national security reasons, the sworn signature on Nosenko's new will registered with the court was not Nosenko's true name. That was the easiest part of the trip, yet I was nervous as hell on the plane down. At that point, not yet thirty years old, I still barely knew any CIA operatives, let alone some hardened KGB turncoat that my new compatriots at the Agency had imprisoned and tormented a decade before. When I got off that little commuter airplane in that little Southern airport, there he was at the gate. Grinning, with that husky Russian growl and a handshake that sent jolts of pain up to my shoulder.

His being there as my welcoming party was not part of the plan. My boss's instructions had been to grab a cab from the airport to the discount motel just outside town to spend the night, and then slip quietly into the courthouse in the morning to do my business with the judge. After that, I was told, I should pay a brief courtesy call on Nosenko, and then fly back home. My other order was even more simple: not, under any circumstances, to engage in any conversation with Nosenko about his years of confinement. I assumed, though no one told me this at the time, the CIA was extremely concerned that Nosenko could still sue for millions, and win. A lawsuit like that was the last thing the Agency wanted splashed all over the newspapers, less than two years removed from the Church hearings.

So there I was, in this big Buick gas-eater, where I absolutely wasn't supposed to be, with this voluble bear of a man behind the wheel insisting that the motel could wait, that I would be his guest for a homemade dinner at his house. The way he barked it out, it was the proverbial offer I couldn't refuse.

Nosenko's home, courtesy of the U.S. taxpayers, was actually a relatively modest bungalow tucked at the end of a dirt road. It was on a lake, and when we first arrived, Nosenko proudly took me down to his dock, where he showed off his little fishing boat. He lived with his relatively new American wife; like a number of defectors over the years, he had left behind not only his old life but his old family when he defected. His wife was a charming, homespun type who looked to be about Nosenko's age—around sixty-five—and seemed to dote on him. She greeted me warmly and sat and chatted for a while. I was vastly relieved at her presence because I had just about run out of noncontroversial material to chat about with her husband. By then, however, Nosenko had retrieved from his basement a sample of what clearly was his most cherished possession—a bottle of his own personally distilled vodka (or "wotka," as he growled with that gap-toothed grin).

More than three decades later, I can still taste the stuff. In those days, I enjoyed an occasional vodka martini, but this was like nothing I ever consumed before or since. After one shot, my hands were tingling; after two, my feet went numb; after the third, I couldn't feel my face. Meanwhile, Nosenko kept belting them down and started talking even more animatedly.

Around my fourth shot, I didn't even notice anymore that he had an accent. And then, out of nowhere, he started talking about his years of confinement. Through my deepening alcoholic fog, I didn't know what to say or do—this was the one subject my bosses had forbidden me to get into with him. His wife, looking at him fondly, glanced over to me and quietly said, "He never has the opportunity to talk to anybody these days about this." So I listened, and no amount of Nosenko's homemade "wotka" could have made me forget what he told me.

Basically, Nosenko said he bore no grudges against anybody. Not James Angleton, not the other Soviet defector who had convinced Angleton that he was a Soviet plant, not his interrogators with all of their brutal deprivations, not the Agency leadership, which stood by and let him rot in that box for three years. "They had do it," he shrugged. "That is the nature of our business and that's what you do to a man like me. . . . I knew I was telling the truth, and I knew that if I didn't break that someday they would believe me. . . . I knew what they wanted, they wanted me to say that I was sent here to lie about Oswald and what KGB knew about him, but I wouldn't do that because if I did, your government would have sent me back to Russia, and KGB would do things far worse to me than what CIA was doing to me. . . . Your colleagues didn't torture me. They don't know what real torture is."

On and on he went, pouring shot after shot. I struggled to recall it all, since even in my increasingly inebriated state I knew I needed to remember all this. "So why," I finally slurred, "are you telling me all this, some young guy you just met?"

"Because," he replied in what to my ringing ears now sounded like the King's English, "you are their lawyer, and I know they never ask me about this because they fear I will sue them. Well, tell them I will never sue them. Never. But you also tell them, I will never forget what they did."

Somehow late that night, I got to my little motel. The most drunken night of my life was followed by the worst hangover of my life. Then Nosenko picked me up at the motel, looking fresh as a daisy, and once again made me an offer I couldn't refuse—he would take me to the judge. And so we walked, me with considerable difficulty, through the picture-book town square to the old courthouse, with Nosenko buoyantly calling out greetings to all the locals we passed. "I don't know that you are supposed to be seen with me," I suggested plaintively. "We look too conspicuous."

"The only one conspicuous is you," he snorted. "You are the one wearing the fancy suit."

After I saw the judge, Nosenko drove me to the airport, but we said nothing to each other about what we had talked about the night before. The flight back to D.C., of course, was bumpy all the way, and I thought I might be about to die for my country, either in a crash or, more likely, from "wotka"-induced nausea.

I did manage to scribble down notes quoting everything Nosenko told me the long night before. After that trip, I didn't have any occasion to think about things like putting somebody in solitary confinement, or trying to get a prisoner to talk, or what is or isn't torture. Not until a quarter-century later, after 9/11.

Another astonishing thing I discovered in my first few years at the Agency was how extensively it interacted with some of the highest-level sectors of American society—the academic, media, and corporate communities in particular. It was not a case of the Agency spying on them; that was clearly verboten in the new post–Church Committee world we were living in. In fact, an outsider might reasonably assume that none of these institutions, in the post-Watergate era, would ever want to have anything to do with the big, bad CIA.

But once I was on the inside, I quickly learned that that was not the case. Some of these folks, mindful of the professional and personal risks of doing so, continued to come forward to offer their services to the Agency—even in the late '70s, when the CIA's reputation and influence had just taken a sustained battering. This realization crystallized for me during yet another lucky assignment that came my way in late 1976. For the first time in its history (and, truth to tell, to forestall potential congressional initiatives in this area), the CIA set out to establish written policies governing the scope and intent of the relationships it would henceforth have with U.S. members of the media, the clergy, and the academic and corporate communities. And I was chosen to draft the proposed policies for the CIA leadership—and ultimately the director—to review and approve. Once again, it was a challenging and infinitely fascinating assignment for a young guy still new to the intelligence world. And, of course, it bore absolutely no relation to anything I ever studied in law school.

I was given only a few basic marching orders: First, no U.S. journalist, clergyman, academic, or businessman was going to be manipulated or duped into any secret work for us. In the unique bureaucratese of the spy business, this was translated into the phrase "no operational use on an unwitting basis." Second, the policies should not be written so as to prohibit any confidential relationships with members of these sectors. But third, the threshold criteria for establishing any relationship should be rigorous and subject to careful internal oversight. No one in the CIA was going to recruit, or accept an offer of services, from a U.S. journalist, academic, businessman, or clergyman on a whim or hunch—there had to be a strong reason to believe that they could provide a real benefit to the Agency's intelligence mission. For use of a journalist or clergyman, the personal approval of the director would be required.

What I found especially surprising was how much people in those professions were willing, and sometimes downright eager, to get into bed with us. Academics and journalists in particular were a strong-willed, independent lot. They had a lot to lose, after all. The universities and news organizations that employed them made it clear that any secret association with the CIA required senior management approval and that any individual who didn't get it risked severe sanctions. In 1977, Harvard University established written policies along these lines for its faculty and staff, and its president, Derek Bok, wrote to Director Turner imploring that the CIA help enforce them by pledging it wouldn't enter into any confidential relationship with a Harvard employee without making sure the employee first cleared it with his/her bosses. Since I was already working on putting together CIA policies in this area, I was told to draft the response.

Now, Stansfield Turner was no hard-core zealot on behalf of the Agency's clandestine side; in fact, he was by nature suspicious of the spy world's mystique. But on this matter he pushed back hard at Harvard: He told me to draft a response stating that he had no intention of forswearing any future secret relationships with Harvard personnel and would certainly not make any of them get approval from their bosses before agreeing to help the Agency in a given instance. He took the same stance the next year when news organizations sought the same kind of commitment. To Turner, and to every CIA director from every administration in the next three decades, the issue was pretty simple: If a U.S. citizen is willing to enter into a confidential relationship with the CIA because he/she wants to help the country, that is between the Agency and the individual, and no one else. And in most cases I would come across over the years, the individual in question would be adamant about keeping the relationship secret, partly because of fears of retribution, not just by U.S. adversaries abroad but also by their own employers, but also partly because they felt strongly—more strongly than the CIA did, actually—that if they wanted to help the CIA, it was their right and no one else's damn business. The policies I helped establish for the Agency in this always-sensitive area remain in effect to this day.

I also was surprised and gratified to discover how much the U.S. corporate sector was (and continues to be) willing to provide secret support to the CIA and its national security mission. American companies—especially those with significant international interests—have far more to lose than to gain in having associations with the CIA. Unlike its counterparts in many other governments in the world, including our European allies, the CIA has never adopted a policy of giving U.S. companies a "leg up" in pursuing overseas business. If they help, therefore, it is simply a matter of their doing so out of a sense of patriotic duty. And if the association is somehow exposed, they are left wide open to charges of being CIA "dupes" or "fronts" and face the real risk of seeing their international business interests dry up or even expropriated.

For the CIA, an internationally connected U.S. company or businessman can be a uniquely valuable resource. They go places and make foreign contacts that U.S. government representatives—whether diplomats or intelligence personnel operating undercover—cannot. And they offer a wide range of intelligence services, from serving as the CIA's "eyes and ears" to letting one of our clandestine officers pose as a company employee while stationed abroad—a so-called nonofficial cover officer (NOC).

In 1978, I was dispatched to meet with the CEO of one of those huge businesses. His company was on the brink of closing a lucrative deal to open a facility in a strategically important foreign country in which the U.S. government had virtually no way of operating effectively. My mission was to explain to him the assistance the CIA wanted him to provide us. The assistance was critical, but highly risky for the company if it ever came to light. Just as important, I was to spell out exactly what we thought those risks were so that he knew exactly what he was in for.

It was my maiden high-stakes venture into the lair of such a big-time corporate mogul, and I was nervous. He had agreed to meet alone with a CIA representative, but he didn't know what we wanted to talk about. For all I knew, he would throw me out, or laugh at me, or both, once he heard the hairy things we wanted him to agree to. I vividly recall walking, as purposefully as my shaking legs would permit, into his top-floor office at the corporate headquarters and having to traverse a carpet about the size of Connecticut to sit in front of his massive desk. And there he was, staring quizzically at me.

Trying not to gape, I dutifully launched headlong into what the Agency wanted his company to do for us, and then pivoted into a laundry list of the risks we thought he could potentially face if things somehow went wrong. He let me ramble on, and then he just raised his hand and spoke for the first time.

"Son," he drawled laconically, "you folks may think you know me, but you have no idea what a rich sumbitch I am. I can figure out the risks. I'll do whatever y'all want."

And the deal was sealed, just like that.

Among businesses in general, the CIA has long had a special relationship with the entertainment industry, devoting considerable attention to fostering relationships with Hollywood movers and shakers—studio executives, producers, directors, and big-name actors. There are officers assigned to this account full-time, which is not exactly a dangerous assignment but one that occasionally produces its own bizarre moments.

In my early years at the Agency, a veteran CIA liaison with Hollywood first explained it to me this way: These are people who have made a lot of money basically creating make-believe stuff. A lot of them, at least the smarter and more self-aware ones, realize what they do makes them ridiculously rich but is also ephemeral and meaningless in the larger scheme of things. So they're receptive to helping the CIA in any way they can, probably in equal parts because they are sincerely patriotic and because it gives them a taste of real-life intrigue and excitement. And their power and international celebrity can be valuable—it gives them entrée to people and places abroad. Heads of state want to meet and get cozy with them. Their film crews are given free rein everywhere, even in places where the U.S. government doesn't normally have it. And they can be the voice of a U.S. message that will have impact with foreign audiences so long as the audience doesn't know it is coming from the U.S. government.

But things can get complicated, as I discovered a few years later when the head of the Agency's Hollywood account came to me with news about his newest potential recruit, a major film star at the time (the CIA won't let me reveal his name). The way our guy explained it, the actor somehow knew that another big star's production company had an association with the CIA's clandestine service over the years (something I didn't know until our guy told me). Now this actor was offering his own name and services to us. Free of charge. Anything he could do. Just out of his patriotic duty.

As our guy related his story, I wondered to myself, why is he telling me this? It all sounded perfectly fine to me. It was kinda cool, actually.

And then he got to the kicker. "There is one little catch," he said. "The actor refuses to take any money, but he told us that instead all he wants is for us to score him the best fifty-thousand-dollar stash of cocaine we can find. He seems to think we can get the real primo stuff. So that's why I'm here. Is it okay for us to do it?"

"Uh, no," I managed to get out of my agape mouth.

"We know a way to get some easily," our guy added hopefully.

I definitely wasn't eager to learn how, so I just repeated my response. "No. No way. Forget it."

"Yeah, well, I thought so, but I thought I'd ask anyway," he said, looking only slightly crestfallen as he left my office.

I later learned that the actor did provide some assistance to the CIA on a particular project. I was assured that his services were totally gratis.

Adding to my portfolio as a generalist, in the summer of 1978 I was handed my first espionage prosecution of a CIA employee. The three-week trial that fall took place in the unlikely locale of Hammond, Indiana, a gritty, blighted industrial town just across the state line from Illinois. It was in the closest federal court to the hometown of the defendant, a twenty-three-year-old second-generation Greek American named William Kampiles.

Kampiles, a fledgling analyst, was charged with selling a top-secret CIA satellite manual to the Russians for the ridiculously paltry sum of $3,000. The manual was a thick, densely worded document stuffed with technical charts spelling out all the details of a newly developed, state-of-the-art U.S. surveillance satellite that represented years of research and that had cost American taxpayers untold millions of dollars. And now, thanks to Kampiles, the Soviets had it dropped into their laps, for a pittance. It was nothing short of a road map for how the Soviet Union could act to shield itself from the U.S. eyes in the sky.

It was a bizarre and tragic case on a number of levels—the golden child of immigrants, he had joined the Agency out of college the year before, with a hopelessly naïve fantasy of a James Bond–style career, only to find himself assigned clerklike duties in the CIA Command Center (the room that actually does have lots of clocks on the wall and rows of furrowed-browed people staring and muttering at their computer screens). Frustrated and bitter, he resigned from the CIA in November 1977 after less than a year, but before leaving he purloined the manual from the Command Center and a few months later walked into the Soviet embassy in Athens to offer his services and, eventually, the manual.

Being not much older than Kampiles nor with much more CIA experience, I was assigned as the point man in the case—the first high-stakes, high-profile espionage case of my Agency career. It was also an experience filled with daily crises and sprinkled with comic and surreal vignettes. A template of sorts for my entire career.

An espionage case is always a crapshoot because of its central paradox: The more egregious and damaging the compromise of national security information involved, the more difficult and risky it becomes to prosecute the wrongdoer, because of the fear that the information will be further spread and compromised during the course of the trial. And yet to not prosecute someone who has sold secrets to the enemy is simply an untenable proposition. Several years after the Kampiles case, Congress passed a law called the Classified Information Procedures Act (CIPA), which established a detailed set of mechanisms designed to protect the excessive or unnecessary exposure of classified information in criminal prosecutions involving that sort of information, while at the same time protecting the defendant's constitutional right to a fair trial. But CIPA did not exist in 1978, so the Kampiles prosecution for me was one long, seat-of-the-pants, *Perils of Pauline* ride.

The Kampiles case was filled with messy, inconvenient facts. First, there was the 68-page KH-11 satellite manual itself. It was indisputably a sensitive, top-secret document. We knew the Soviets had it—Kampiles himself had admitted to the FBI that he gave it to them (although he tried to recant that at the trial). However, it turned out that for months after Kampiles filched it from the Command Center, no one noticed it was missing, even though it was the only copy there. In fact, the Agency started looking for it only after Kampiles's admission under quietly relentless FBI questioning. On top of that, when an Agency-wide inventory was belatedly conducted, about a dozen other copies could not be accounted for. What did that say about the supposed sanctity of the information inside it, and the CIA's competence in keeping track of its secrets? It was left to me to deliver that unpleasant nugget of news to the Justice Department in the run-up to the trial. For the first of what would be far too many times in my career, I was in a room with a bunch of prosecutors giving me a collective eye-roll after I gave them news they did not want to hear.

But the contents of the KH-11 manual weren't the biggest secret the Agency sought to protect in the prosecution. After all, the Soviets already had it—although none of our other adversaries had it, as far as we could tell, so it was still well worth protecting from public exposure. But that concern paled beside another secret, known to fewer than a dozen people in the government. It was a secret that the CIA told Justice from the outset had to be protected at all costs, up to and including aborting the prosecution if there was any risk of its being exposed. It was the type of secret that the CIA has always kept, as an article of faith, above all others: the identity of a human source. In this case, a penetration—a mole—inside

Soviet intelligence, who gave the CIA the first lead in the investigation that would lead to Kampiles. The lead, as most explosive leads are, was fragmentary: Sometime in the winter of 1978, a young American had met with a Soviet official in Athens and provided a top-secret document on a U.S. spy satellite. And a name, maybe not a true name and maybe garbled: Ruggerio or Ruggeri, something like that. That was it. And that's how the investigation got under way.

It was the first big secret I learned at the CIA. The kind of secret that gets someone killed if it gets out. And I was the guy ordered to protect it at all costs.

For the government, every espionage prosecution has two focal points. The first is in Washington, where the senior leadership of the various stakeholders—Justice, the FBI, and the intelligence community—resides and makes the strategic and policy decisions for each prosecution. The second focal point is where the prosecution is happening, where staffers from each of the concerned agencies are in the courtroom every day for the pretrial proceedings and throughout the trial. For the Kampiles case, that group consisted of Dave Homer and his boss, John Martin, from the DOJ's Internal Security Division; Don Stuckey and John Denton from the FBI's Counterintelligence Section, who were the investigating agents on the case; U.S. Attorney Dave Ready and Assistant U.S. Attorney Jim Richmond, the local federal prosecutors who were the lead government attorneys in the courtroom; and me, representing the CIA and the rest of the intelligence community. Only those in these tight, hermetic groups knew about the big secret in the Kampiles case.

Every espionage case also has the same dynamic. Justice pushes to cross every "t" and dot every "i" to guarantee a conviction and preclude a reversal on appeal, which in turn causes them to instinctively want to use every piece of intelligence information the government has, no matter how sensitive, to ensure a conviction, or at least not screw one up. We on the intelligence side refer to this, perhaps unfairly, as the "kitchen sink" approach to prosecuting a case. The CIA, on the other hand, while equally focused on securing a "clean" conviction, traditionally pushes for a more nuanced approach: We tell the DOJ that we will turn cartwheels to provide our intelligence secrets necessary to get a conviction, but we are going to push back hard if we think the DOJ is going for "overkill" by putting sensitive information into jeopardy when it doesn't have to.

Shortly after Kampiles's arrest on August 17, 1978, the CIA's leadership—in the persons of Director Stansfield Turner and my boss, General Counsel Tony Lapham—laid down a marker with Attorney General Griffin Bell: The existence of our source must be protected at all costs, including abandoning the prosecution, if necessary. Bell's response was measured: Justice would do "all in its power" to protect the information. And that's how it was left, with the trial looming three months later.

One favorable factor was that the investigative trail did not lead in a straight line from the source to Kampiles. In fact, Kampiles came onto the screen only when he began bragging to former CIA co-workers that he had recently met with the Soviet intelligence officers in Athens and had "conned" them into paying him $3,000 by just telling them he was a CIA official with access to classified information. An astoundingly stupid and ignorant move on the kid's part, of course—the first tenet of Cold War Counterintelligence 101 is that the Soviets never, ever paid something for nothing in return. So Kampiles's story was quickly relayed to the FBI, where it dovetailed with the fragmentary source lead that the Bureau was already chasing. Kampiles voluntarily agreed to an interview with FBI special agents Stuckey and Denton, initially repeated his "something for nothing" story, was challenged on it, agreed to take a polygraph, flunked it, and ultimately confessed to the entire thing. All within a couple of days, and Kampiles never once invoked his Miranda rights to counsel. If his crime hadn't been so serious, his naïveté would have been comic.

The confession stood on its own, but the worries we in the CIA had were nagging and persistent. At the time that the hapless, dumb Kampiles wandered into the crosshairs, the FBI had focused on another suspect. Someone who was living in a midwestern city whose name was quite close to "Ruggeri/Ruggerio," that tantalizing shard of a clue passed along by our source. The Bureau was, in fact, about to get a court order to wiretap the poor guy and secretly search his house. Once Kampiles confessed, the FBI dropped its plans. To this day the anonymous, law-abiding Mr. Ruggeri/Ruggerio doubtless has no clue how close he came to being sucked into an international espionage case.

But the mysterious Ruggeri/Ruggerio bell could not be unrung. In all of his otherwise self-incriminating statements, Kampiles insisted he never gave his Russian handler any name, real or bogus. What made the Russians think that was what his name was?

It was much more than a curiously loose end to the case against Kampiles. It was potentially Brady material—*Brady* being a landmark Supreme Court case compelling the government in any criminal case to turn over to the defense any information in its files potentially exculpatory to the defendant. And surely we were in that territory here—the FBI not only had that lead, but had been chasing it down right up to the moment Kampiles obligingly popped up. And it seemed to point to someone other than Kampiles as the culprit.

The thought of providing to the defense any information that could conceivably be tied back to our source was, well, inconceivable to the CIA. Director Turner would have gone to President Carter—and that's what it would have taken—to get him to order the attorney general to abort the prosecution. And a confessed traitor—a CIA employee, no less—would get away with what he did, courtesy of the CIA's intercession. It would have ignited a huge, unprecedented firestorm. But it was conceivable.

The sense of dread and impending doom haunted me for weeks. The defense was filing a blizzard of motions asking all sorts of open-ended questions, and every week or so my boss, Tony Lapham, and I—the only CIA lawyers knowledgeable about the source—would agonize over a particular query that seemed to come close to the verboten area. Meanwhile, those cleared at the DOJ—the "kitchen sink" boys—were warily watching, too, seemingly all too ready to say "Okay, guys, that's it. We gotta tell the defense." Kampiles's defense counsel sensed something was up, even if he didn't know what, and kept probing. We kept dodging every bullet, but I thought it was only a matter of time.

But then, a few days before the trial was to begin, with CIA and FBI agents knowledgeable about the source slated to testify, a miracle happened.

Someone in the small circle of government officials clued in to the source—I'd like to say it was me, but it wasn't—remembered seeing something at some point in the thousands of pages that made up the Kampiles investigative file. It was only a sentence or two, buried in the huge pile. Kampiles happened to mention to somebody, either his FBI interrogators or the people in the CIA to whom he confided, what clothes he was wearing when he met with his Soviet handler in Athens. He purposely dressed like a tourist, he said. Khaki pants and a rugby shirt. Not just any rugby shirt, he added, but one made by Rugger. With "Rugger" stitched on the left breast.

The nagging mystery was finally, suddenly solved. Kampiles's Soviet handler must have figured the thing was a damn monogram. And no doubt proudly so reported it up his chain of command. With a little bit of mangled spelling.

Well, I thought for the first but far from the last time in my career, everybody in the spy trade screws up once in a while. And then I thought, also for the first but not the last time in my career, this is the kind of stuff I could never make up.

After that, the trial was almost an afterthought. With the Justice Department's prodding, we grudgingly agreed to let the presiding judge, a no-nonsense midwesterner named Phil McNagny, look at the "Ruggeri/Ruggerio" information alone inside his chambers. I hand-carried the documents to him myself and waited outside to retrieve them when he was done. He confirmed what we knew already: The information was extremely sensitive, and extremely inculpatory to Kampiles. The defense would not see it, and nothing in the trial would get anywhere near it.

The trial lasted a week, and the jury came back after ten hours. Kampiles was found guilty of espionage and subsequently sentenced to forty years.

As for our source, I heard nothing more about him until a number of years later, when I learned that the Agency had just safely brought him in from the cold and resettled him in the United States. Which made me happy.

By 1979, Carter—despite his earlier stance, and like all presidents of all political stripes before and after him—was turning to the CIA as a uniquely valuable tool when unpredictable and ominous events in the world forced his hand. The Soviet Union had not only invaded Afghanistan but encouraged and supported, via weapons and advisors, proxy regimes there as well as in Africa and, especially, Central America, where the Sandinistas seized control in Nicaragua and fomented leftist insurgencies in its neighboring countries. Meanwhile, the shah of Iran was overthrown by the virulently anti-American forces of Ayatollah Khomeini, culminating in their November 1979 seizure of the U.S. embassy, with 52 U.S. Government employees (including CIA personnel) held hostage.

As it happened, this was also about the time when I received what turned out to be my career-making job assignment: I was named to the post of legal advisor to the Directorate of Operations (DO). The DO was shorthand for the CIA's clandestine service, the entity responsible for all undercover activities. For someone with less than four years of Agency experience, it was a plum position. I was given an office situated inside the spaces of the DO, working literally in the midst of the covert or "dark" side of CIA. At the time, it was the only legal assignment in the CIA located outside the physical confines of the OGC. (Today, there are about sixty such "on-site" lawyers scattered throughout virtually every component of the Agency.) I was never really told by my boss, Dan Silver (who had succeeded Tony Lapham as general counsel the year before), why he chose me for the job, but one reason quickly became apparent as soon as I settled into my new digs. My predecessor in the position was seen by many as brusque and condescending, and the word had been passed through the DO "rat line" (these guys were spies, after all) to avoid dealing with the DO lawyer if at all possible. So for the first few weeks after I arrived, I was the proverbial Maytag repairman from those old TV commercials—sitting in my office waiting in vain for my phone to ring.

Gradually, as I doggedly engaged in a sort of missionary work inside the cloistered environment of the DO, the tide began to turn, and I started to get phone calls and "walk-in" office visits by the clandestine service officers. I did my best to put them at ease and be responsive to all comers, whether junior or senior in rank. (I was told that my predecessor in his final months had taken to demanding to know the salary level of every DO caller before consenting to take the call.) In those early weeks I learned a lasting lesson about the psyche of CIA covert operatives, at least as far as how they relate to lawyers: They are totally focused on the mission but completely un-Machiavellian when seeking legal advice (otherwise, they wouldn't be coming in the first place). They ask only that their lawyer not look or act like he thinks they are idiots, lunatics, or criminals.

And as 1979 turned into 1980, with the Carter administration finally rebooting the moribund CIA covert-action capabilities, my job as the DO legal advisor began to have booming business. I had to engage in crash, on-the-job training as the architect of another arcane CIA legal art form: Presidential Findings. These are the instruments, mandated by Congress in the mid-'70s, by which the president is required to personally approve in writing all covert-action programs. Congress created this process to end forever the practice of undocumented, "wink and a nod" marching orders that presidents issued to the CIA in the halcyon years of the '50s through the early '70s, leading to everything from foreign coups to assassination plots.

From the time the congressional requirement legally kicked in, in the mid-'70s, up to 1979, covert action was virtually nonexistent, so I was operating on a largely blank page in trying to figure out how to write a Finding. The process would always begin the same way: A directive would come from the National Security Council (NSC), or sometimes the president himself, to draw up a covert-action proposal (defined as an activity designed to influence conditions abroad so that our government's hand is not acknowledged or apparent) involving a particular objective. The CIA would then come up with a menu of options—it could run the gamut from a propaganda campaign to organizing an armed insurgency. The White House would pick and choose the options it was prepared to endorse, and that's where I would come in. I would draft the Finding for the president's signature, incorporating the White House's wishes in language specific enough to accurately convey the mandate but broad enough not to require going back to the president for a new imprimatur for every new "wrinkle" after the program was launched.

Writing a Finding was thus a delicate and tricky endeavor, and I had no road map to follow. But orders for covert-action campaigns in Afghanistan and Central America first came out of the chute from the White House in late 1979, and they came quickly, so we at the CIA had to move quickly. Those first Findings were terse—two or three short paragraphs at the most—because the Carter White House was cautious about letting out too much "leash" to the CIA, and because we at the CIA had never really written any of the damn things before, so we erred on the side of brevity. Beginning in the mid-'80s, Findings would expand in length to more than a page, and they would keep getting longer, becoming almost mini–white papers in later years. But at the beginning, they were short and to the point. On one side of the page, the target country or region would be identified. On the opposite side, the actions the CIA would be authorized by the president to undertake.

Dan Silver and I cobbled together a shorthand vernacular for particular kinds of actions, the idea being that they could be plugged in as appropriate in all future Findings, thereby developing a glossary for covert action. When "political action" is authorized, that means influencing a foreign government's viewpoint toward the United States and/or U.S. policy objectives. It could include buying the favor of a local politician or creating a political movement abroad (the phrase does not include, however, the CIA effecting an outcome in a foreign election; something that aggressive and risky, we decided, required explicit presidential authorization). Some of the phrases we came up with were admittedly a bit sanitized, largely because we recognized that it was unlikely that any White House, and in particular the Carter White House, would countenance the president signing a directive to the CIA authorizing deception and misinformation campaigns or, in the ultimate case, killing people. No president would affix his signature to a piece of paper that contained the words *lie* or *kill*, so the former sort of activity was dubbed "all forms of propaganda," while the latter was described as "lethal action." Nonetheless, everyone involved would know what those terms meant, from the president to the congressional intelligence committees that receive copies of Findings.

Afghanistan was a particular challenge. President Carter ladled out our authorities carefully and incrementally, Finding by Finding. At first, we were not permitted to give arms or ammunition to the Afghan resistance ("lethal equipment" in Finding-speak), only "cash" and "logistical support." This sort of calibration worked much better for us desk jockeys in Washington than it did for the CIA people in the field. I remember a visit early on from the chief of the CIA's Afghan Task Force, who had a bewildering question about, of all things, mules. It seemed that the Afghan resistance fighters were in dire need of them to navigate the rugged Afghan topography and, in particular, to carry arms and attack the Soviet-backed forces. So, would the CIA's providing them constitute "logistical support," which was permitted, or "lethal equipment," which was verboten? And the chief said he needed an answer right away—time was of the essence. As for almost every other question I had to confront as the DO lawyer, there was no statute or court precedent to help guide me on the appropriate legal status accorded mules. So I paused briefly, pondering whether or not a mule could be "lethal" in circumstances other than kicking some poor guy in the head. Deciding on pure gut instinct that a mule more properly belongs in the "logistical" category, I told our guy that we could provide the mules.

Navigating the Carter Findings on Central America, and Nicaragua especially, presented much more significant obstacles. In Afghanistan, at least the objective was clear from the outset: Get the Soviets, and their puppet government, out. In Central America, the objectives were sub-tler: deterring the Soviets, the Cubans, and their Sandinista acolytes from spreading their influence throughout the region. Our authorities stopped short of overthrowing the Sandinista regime in Nicaragua. That meant making a Nicaraguan resistance movement viable—hence, the Carter Findings authorized "political action"—but not strong enough militarily to force a change in government. And that's what the Nicaraguan resis-tance (soon to be forever known as the "contras") wanted and needed from the United States—because otherwise the contras knew they would be crushed by the increasingly despotic and brutal Sandinista regime. Regime change was their objective, but not the U.S. Government's.

Another huge factor in the disparate ways the Agency had to treat Afghanistan and Central America—and how I had to interpret the covert-action authorities Carter gave us—was Congress. There was total consensus in Congress that the United States needed to get the Soviets out of Afghanistan, so the administration had almost a blank check. Put another way, I could have legally categorized mules as anything I wanted, secure in the knowledge that no member of the congressional intelli-gence committees would have cared. In Central America, by contrast, there was no congressional consensus—sentiment there toward the San-dinistas ranged from apathy to mild annoyance, up to considering them an existential threat to the Western Hemisphere. And so from the begin-ning, the intelligence committees were watching closely, scrutinizing our activities piece by piece, dollar by dollar. This congressional ambiv-alence toward U.S. policies in Central America (which were themselves ambivalent) would haunt the CIA for years. For my part, I would spend far more time over the next several years walking on eggshells in giving legal advice on the Central America program than I ever would on the Afghanistan program, which was exponentially larger in terms of fund-ing and sheer violence.

Still, those last two years of the Carter administration were exhilarat-ing for me professionally. The Afghanistan Findings kept coming, albeit in bologna-slicing style, and I was the guy who was putting them together. The Central America program, meanwhile, was also gradually expanding, and to top it off, the White House ordered up a covert-action program in response to the November 1979 hostage crisis involving the U.S. embassy in Iran. By 1980, the White House counsel, the legendary D.C. superlawyer Lloyd Cutler, became so concerned about the perception of Carter signing so many Findings that he directed my boss, Dan Silver, and me to create a different name for a Finding that simply expands or otherwise changes the scope of a preexisting Finding. We came up with the deceptively innocuous term "Memorandum of Notification"—MON for short. It was purely a cosmetic move, since an MON was the same as a Finding in everything but name. Still, Cutler was happy, because it kept the number of Findings down, and from his perspective, protected his client from being accused by critics, or later by historians, of being a late-blooming, covert-action-addicted president. Never mind that Carter signed all MONs, as well as Findings, so his fingerprints were all over both. Nonetheless, notwithstanding their rather disingenuous provenance, MONs have endured, and have been regularly issued by presidents to this day.

For me, what the Carter White House preferred to call all these covert-action authorizations didn't really matter. What did matter to me is that I was the one tasked to draft them. And it was pretty heady stuff, composing documents describing all sorts of derring-do that was classified above top secret and knowing that the president of the United States would be personally reading my words and putting his signature on the bottom of the page (no autopens allowed). Shallow, maybe, but I was still in my early thirties.

CHAPTER 3

Enter William Casey
and a Whole New Ball Game
(1981–1984)

Following Carter's loss in November 1980 was a rocky transition from his administration to the incoming Reagan team. Stansfield Turner, the four-year incumbent DCI, was number one on the target list for the Reagan national security team. It was the second transition between a defeated incumbent and a newly elected president from the opposite party that I had witnessed at the CIA, the first following Gerald Ford's loss to Jimmy Carter four years earlier. But that change hadn't seemed nearly so rancorous.

I had found Turner to be an impressive and admirable man in many respects. But with his military bearing, he had alienated most everyone in the CIA rank and file early on and never recovered. And the Reagan national security transition team—composed exclusively of staunch conservative hawks—made no effort to hide their contempt for him (and by extension, Carter) in their visits to the building. Which in turn prompted Turner, a proud and prickly man, to abruptly stomp out of the CIA midtransition.

Enter William Casey. He would turn out to be the toughest, smartest, most complex, and most enigmatic of the dozen CIA directors I served under.

Casey arrived as CIA director in early 1981 with eclectic credentials, to say the least. A lawyer by background, he was a veteran of the Office of Strategic Services (OSS), the predecessor of the CIA in World War II. He then made a fortune on Wall Street but in later years would serve as a tough, aggressive enforcer as chairman of the Securities and Exchange Commission. He was Reagan's 1980 campaign manager and likely could have had his pick of numerous senior posts in the new administration. But he wanted to be the CIA director. Badly.

Casey made it immediately clear to the workforce, especially the Directorate of Operations, that the Reagan administration was going to take the gloves off against America's adversaries around the world. (He made it clear by deed, since his gruff demeanor and mumbled speech pattern hampered communicating anything orally to large CIA audiences.)

I met Casey for the first time a couple of weeks after he took office. It was not an auspicious beginning to our relationship.

I was summoned to the director's suite on the seventh floor for what his secretary cryptically described as a background briefing on covert action. The meeting was scheduled in fifteen minutes, she said. That's all the notice I was given. I took the elevator from my office in DO on the second floor, a little nervous about meeting Casey for the first time. But I also assumed there would be others attending the meeting—the deputy director for operations, the chief of the DO covert-action staff, perhaps a couple of Casey's new aides. But when I arrived, his secretary pointed to his closed office door and simply told me he was waiting. In I walked, and there he was sitting alone at his desk, surrounded by boxes, with papers scattered all about him. He simply looked up through very thick eyeglasses, grunted at me to sit down, and kept on reading a stack of documents in front of him. I could see they were copies of all the existing Presidential Findings. I couldn't help noticing that he was wearing what looked to be an expensive bespoke pinstripe suit, one with buttons on the sleeves that actually could be buttoned. I also couldn't help noticing that it looked like he had slept in it.

After a few very long minutes, he addressed me for the first time. He made no pretense of knowing my name. "Did you write these?"

"Uh, yes, sir."

"Why does a lawyer write up covert-action programs?" Casey made it sound like an accusation.

"Well, sir, the law mandates that the president must issue a directive to CIA—"

He cut me off. "I know what the law says," he said impatiently while pulling out of his drawer a maroon book that I recognized as Title 50 of the United States Code, containing all the existing statutes and legislative history relating to the CIA and national security. "I'm a lawyer, too, you know." I remember thinking, I don't have a copy of that thing anywhere in my office. I felt the onset of flop sweat. This scowling old guy was twice my age, and I was sure he was about to give me a pop quiz.

But mercifully, he put Title 50 aside and returned to looking at his stack of Findings.

"There's not much in these," he said dismissively. "Not very tough."

I didn't know quite what to say, if anything. Was he somehow blaming me for that? I wasn't about to suddenly become an advocate for the Carter administration's record on covert action, but the thought did occur to me: If this guy thinks these Findings are wimpy, he should have been here two years ago, when we hardly had any at all. And the thought also occurred to me: Why am I the only one here listening to this?

Casey then looked at me and simply said, "You're going to be writing Findings that are a lot stronger than this." And then he mumbled, "Thanks." And that was it. I was dismissed. The "briefing," if that's what it was, was over.

Taking the elevator back down to my office, I wondered, a bit shellshocked: What is the Agency in for? What am I in for?

Casey soon started to assemble his own team. Mostly, he moved and promoted people from within, but he did bring in a couple of newcomers to the CIA to serve atop his management team. One of them directly affected me: He recruited an old friend and colleague from his SEC days in the 1970s, Stanley Sporkin, to be the general counsel. (Stan replaced Dan Silver, who returned to his private law practice, as Dan's predecessor, Tony Lapham, had done two years before.) It was an unorthodox choice. As the SEC's head of enforcement, Stan had earned a nationwide reputation for being a tough, relentless antagonist of Wall Street corporate barons. I had read about him and his investigative crusades in recent years and learned even more from one of my best friends from law school, Ed Herlihy, who had joined the SEC after graduation and quickly became one of Stan's most dedicated young protégés. Ed had spoken to Stan about me, and one of the first things Stan did when he arrived was reach out to me, to seek my help in learning the ropes at the CIA. It was the beginning of a close working relationship, one in which he showed me unstinting kindness and support, and a friendship that has lasted to this day.

Both Stan and Casey were perpetually rumpled and seemingly oblivious to what they were wearing (although Casey's clothes were considerably pricier). I would witness both of them carelessly devouring their lunches, crumbs spilling out everywhere. And then there were their conversational traits. Casey was a notorious mumbler, while Stan tended toward a pattern of elliptical, often sports-related metaphors uttered in cadences that could range from guttural to high-pitched. On many occasions, I would attend meetings between them, sometimes alone and sometimes with others, and come away utterly convinced that they were the only two people in the room who could discern what the other was saying—which could be disconcerting when the subject was some highly complex, highly risky covert operation. But they certainly were on the same wavelength, and they clearly trusted each other completely.

Still, as much as Casey wanted Stan on board, Casey's first priority was not overhauling the Agency's legal shop. What Casey really focused on, what really drove him from the start, was shaking up and energizing the CIA's covert-operations side. First, however, this otherwise brilliant, shrewd man pulled one of those occasional inexplicable boners that would mark his tenure and make him such an intriguing, perplexing figure. For reasons known only to him, Casey recruited one of his gofers from the Reagan campaign, an obscure New Hampshire businessman named Max Hugel, to take over the CIA's most venerable and sensitive career post—deputy director for operations. In other words, head of the Agency's clandestine service. Not only was Hugel a novice to the spy world, he was, it turned out, a buffoon. Thankfully, after a couple of articles in the *Washington Post* (co-written by Bob Woodward, Casey's future Boswell) exposing the hapless Hugel's checkered past, Casey quickly jettisoned him and turned the DDO job over to a respected Agency veteran, John McMahon.

At the next level down at the DO, Casey would make his real mark. Late in his term, Carter had cautiously authorized the first, limited covert-action forays into Afghanistan and Central America. Casey signaled almost from the outset of his tenure that Reagan and he, as their first order of business, were going to up the ante. And to do that, Casey looked to his new chiefs of the DO's Near East and Latin America divisions: Charles (Chuck) Cogan and Duane (Dewey) Clarridge, respectively. The two had entered the Agency as young officers a quarter-century before, and they had remained close friends over the years. They could not have been more different in personality, but they shared almost a cult-figure status inside the closed world of the DO. They were the two guys I probably worked closest with during the Casey years, and I came to respect and like both of them immensely.

Of all the Agency operatives I dealt with in the course of my career, Chuck Cogan most looked the part. That is to say, he looked the way people on the outside imagine a CIA spook to look. (In reality, most of them look like insurance salesmen.) *Veil*, Bob Woodward's chronicle of the Casey years, captured Cogan perfectly: He could have been the model for the "Hathaway Man" from those vintage shirt-maker advertisements. A native New Englander with a patrician air, Chuck was tall, ramrod-straight in bearing, impeccably yet conservatively dressed, with slicked-back graying hair and an elegant mustache. And then there was his voice—clipped, soft, almost gentle, yet with an unmistakable (if misleading, once you got to know him) trace of quiet menace. Chuck had spent most of his career in and around the Arab world, where words are chosen carefully and often with seemingly hidden meaning. He had picked up that tendency, which, along with his New England reserve, made him a distinctive, intimidating communicator. I remember once accompanying a senior career Justice Department prosecutor to meet with Chuck about an investigation he was working on against two shady Iranian American businessmen. The DOJ guy, who prided himself on his toughness, came out of the meeting shaken. "That is the scariest guy I have ever met," he muttered. Chuck had been unfailingly polite, but he hadn't uttered more than a few sentences and otherwise stared impassively at the cowed DOJ prosecutor.

Chuck had the Afghanistan account and was also responsible for overseeing covert operations against two blossoming bogeymen in the region: Khomeini in Iran and Qaddafi in Libya. These represented three of Casey's four biggest priorities when he became DCI, and he came to rely on Chuck heavily. I would see them interact frequently, and the chemistry between the two was fascinating. They never seemed to develop a personal closeness—Cogan was too reserved and Casey by nature was not much of a schmoozer—but Chuck was so unflappable, so quietly self-assured, and exuded such a sense of command that Casey could not help being drawn to him.

And then there was Clarridge. Duane was his given first name, but everyone knew him as Dewey. He was the most swashbuckling, colorful character I ever met at the Agency. If the Reagan White House and Casey were determined to mount a full-scale covert assault on the Sandinista regime—and they were—they couldn't have found a CIA guy more suited to it. Never mind that in his previous quarter century in the Agency, Dewey had never served anywhere in the Western Hemisphere, let alone Central America. He didn't know the region, he didn't know Spanish, and I doubt he ever gave Nicaragua a second thought before he got the job of chief of CIA covert operations for all of Latin America. But he was by nature aggressive, imaginative, and largely uninterested in cushy and career-enhancing assignments. And personally, he had a flair that bordered on the flamboyant. An aficionado of flashy clothes (he especially favored white suits accented with a colorful handkerchief cascading out of his breast pocket), fine Cuban cigars, and expensive Italian wines, he was everything his friend Chuck Cogan was not—exuberant, occasionally bombastic, and flowing with joie de vivre.

Dewey and I instantly bonded. In his 1997 memoir, *A Spy for All Seasons*, Dewey gave me my first, albeit brief, mention in the media. "I always liked John Rizzo," he wrote, "perhaps because he is smart, smokes cigars, has a fine sense of humor, and dresses well." Years later, I would get far more coverage in the media than I ever expected, but Dewey's short, tidy description was more accurate—and generous—than any of the coverage I would get elsewhere.

Casey also quickly came to be smitten with the irrepressible Dewey. Frankly, it was and is almost impossible to dislike Dewey—he is an impish, charmingly roguish guy, with no pretense and, most tellingly, no particular interest in whether you like him or not. And despite the public persona that would develop around him in the Iran-contra investigation as an arrogant, Machiavellian schemer—an image, I think, that did not entirely displease him—I had almost daily contact with Dewey from 1981 through 1987 and found him to be honest and candid in all of his dealings with me. For instance, he came to me promptly one day in 1984 when he first came up with the notion of mining the harbors of Nicaragua. Dewey told me that he had conceived the risky and controversial idea (he always seemed to gravitate toward anything risky and controversial) while sitting alone the night before with a glass of gin on the rocks. I was momentarily disconcerted—is that how he comes up with most of his gung-ho epiphanies?—but I never doubted he was telling me the absolute truth.

The Casey-Clarridge bond was strengthened by their common contempt for the CIA's congressional overseers, a lot of it fueled by the skepticism expressed on Capitol Hill about the Reagan administration's true objectives for the stepped-up covert action in Central America. A couple of months into the administration, Casey passed the word down from the seventh floor that I should write a new, broadly worded Finding for Central America to supplant what he viewed as Jimmy Carter's equivocal, feckless authorizations of 1979–1980. So I came up with something short—just a few sentences—and as expansive as I could make it: The CIA would be authorized to provide cash and training to the region. The immediate focus was on El Salvador, where a right-wing but pro-U.S. regime was being challenged by a leftist insurgency armed by the Sandinistas and their Soviet sponsors. Reagan signed the Finding less than a week after I finished it and sent it up to Casey, which was in sharp contrast to my experience in the Carter years, when the language of Findings was fretted over and massaged by the White House seemingly forever. Casey told a few of us that he was there when Reagan signed it, and that the new president did it quickly and with a dramatic flourish: "Victory in El Salvador!" Reagan exulted as he affixed his name to the one-page paper.

Still, while the Finding fell short of authorizing the overthrow of the Sandinista regime, senior House Democrats, notably Speaker Tip O'Neill and the intelligence committee chairman, Edward Boland, were convinced that was the Reagan administration's hidden agenda. And so in 1982 they engineered a law prohibiting any U.S. efforts toward that end. This infuriated Casey and the newly arrived Clarridge—the fact was, they decided early on that the Sandinistas were the true cancer in Central America, and that they had to be stopped. Not dissuaded or discouraged, because the Sandinistas were committed Marxist revolutionaries who would not be deterred. And Congress, in the Casey-Clarridge view, was too obtuse or gutless to recognize that. In meetings inside the Agency, they would feed off each other on this notion and before long it spilled out in barely disguised contempt in their dealings on the Hill.

I accompanied Casey and Clarridge, who usually appeared separately, to numerous closed hearings before the congressional intelligence committees. Whereas Casey gave the unmistakable impression of impatience, Dewey seemed to view his appearances as performances, where he would revel in sticking it to his congressional inquisitors, be it through word or gesture. I remember one session before the Senate committee, when Dewey came armed with a series of large charts mounted on an easel. Wielding a pointer like it was a dueling sword, Dewey stood right up close to the dais within inches of the committee members. Speaking loudly in his native New Hampshire accent, he would suddenly punctuate an assertion by smacking his pointer on one of the charts, then flinging it down and going on to the next one. With each loud "thwack," the senators would instinctively cringe; Bill Cohen of Maine, a Republican, had the misfortune to be sitting closest to the charts, and he visibly jumped at the first "thwack." It was wonderful guerrilla theater, but I wondered about the impression Dewey was leaving with our congressional overseers. "Who cares?" he said, shrugging, when I asked him about it afterward. "It was fun."

On another occasion, Dewey was even less subtle. Daniel Moynihan, the colorful and voluble New York Democrat, once arrived late at a briefing Dewey was giving one afternoon to the Intelligence Committee. Dewey, without a care in the world, casually perched his leg on one of the adjacent witness chairs, causing a red-faced Moynihan to loudly chastise him for his disrespect to the committee. Slowly, very slowly, Dewey brought his leg down. Everyone there was uncomfortable and embarrassed about the awkward scene. Everyone except Dewey. "Moynihan was probably drunk," he simply said in the car on the way back to the CIA.

As the early '80s wore on, my workdays as the DO lawyer were growing increasingly unpredictable and frenetic. Handling the regular stream of questions coming in from officers on the Afghanistan and Central America accounts was more than enough to fill my plate; Chuck Cogan and Dewey Clarridge had passed the word down through their staffs that virtually every proposed operation of any significance had to be run by me first. (Chuck and Dewey, despite their long careers as hardbitten "street" operatives, seemed to recognize from the start that a lawyer needed to be involved in everything they were now doing.) But my assigned responsibilities were broader than that—I was the legal advisor for all CIA covert-action programs worldwide. And Casey was hell-bent on generating new Findings on places I knew about and other places I had barely heard of.

I was beginning to get worn down by the sheer number and pace of the programs. One morning in 1983, I was awakened at 3:00 by an emergency call from the White House Situation Room. A young, military-sounding voice crisply advised me that an emergency planning meeting scheduled for 8:00 that morning had been canceled. I had no idea that any such meeting had even been in the offing. The voice then apologized about calling at that hour, and quickly hung up. About five o'clock, I snapped awake from a fitful sleep, convinced the whole thing had been a bad dream. It hadn't.

It didn't help my workload that by this time I was the only CIA lawyer left in the Agency headquarters building. In 1982, the rest of the Office of General Counsel (about fifty lawyers at that point) was uprooted and dispatched to another Agency-leased building several miles away. The official reason was overcrowding in the headquarters spaces, but there was much speculation in the corridors that Casey had signed off on the move because he wanted to get the lawyers out of his way. I didn't believe that—if true, then why was I, of all people, left untouched? General Counsel Stan Sporkin, a good soldier and ever loyal to his friend and patron Casey, did not raise much of a fuss, so off all the lawyers went, except for me.

Meanwhile, I had more and more opportunities to see Casey up close, and the old man was a wonder to behold. He worked endlessly, tirelessly, firing off short memos in every direction to all parts of the building. His range of contacts was eclectic—his invited guests would include not only corporate titans from his Wall Street days but also such unlikely visitors as Ralph Nader. ("Only in America," Nader said as he was escorted into Casey's office.) The Agency careerists he nurtured and promoted from the inside ranged from legendary, risk-taking operatives such as Clarridge and Clair George (a blunt, wisecracking, but brave overseas veteran whom Casey named to be his congressional liaison, of all things) to more buttoned-down, cautious types such as John McMahon and Bob Gates (a particular Casey favorite, he was then in his thirties, and Casey leapfrogged the precociously self-assured Gates over more senior analysts to the post of deputy director of intelligence in 1982).

As Casey kept ordering up new covert-action Findings, every one of them, from the most portentous to the least seemingly significant, had to be written up right away. His operating style tended to be ad hoc, to put it mildly. The Reagan White House, like every administration I worked in before and since, set up a layer of review entities to discuss and approve proposed Findings on their way up to the president. The most senior layer—a group consisting of the national security advisor, the secretaries of state and defense, the attorney general, the chairman of the Joint Chiefs of Staff—has been called different things over the years; under Reagan, it was called the National Security Planning Group (NSPG). Sometimes Casey would adhere to the process, but sometimes he would blithely ignore it, up to and including the NSPG.

On one occasion in the early '80s, the word came down to me from a Casey aide: The director wants you to write a proposed Finding regarding a country in the Mideast. I was given details about the aims, and he needed it in an hour. So off I sped to NE Division to huddle with Chuck Cogan and his people. I emerged with some hastily crafted language, which I hoped reflected the operational realities yet satisfied Casey's dictates, and hightailed it up to Casey's office, where he was waiting. He looked at it, grumbled something that sounded like assent, stuck it in his briefcase, and got into his private elevator down to the garage, where his car was waiting to take him to the White House. An hour after that, he returned to headquarters with the president's signature on the thing. "Send this to the people who need to see it," said the cryptic note he sent me, as best I remember. Turns out Casey had just marched into the Oval Office and stuck it in front of the president. The entire thing had unfolded between lunch and dinner. I have never seen anything like it, before or since.

Another time, Casey's unique sense of what constituted collegiality with his colleagues presented me with an unusual, and uncomfortable, legal dilemma. By the beginning of 1984, the texts of Presidential Findings were becoming longer. Two or three short paragraphs, the norm in the late Carter and early Reagan administrations, were now morphing into a dozen or so paragraphs that would extend the length of the Finding to two or even three pages. Over time, the Reagan White House began to view Findings not just as operational directives—a laundry list of the sorts of activities the CIA was to undertake—but as presidential policy documents. So more and more, staffers on the National Security Council would stick in sentences as the Finding wound its way through channels up to the president. Second, the scope of the Findings began to expand. Instead of being limited to a particular targeted country or region such as Afghanistan or Central America, some of the Findings were now "worldwide" in scope, meaning that the objective was to counter and combat an international threat, such as terrorism or narcotics trafficking, that transcended national boundaries and continents. Casey, a man who liked the Findings to be terse and unadorned of verbiage, was not happy about this increasing word creep, but mostly he would just grumble about it and go along.

That is, until one day in 1984 when the National Security Council staff forwarded one of the first of those multipage Findings to the Oval Office. If memory serves, the Finding was three pages long. Once President Reagan affixed his requisite signature, it was, per regular procedure, sent back promptly by courier to the CIA for implementation and transmission to the congressional intelligence committees. But when I saw it, I was confronted with a problem I had never encountered before: The president had signed at the bottom of the first page rather than at the end of the text, two pages later. This was not a matter of lawyerly nitpicking—the entire legal rationale for requiring written presidential approval of all Findings is to hold him accountable for *all* the covert-action activities set forth in the text. There had to be a documented record of the presidential imprimatur—no more of those "wink-and-a-nod," "plausible deniability" shenanigans of the sort practiced by presidents from Eisenhower up through Nixon. For its part, the CIA cannot lawfully undertake any covert action that the president has not authorized. In short, with Reagan's signature only at the bottom of the first page, there was no record, no critical documentation, that he had approved the activities set forth on pages two and three.

Somebody had to tell Casey, and right away. My first (cowardly) thought was to buck the odious task up to my boss, Stan Sporkin, who was much closer personally to Casey and thus hopefully better suited to soften the blow. But then I realized Stan was out of town. So with considerable trepidation, I called Casey's secretary and asked for two minutes of his time. I figured it would take me one minute to tell him the problem, so that would leave only one minute for him to yell at me.

In I walked, and there he was slouched behind his desk with the usual stack of papers and books scattered seemingly haphazardly around him. Desperately trying not to let my voice quaver, I blurted out as quickly as I could why, essentially, I had concluded that a document the president of the United States—a man Casey deeply revered—had just signed was not legally worth the paper it was written on.

As was his wont, Casey sat there for a moment, just taking it in, staring back at me through his thick glasses. I started to feel the flop sweat coming on. Then he said, "I'm a lawyer, too, you know." (Where had I heard that before?) I braced myself for the barrage that I knew was coming.

But then Casey did something of the sort that would make him such a fascinating, enigmatic figure to me. He got mad, all right, but not at me. Instead, he vented against the NSC staff, angrily muttering that their sloppiness had let the president down and left the Agency out on a limb. Casey didn't once question my conclusion, let alone the presumption of some pissant staff lawyer like me throwing sand in the wheels of an important covert-action initiative just because of a quibble about where the president had signed his name. Casey just grunted that he would take care of it. Then he went back to reading what he was reading.

I got word later that day that Casey had ordered that no action be taken under the Finding and that the few existing copies at the CIA be destroyed, and that he then went to the White House for what I later heard was a reaming of the NSC staff. A new Finding, with President Reagan's signature duly inscribed on the bottom of the last page, arrived a day or two later. I was told by a friend at the NSC that Casey had insisted on watching Reagan sign it.

By October 1984, I had been the DO lawyer for five years, and at the CIA for nearly nine years. Five very eventful, fascinating years spanning two administrations. But they had been increasingly pressure-packed and frenetic, and I was starting to get worn down by the sheer pace and responsibilities of the job. And five years is too long for anyone to stay in one position at the Agency. You become not only weary, but stale. That's why it's always been CIA policy to have its senior career cadre in the DO and the DI rotate into new jobs every two or three years. Also, if you stay in one assignment too long, inevitably you lose your perspective and become too wedded to the policies and programs that you have developed and overseen. And, of course, above all others, a CIA lawyer over-seeing covert-action operations must maintain that sense of perspective.

No one is irreplaceable at the CIA, least of all a lawyer with less than a decade of Agency experience. And John McMahon, the recently appointed CIA deputy director, recognized that better than anyone else. A CIA veteran of over three decades, McMahon was a burly, convivial, and sometimes profane Irishman who had started his Agency career as a file clerk and steadily rose through the ranks to senior positions in each of the four CIA directorates—Administration, Intelligence, Science and Technology, and Operations. No other Agency officer in my career was as experienced, and as successful, in so many disciplines. He was known and revered inside the CIA as a tough but fair manager. And by mid-'84, he wanted me out of the DO lawyer job.

It was nothing personal. I had first come to know McMahon well when I came to the job five years earlier, when he was the deputy director for operations. He was enormously supportive and patient as I learned the ropes as a DO lawyer, and he was one of my biggest boosters inside the CIA. We always got on extremely well. But what made him such a successful manager was his ability to see beyond his personal friendships with Agency employees—and he had hundreds of such friendships—and make cold-eyed personnel decisions. He had concluded, by mid-'84, that I had been in my job long enough and needed to move on.

I resisted, of course, for as long as I could. But by October 1984, I was reconciled to moving on. I had no interest in taking another position in the Office of General Counsel, particularly when it would have necessitated me leaving headquarters for the OGC's digs several miles away. John Stein, then the Agency's inspector general, came to my rescue. Stein was a career DO officer who rose to the position of DDO after Casey's abortive fling with the hapless Max Hugel, and thus he became not only my most senior client but a trusted friend. Casey had recently moved Stein to the IG job—the IG is basically an internal watchdog and ombudsman—and Stein invited me to join his staff for a year or two as an investigator/inspector until I figured out what I wanted to do next in my legal career. "It'll be good for you," he suggested in his usual casual way. "I'll give you some interesting cases, you'll get to travel some, and there's no heavy lifting." I knew already he was right at least about the last part. In those days, the Office of Inspector General was a small, low-key place with a decidedly studied pace—it was well known inside the building that by 5:00 p.m. each day, the OIG was a ghost town. There seemed to be nothing it did—whether it was an inspection or audit of a CIA component, or an investigation of an employee's personal impropriety—that the OIG management thought couldn't wait until another day.

As I mulled it over, the notion of retreating to a quiet sinecure was more and more appealing. I had gone through a divorce three years earlier, and my ex-wife and I shared custody of our son, Jamie, who was about to turn seven. Which in my case meant having him stay with me two weeks out of every month, no matter what. Maintaining that regular routine with him was paramount to me, but it did get a bit frantic at times—racing out of meetings at the White House to pick him up at the school car pool, scrambling to find someone to watch him or take him to his soccer or Little League game on a Saturday morning when I would be unexpectedly summoned into work, and so on. The poor little guy had spent most of his young life watching his dad breathlessly picking him up or dropping him off somewhere. Moving to a more predictable, sedate schedule meant more time that I could devote to being a father, and that was very big to me.

CHAPTER 4

The Calm Before the Storm (1985)

At the beginning of 1985, I settled into my new surroundings in the OIG, located on the sixth floor of the headquarters building. It would be several years before Congress would designate the inspector general's position as a "statutory," meaning a person nominated by the president and confirmed by the Senate. In practical terms, the change would turn the incumbent, and the rest of the office, into a much larger, more independent—and adversarial—entity vis-à-vis the rest of the CIA. But in 1985, the OIG was still what it had always been up till then—a sedate, relaxed group of about three dozen people either taking a midcareer break from their regular CIA duties or older Agency veterans who had come to the office essentially to wind down their careers. John Stein, the incumbent IG when I arrived, like all his predecessors, had been appointed to the post by the CIA director.

Casey had put Stein into the job several months earlier. Until then, Stein had served in the Directorate of Operations for his entire CIA career, having entered the organization a quarter century earlier following Yale and a stint in the military. He, Dewey Clarridge, and Chuck Cogan had all arrived at the CIA as young men at about the same time, and the three would remain close friends for their entire careers, notwithstanding their widely disparate personalities. Stein was somewhere in between the flamboyant and voluble Clarridge and the measured and reticent Cogan. A large, bearlike man, Stein dressed mostly in tweeds and cardigans that had a rumpled elegance. He had an impish, sometimes mordant sense of humor, fond of tossing off one-liners in meetings large and small, and had one particular habit that I found curious but endearing: He always had a TV in his office that was turned on, with the sound off, either showing episodes of *Sesame Street* or cartoons. Before becoming the IG, he had risen to the top of the DO, holding the iconic position of deputy director of operations (DDO, the top career spy in the CIA).

He was, in short, an immensely likable, accomplished man. However, Casey's decision to move him to the IG job was abrupt and took everyone by surprise, including Stein. In effect, he was pushed aside to make room for his onetime deputy, the equally accomplished but far more irascible Clair George. The word inside the DO was that Casey had decided that Stein was too laid back (for example, Stein had largely stayed out of the burgeoning covert-action program in Central America, leaving Clarridge alone to work directly with Casey), too nice a guy to be Casey's DDO.

Stein accepted his fate with his usual equanimity, but he was also a realist. When he recruited me to join the OIG, he told me he would probably retire in a year or so, and that in the meantime we could both relax and do some fun and interesting work.

The OIG is made up of three divisions: Audits, Inspections, and Investigations. On the inspections side, the work involved being part of four- or five-person teams, reviewing whether a particular CIA unit was operating in an effective, efficient manner in compliance with the law and Agency regulations. Each inspection would take several months, usually included a number of trips overseas, and culminated in a detailed report containing a list of conclusions and recommendations. I took part in two such inspections while in the OIG. Stein was right: They were interesting, and far from taxing.

Stein handpicked me to work alone (which pleased me, because it was my preferred way of operating) and look into possible malfeasance by a couple of overseas chiefs of station (COS). A COS is the chief U.S. intelligence official in a foreign country, a position of considerable responsibility and sensitivity, since each COS operates undercover, overseeing all sorts of clandestine activities. A COS must exhibit tact and discretion and be above personal reproach. In both cases I was asked to look into were allegations that the COS was lacking in these areas. Each man adamantly denied the allegations.

The first case involved the COS in a middle-sized station in a Western European country. Such an assignment in a nominally friendly environment, working in cooperation with an allied foreign intelligence service, is usually relatively placid. But not this time. The COS had managed to totally alienate his foreign counterparts, in part because of a botched intelligence operation conducted without the knowledge of the host government. As a result, the COS suffered the ultimate sanction from the host government—he was PNGed (declared "persona non grata") and ejected from the country. Back in the United States, the COS was bitter and came to the OIG, claiming he had been wronged. However, his ire was not directed against the foreign government. Instead, he blamed Dewey Clarridge.

Yes, there was Dewey again. Several months before, Clarridge had been moved from his position as chief of the Latin America Division to take over DO's Europe Division and thus was now the COS's superior in the chain of demand. Casey had made the change because he had come grudgingly to the realization that Clarridge had become a lightning rod for Congress's growing opposition to the expanding covert war in Central America. It was a role that Dewey rather enjoyed, but he understood the realities and accepted the move to the Europe Division—basically, a lateral assignment—without complaint.

According to the COS, Clarridge had begun to undermine his authority as soon as Clarridge took over the division and had done nothing to defend him when he came under attack from his foreign counterparts, who the COS claimed were almost impossible to deal with in the first place (in this latter regard, the COS had a point—despite this being a putatively friendly Western European government, the COS's two predecessors encountered rocky if not outright hostile relations in dealing with the government). Clarridge, he basically claimed, had a vendetta against him because he wasn't one of "Dewey's boys."

I went to get Clarridge's side of the story, and in the process saw another aspect to his complex, fascinating personality. I fully expected Clarridge to trash the COS for attacking his motives and actions. But he didn't. He not only denied any personal animus toward the COS, he expressed what I considered genuine regret about the COS's expulsion and praised him as a hardworking, dedicated officer. It wasn't personal, Clarridge said, it was strictly business—he realized that the people the COS had to deal with were a pain in the ass, but the fact was that if you are a COS in a country and the country wants you out, you have to leave.

Your continued effectiveness, your continued viability, is irredeemably undermined. Simple as that.

I then interviewed about a dozen Agency officers and found no substance for the COS's charges against Clarridge. In fact, the COS's former subordinates in the station talked about his abrasive personality and management style and said it served to make his relations with his admittedly difficult foreign counterparts even worse.

Case closed. And after I interviewed Clarridge, he never asked me about it again.

The second case was trickier. The COS in question was serving in a small country, and it was his first time heading up a station, which is a critical test for any up-and-coming, ambitious DO officer. He was in his late thirties and had done well in his previous assignments, most of which were at headquarters. He was also a racial minority, and racial minorities were then in woefully short supply in the DO management ranks. Everyone wanted him to succeed in his new posting.

After about a year, however, some reports began to trickle in from his subordinates. There were questionable accountings for meals and travel he had incurred ostensibly for official purposes. The expenses claimed were massive—far more, on their face, than would be expected for a station that small. What's more, a large portion of the expenses was spent on local women, some of whom were well known in the community. In and of itself, not necessarily verboten—case officers in a foreign country are supposed to "develop" for possible recruitment local citizens who may be valuable sources of intelligence. But the initial reports vaguely intimated that the meetings were not about business, but rather romance. The COS was a married man, and he was on an "unaccompanied" tour, meaning his wife had stayed behind in the States. Again, not an unusual occurrence in the DO, especially when the COS is serving in a remote area.

I first plowed into the COS's accountings. It indeed showed a number of trips out of country and lots of meals in-country with a slew of people, mostly the same lineup of local women. There should have been accompanying reports, recounting what the expenses were for, the potential intelligence value of the women, how the "development" was progressing. I found little of anything in the records on that score. I tracked down the COS's subordinates, not just the ones who had flagged possible improprieties, but others who hadn't said anything up to then and were now scattered around the world. It was awkward for all of them. But the reaction was unanimous: the COS had been financing his love life with foreign women—about whom the CIA knew nothing—with Agency funds, and had been rather brazen about it.

For his part, the COS denied everything, but the evidence was overwhelming. With absolutely no enthusiasm, I dutifully wrote up the report and sent it forward to his management. He was reprimanded and demoted, effectively derailing his once-promising career. He resigned shortly thereafter.

My time in the OIG was not without its surreal moments.

On one occasion, I was transferring through a major European capital on my way to another destination and, as my usual custom, I had alerted the station in advance that I would be in town and would be happy to make a courtesy call. The COS sent word that he would welcome my coming by the office.

I expected a brief visit, a little gossip about what was going on at headquarters. When I arrived, we did all that, but then the COS asked me if I would be willing to do him an unofficial favor, totally informal and off the record. The station had been meeting with a well-placed foreigner—it wasn't a local, but a third-country national—whom it was "developing" for recruitment as a source. Among the enticements being offered was eventual resettlement in the United States, and the guy was apparently asking questions about his legal status here, how he could safely and legally acquire a driver's license and professional credentials, what his new name would be, things like that. The COS asked if I would be willing to meet with the target in a quiet, out-of-the-way spot in the city to answer some of his questions. It was an irregular thing to ask me to do—I was no longer working as a CIA lawyer and was certainly not a trained DO officer—but it just sounded too intriguing, so I said okay.

The meeting was held in a small, somewhat seedy bar on a backstreet in a part of the city I didn't even know existed. I will not describe the guy I was meeting, other than to say he was furtive and understandably nervous, his eyes constantly darting around the near-empty bar. And then, seemingly out of nowhere, a couple walked in and sat at a table a few feet away. They were Americans, and they looked to be about my age. I was taken aback, but tried my best to ignore them, and, more important, to get the target to ignore them.

That amateurish facade of indifference to their presence crumbled into a heap a couple of minutes later when the guy suddenly called out to me. "John Rizzo? Hey, is that you? I can't believe it!" Neither could I. Who was this character? I desperately wondered as he ambled over and stuck his hand out.

"So, what are you doing here?" he asked jovially. I was momentarily frozen. I couldn't bear to look at my target sitting next to me, but I could sense the panic-stricken vibe emanating from him.

And then it hit me. The boisterous American was a guy I had gone to college with at Brown, where the class population was small enough that everyone pretty much knew everyone else by sight. This guy and I had attended a few classes together and had a nodding acquaintance, but that was it. I hadn't seen him since my graduation fifteen years before. Of all the gin joints in all the world, he had to walk into this one.

He waved his female companion over and introduced her as his wife. I jumped up from my chair, not out of politeness but to try to forestall them from plopping down at the table. I rattled off something about being amazed (true) and delighted (untrue) to see him after so long and in such unlikely surroundings, all the while stealing glances at my target to see if he was about to bolt. The target, however, seemed paralyzed, simply staring down at his drink.

"Yup," he responded, "we wanted to find some place without all the usual tourists, and there you were sitting there." He glanced at my catatonic tablemate with obvious curiosity and then asked, "Are you here on business?"

"Uh, yes."

"So, remind me what you're doing now." Mercifully, few of my college friends knew I was at the Agency, and this guy was most certainly not one of them.

"I'm a lawyer."

"Great. Where?"

"D.C.," I responded, doing my best not to stammer. I figured that if I made up a phony hometown, my luck would be such that it would have been where this guy was living.

"You with the government?"

Jeez, I thought.

"Private practice. Solo practitioner. Real estate law." Thankfully, this had the intended effect—I had made my job sound so boring the guy stopped peppering me with questions. And I wasn't about to start asking him about his life after Brown.

I seized the awkward pause that followed to blurt out something like, "My friend and I"—gesturing at the target, who was still staring into his glass—"are late for an appointment across the city," or some such lame story. I then hustled him out of the bar.

"I am so, so sorry," I finally told him when we were safely a couple of blocks away. The target just stared balefully at me, gave me a perfunctory handshake, and disappeared into the gathering evening crowds.

I learned much later that the target rejected the Agency's "pitch" the following week. I never wanted to know why. And I have never seen that old classmate again.

A few months after that fiasco, I had IG business that took me on several stops to stations in central and southern Africa. I had never been there before, so I was looking forward to what I hoped would be a memorable experience. It was that, and then some.

At one of the stops, the COS booked me into a hotel right on the shores of a tranquil lake. The hotel was a sprawling, stately, white-columned structure, in the middle of nowhere, that dated back to the colonial era, with exotic tropical plants and fauna all around and staffed by what seemed like dozens of white-liveried locals constantly scurrying about on the polished stone floors in the vast lobby. The whole scene was just spectacular and unreal, especially since, from what I could tell, I was the only guest there.

I had checked in at midafternoon, and I had a few hours to kill before meeting the COS for dinner. With the hotel literally carved out of a jungle, the only place to safely walk was on the small white sand beach behind the hotel. At that hour, the lake looked ethereal—still deep-blue water as far as I could see. I stuck my hand in, and the water was bathtub-warm. Looking around, totally alone, I suddenly thought: Here I am, by myself in this mysterious, magical setting thousands of miles from home, someplace I will never come to again. By God, I impulsively concluded, I am going to take a swim.

So I went back to my room, changed into some Bermuda shorts, returned to the beach, and waded in. There was still no one around anywhere, not in the lobby and not on the beach. I had to walk out about thirty yards before the water was chest-deep, and then I began a leisurely backstroke, gazing up at the cloudless sky, still not quite believing I was where I was.

My reverie was soon interrupted, however, by the distant sound of an excited voice coming from the beach. I flipped over and saw a couple of the white-liveried hotel attendants running down to the water's edge, waving frantically in my direction. My first thought, as I swam back toward them, was that I had gotten some sort of phone call, probably from the COS.

That wasn't it.

Instead, one of the white-liveried guys hauled me out of the water a few yards from shore, simultaneously pointing back behind me and excitedly yammering something I couldn't quite understand. I looked back at the lake, and in the general area in the distance where I had been floating I saw several indistinct bumps on the lake's tranquil surface. I then understood one of the words the guy was saying: *hippopotamus.*

Evidently, I had blundered into the part of the lake, and at the time of day, when the hippos go cruising for dinner. Hippos, who knew? Anyway, a worried-looking hotel manager, who had arrived by then, assured me that hippos do not attack humans. Unless, of course, it is some idiot who is screwing up their feeding areas. Suddenly very wobbly, I returned to my room and sprawled on the bed, but not before ordering the stiffest drink the hotel bar had to offer. I lay there, wondering how the poor COS would have crafted a cable to headquarters trying to account for how his OIG visitor had been gnawed to death by hippos; wondering how my obituary would have read, and what my parents and sisters would have thought, how they would explain it to my eight-year-old.

It would have been a hell of an obituary, though. Doubtless, it would have generated a lot of lawyer jokes.

I had seen a few interesting things in the OIG, but as I approached the one-year mark in late 1985 I decided it was time to move on. I missed being a lawyer. Even more, I missed being in the mainstream of the Agency's day-to-day mission. I was in my late thirties, about to mark a decade at the CIA. Much as I enjoyed the freedom and independence of operating on my own, I realized that the logical next step in my career progression was to assume some sort of supervisory management position. The problem lay in figuring out where to go.

The OGC's main office, where all the management positions were, was still located in a building miles from headquarters. Residing there had absolutely no appeal, and neither did any of the available positions. There was one job at headquarters, however, that did fill the bill. The number two position in the Office of Congressional Affairs (OCA) was historically held by someone with a law background, in most instances a refugee from the OGC. And the good luck I had enjoyed since entering the Agency continued to hold: The job came vacant at the end of 1985. The ever-loyal and supportive Stan Sporkin endorsed me, as did Deputy Director John McMahon. Director Casey, who I was told was oblivious to the fact that I had moved to the OIG the year before (so much for my indispensability as the DO lawyer), signed off on the appointment, and I started my new job in November 1985.

The OCA director, Dave Gries, was also newly appointed. A longtime CIA veteran whose area of expertise was in Far East affairs, Gries had previously held senior positions in both the DO and DI. Trim, and with thick curly hair and tortoiseshell glasses, he had a professorial look and manner. He could be intense at times, but he was very smart and hardworking, with a dry sense of humor. Dave was a good fit for me. So was the OCA—I had always followed Washington politics, and I was already familiar with many of the personalities on the congressional intelligence committees because of my previous job as the DO lawyer. Moreover, it gave me my first shot at managing others—the OCA had a staff of about two dozen, including a small group of OGC lawyers detailed to the office.

During my year in the OIG, I had been pretty much divorced from the major developments and programs involving the Agency, so in my first couple of weeks in the OCA I tried to catch up. The septuagenarian Casey, now entering his fifth year at the helm, was still operating at his breakneck pace. But he was beginning to show signs of wear—he never was a picture of physical health, but the first time I saw him after my year away, he looked to have aged considerably. And no wonder. His two pet covert-action projects—Afghanistan and Central America—were going in different directions, Afghanistan extraordinarily well and Central

America increasingly badly. The former program had huge, bipartisan congressional support, while the latter was drawing increasing fire from prominent Democrats such as Speaker Tip O'Neill, which had culminated in the passage of a law at the end of 1984 essentially barring any U.S. funding of the Nicaraguan contras.

Meanwhile, there was a new, alarming threat growing exponentially. It had begun in 1983, with the bombing of the U.S. marine barracks and the U.S. embassy in Lebanon. Now American civilians abroad were becoming terrorist targets: commercial airline hijackings, commando-style attacks inside airports in Rome and elsewhere, kidnapping of U.S. citizens living and working in the Mideast.

Although I didn't realize it at the time, the seeds of what would become the Iran-contra affair were already being sown.

CHAPTER 5

The Wheels Come Off
(1986)

During my yearlong sabbatical in the OIG, I was basically cut off from the CIA's day-to-day activities. But it was impossible to avoid the media coverage of two of the Agency's central operational priorities: terrorism and the conflict in Central America. What I didn't realize was how the two were connected.

The early '80s saw the rise of an especially violent Middle Eastern terrorist organization named Hezbollah, led by a particularly bloodthirsty thug called Imad Mughniyah. The new Khomeini regime in Iran bankrolled Hezbollah and sheltered Mughniyah, and Americans in Lebanon were promptly put in the crosshairs. In 1983, Hezbollah carried out spectacular mass-casualty bombings at the two most important U.S. government facilities in Lebanon: the U.S. embassy in Beirut, where 63 people died (including 7 employees of the CIA) and U.S. military barracks at Beirut International Airport, killing 241 marines. Hezbollah then switched tactics, targeting individual U.S. citizens living in the country.

By the time I arrived in the OCA at the end of 1985, kidnappings of Americans were becoming depressingly routine, with the grainy hostage videotapes played and relentlessly replayed on the TV networks. I had gotten a first bitter taste of the growing terrorist threat in the final months of my tenure as the DO lawyer in 1984. A gentle, quirky Boston-bred Irishman named William Buckley had been snatched off the streets and disappeared one morning on his way to work in downtown Beirut. He was the local CIA station chief, whom many at the CIA, including Casey and me, knew as a colleague and a friend. And, unlike most of the other Americans—businessmen, clergymen, and journalists—who would be captured in the months ahead, Buckley was tortured for months before finally dying at the hands of his captors, Hezbollah. He was the first CIA employee I knew well who was murdered in the line of duty.

I had first met Bill Buckley in 1980 when he was heading up the counterterrorism "group" at CIA Headquarters, which in those days numbered only a handful of people. Soon after we met, when I was still learning the ropes in the DO, I asked him what his counterterrorist duties entailed. "Pretty simple," he replied. "I travel around the world giving briefings, and I write up reports, basically blaming Qaddafi for everything, including the weather." In his own low-key, undemonstrative way, he was a wonderful fellow. When I was selected to join the Agency's top executive ranks in 1981—called the Senior Intelligence Service—Bill was the first guy to call and congratulate me. Equally surprising and endearing to me, I came to learn that this quiet, nondescript bachelor was actually quite a ladies' man.

When Buckley disappeared, Casey ordered that all the stops be pulled out to locate him—wiretaps, bribes, satellite surveillance. I gave immediate legal approval for everything Casey wanted. All to no avail. At one point, the CIA got a briefing on the details of his torture. I listened, as did Casey and a few other top CIA officials. It was an indescribably chilling and heartbreaking experience. The memory of it and of Bill Buckley would stay with me for the remaining quarter century of my career.

I was told that, during the time I was at the OIG, Casey was almost obsessively focused on the hostage issue and would frequently hark back to the Buckley case in internal Agency meetings. The word around the senior management ranks at Langley was that President Reagan, not the most inquisitive type when he was getting intelligence briefings, would consistently press in NSC meetings for the latest information on what was being done to locate the hostages.

In early 1986, shortly after I arrived at the OCA, Casey created a large new component to deal with the escalating terror threat. It was called the Counterterrorist Center (CTC), and it was designed to put everything the CIA was doing in the area—both in operations and analysis—under one roof. Casey picked Dewey Clarridge to head the CTC. He was to report directly to Casey.

It soon became apparent to me that helping manage William Casey's relationship with Congress was going to be a thankless task. By the beginning of 1986, the relationship was poisonous, a state of affairs largely attributable to the CIA's covert war in Central America. Things had begun to go downhill in 1984, during my last year as DO lawyer, when Congress barred the Agency from expending any funds whatsoever to support, directly or indirectly, the contras. Casey had taken the action as a personal repudiation, and it seemed intended as such, at least in part.

Congress's action was in reaction to a rancorous dispute Casey had with the Senate Intelligence Committee chairman, Barry Goldwater, over whether Congress was given adequate notice of Clarridge's efforts to mine the ports of Nicaragua. Goldwater was an influential senior Republican who supported the war, but he and Casey were both stubborn and crusty enough to get into an ugly public dispute.

In the year I had been gone, Casey and Goldwater had slowly repaired their relationship. The two curmudgeons had, deep down, an abiding affection and respect for each other. In fact, in the summer of 1986, Casey insisted on holding a large ceremony in the CIA employee cafeteria to personally award Goldwater the Agency Seal Medallion, the highest honor the CIA bestows on a nonemployee. My boss, Dave Gries, was away on vacation, so I got to be the emcee at the ceremony. Goldwater by that time was in declining health and walked with a cane, so I met him at the front entrance and escorted him—slowly—to the large, packed cafeteria. As we inched along, I nervously tried to make small talk with this venerable, storied figure. "The director is so pleased and honored you could come here today," I told him deferentially. Goldwater abruptly stopped and glared at me through his trademark horn-rimmed glasses. "Why the hell wouldn't I come?" he barked. "I love the old bastard!"

But as 1986 unfolded, Casey's contempt for Capitol Hill only grew. There had been a string of media leaks describing various CIA secret operations against terrorist organizations, and Casey placed the blame squarely on Congress. Inevitably, the word got back to the committees, exacerbating the rancor on both sides.

Despite everything, Casey was savvy and self-aware enough to recognize that he had to try to make some effort to fix his terrible relations with the Hill. A few months after my arrival in the OCA, he asked me to start inviting individual key members of the intelligence committees to Langley for breakfast or lunch with him in his private dining room. The initiative proved to be of limited value, to say the least—in most of the sessions, Casey would mumble incomprehensibly with his mouth full and, after a few minutes, would start to squirm around in his chair, making absolutely no effort to hide his impatience and boredom.

I vividly recall the day when Senator Bill Bradley, New Jersey Democrat and basketball legend, came to lunch. Bradley certainly was no friend of the Reagan administration, yet Casey and others of us at the CIA respected him greatly. He was a conscientious member of the Intelligence Committee, attending all of the hearings (virtually all of them "closed," meaning there was no opportunity to play to the cameras). He could be a withering, acerbic questioner, but he always did his homework—which, frankly, was not the norm for most of his colleagues.

However, even with Bradley, who shared his disdain for fluffy chitchat, Casey couldn't contain his fidgeting and ennui for very long. As I escorted Bradley down Casey's private elevator after the session mercifully ended, the towering senator glanced down at me and wryly observed, "You know, I think I could actually like the guy if I could understand a word he was saying and he didn't act like he was late for a plane."

Serving as the conduit between Casey and Congress was a challenge, to put it mildly. But I was happy. I felt like I was back in the loop.

Meanwhile, the controversy over Nicaragua had continued to swirl, even after Congress cut off funding in late 1984. While I was still at the OIG, I had begun reading in the press about White House efforts to encourage private fund-raising efforts to support the contras, said to be led by an obscure and shadowy NSC staffer named Oliver North.

Ah, yes, I thought. I remember Ollie North.

I had first met him in the early '80s through Dewey Clarridge as the covert-action program in Central America was picking up steam. At that point, the NSC staff had no in-house lawyer to speak of, so Dewey took me to many of his meetings with North, who was his point of contact at the White House. "He's not your normal NSC bureaucrat," Dewey told me before our first meeting. Dewey meant that as high praise.

He was right. I had never seen or dealt with anyone quite like Ollie North. Not at the White House, and not at the Agency, for that matter. He would subsequently become hugely famous, but in 1982 very few people at the CIA, let alone anyone else, knew anything about him. He made a startling and vivid impression on me. Ramrod-straight in bearing (he was always in civilian clothes in those days (although Dewey told me he was on loan from the marines), he immediately set out to charm, flatter, and above all influence me in a way that I had never been "worked" before, not even from any of the hardened and cynical DO operatives who were then my clients.

At the same time, for all his blather, there was much to admire about Ollie. He was very smart and always willing to listen. His energy level was nothing short of phenomenal; he seemed to be churning out memos or talking on the phone constantly, mostly with Dewey at first, but then with me and, I came to learn, with many other people inside and outside the intelligence community. He seemed to be everywhere, under the radar.

There was another striking thing about being around Ollie North in those days. Every time I went to his cramped office at the Old Executive Office Building, and it could be early in the morning, late at night, or on a weekend, a ubiquitous, hovering presence was his stunningly attractive assistant, a woman named Fawn Hall. Like Ollie, she was destined for fame (or infamy) in later years, but in those days she was anonymous— all I knew at the time was that she was efficient, cheerful, and gorgeous, with her flowing Farrah Fawcett–like mane and long, model-worthy legs. I confess that her evident devotion to Ollie caused me to wonder at first if there was something more than business going on between them. My curiosity (and possibly envy) finally got the best of me, so I asked Dewey about it one night when we were driving back to the CIA from Ollie's office. He was typically direct and unvarnished in his response: "Believe it or not, no. Never. Neither of them is that type."

Dewey had left the Latin America Division at the end of 1984, and Ollie's principal interlocutor at the Agency then became Alan Fiers, chief of operations for Central America. While I was away, OGC had decided—sensibly, given the controversies, the congressional prohibitions, and the increasing complexity of the Agency's actions in the region—to put a couple of very capable lawyers to work directly with Fiers and his staff. So when I arrived in OCA, I trusted that Ollie North's activities notwithstanding, the CIA was playing inside the legal lines. Besides, I soon realized that Alan, unlike Dewey, didn't especially like or trust Ollie very much. It wasn't all that surprising: Both men were in their early forties, ambitious, with the same driven, intense personality.

I actually found that rather comforting—Ollie wasn't about to roll Alan on anything dicey.

What I didn't realize was that Ollie was now a full-fledged protégé, and surrogate, of Casey's. In fall 1986, less than a year after I joined the OCA, there were lots of things I didn't know.

On October 5, the Sandinistas shot down an American C-123 cargo plane carrying weapons from El Salvador to the contras. The only survivor in the crash was an American named Eugene Hasenfus, and the Sandinistas promptly displayed Hasenfus, bedraggled and scared, in a chaotic press conference, where he made vague statements about working for the CIA. And so the scramble inside the CIA was on: Who was this Hasenfus guy (a records search turned up nothing), and why was he on that plane? Was anyone in the field aware of any of this? And what was North up to, anyway? At least those were the questions people like me, people who weren't in the know, were asking. Congress was also demanding answers. The CIA inspector general launched an investigation. Soon enough, the IG started discovering North's name in the CIA's Central America cable traffic dating back to 1984–1985. At that time, the Agency was barred by Congress from assisting the contras, but there was North, over at the NSC, apparently in contact with CIA people in Langley and in the field, pulling strings. How long the strings were, and where they would lead, were not yet clear.

Barely a month later, there was another bolt out of the blue. A small weekly magazine in Lebanon, known to be well wired into the Khomeini regime, published what seemed to be an unbelievable story: The United States had for some time been secretly supplying arms to the Khomeini regime in Iran as part of some sort of Faustian bargain to secure release of the U.S. hostages being held in Lebanon. After initially stonewalling, the White House came clean—sort of. President Reagan went on television acknowledging the arms sales but strongly denying they had anything to do with the hostages. And the ensuing uproar intensified when the congressional leadership was called to the White House and informed that the whole thing had been authorized by Presidential Findings. Though drafting them had been my bread and butter from late 1979 through 1984, I knew nothing about the existence of these Findings. They had been drafted, under the supervision of my former boss, Stan Sporkin, by lawyers in the OGC, miles away from headquarters, who had never before been involved in the Finding process.

The Wheels Come Off (1986)

I first saw them the day after the president's TV appearance. Casey had kept the OCA out of the loop about the existence of the Findings, but now they were provided to me for transmission to the Hill. As soon as I read them, my heart sank. In the first place, they contained language, approved by the president, linking the arms sales to Iran to the release of the U.S. hostages. This starkly contradicted the avowed policies of not only Reagan but also presidents going back to the dawn of the terrorism era: no ransom or bargaining for the release of hostages. They also gave the lie, in black and white, to what the president had just told the American people.

Second, the first of the two Findings—signed by Reagan on December 5, 1985—seemed intended to secure presidential approval for activities the CIA had already undertaken. Specifically, it had the following sentence: "All prior actions taken by U.S Government officials in furtherance of this effort are hereby ratified." The notion of the president giving retroactive approval for covert action flew in the face of the law, not to mention all precedents the Agency had followed since Congress established the Finding process in the mid-'70s. I had drafted dozens of Findings in my time, and it was inconceivable to me that a retroactive Presidential Finding could be considered legally valid. Notwithstanding my enormous admiration for Stan Sporkin, I thought he made a huge mistake here.

But that wasn't the most politically explosive element of the Findings. Each contained a sentence I had also never seen before: "I direct the Director of Central Intelligence not to brief the Congress of the United States . . . until such time as I may direct otherwise." In every other Finding I was aware of during my career—before or after this time—Congress was notified of the Finding within forty-eight hours after the president approved it. In the overwhelming number of cases, it was the full membership of the intelligence committees. In a few cases, for extraordinarily sensitive Findings, it was the so-called Gang of 8—the bipartisan leadership of the House and Senate.

Does the president have the legal authority to delay congressional notification of a Finding when he concludes that national security considerations require it? Absolutely. Every president since Ford has gone on record in support of that proposition, and Congress has basically—if grudgingly—accepted it.

But can a president withhold notification forever? On that, constitutional scholars have long disagreed. In the real world of intelligence, however, I can tell you it never has been seriously contemplated in an actual case. True, the Findings in question didn't rule out congressional notification forever, but it did leave the delay open-ended. And Congress found out about the Findings, a year after the president signed them, in the worst possible way: after the program was basically blown in a magazine—a tiny foreign magazine, to boot. If that hadn't happened, when would the Reagan administration have told Congress? Ever?

If there is one lesson I ruefully learned in my decades of dealing with Congress, it's that nothing pisses the members off more than learning about a CIA covert operation for the first time by reading about it in the media. Suddenly, as the number two guy in charge of CIA congressional relations, I was plunged into a maelstrom of Capitol Hill fury. The intelligence committees both immediately launched investigations, demanding Agency witnesses, beginning with Casey, whom they despised and distrusted as much as he despised and distrusted them.

By this time, in mid-November 1986, I didn't think things could get any worse. Less than two weeks later, they did.

On the long Thanksgiving weekend, I was visiting my parents in Massachusetts, a custom I followed on most major holidays. This time it was an especially welcome respite from my work at the Agency. I had spent the previous couple of frantic weeks helping to organize the Agency's response to the furious congressional reaction to the revelations about the arms sales. I had found there was so much that most of us in the Agency didn't know, and those who did seemed to know only pieces of the story. Casey, of course, was at the center of the storm, and he already had faced a series of grillings at hearings held by the two intelligence committees. At a number of confused and chaotic preparatory sessions held in his office and conference room, Casey appeared increasingly unfocused and exhausted, looking even older than his seventy-three years. We kept trying to put together a comprehensive "timeline" on who knew what when in the CIA about the arms sales and also about the separate (or so I still thought) controversy over Ollie North's efforts to aid the contras that had been set off by the downing of the C-123 carrying

Hasenfus. And we had to keep changing the chronology as pieces of new facts emerged from the bowels of the building.

On November 25, I learned about the most astonishing new fact of all, and I learned about it by watching TV. First, standing at the podium in a raucous White House pressroom, an atypically flustered Ronald Reagan was announcing the resignations of Ollie North and his boss, National Security Advisor John Poindexter. He then hastily departed, leaving the podium to the attorney general of the United States, Ed Meese. Meese blandly announced to the country that his investigators had just discovered a document in North's files indicating that proceeds from the arms sales to Iran had been diverted to support the contras. There had been no reference to this in the arms-sales Findings. Worse, the diversion of the proceeds seemed to be a blatant violation of the existing congressional prohibition on any U.S. funding, "direct or indirect," to support the contras. The raucous pressroom turned into total pandemonium.

Right at that moment, my parents' phone rang. It was the CIA Operations Center, with a message from my boss, Dave Gries. The message was terse: You need to get back here. Now.

When I returned to the office the next morning, Dave looked understandably shaken. "Look," he said, "this thing now could be a criminal case. The Hill is talking about creating a special committee and hiring a slew of lawyers to investigate it." I knew what was coming. "I want you to take over the lead in dealing with Congress on it." Dave said he had to recuse himself from the case. "Some of the Agency people who could be implicated in this are my friends," he explained.

Some of them were my friends, too, I thought to myself. No matter. "It's all yours," he told me with finality.

I was not yet forty years old.

In the late morning of Monday, December 15, I sat alone in the reception area in the CIA director's office suite. It was (and is) a surprisingly modest space as far as offices of Executive Branch bigwigs go, with only a few chairs and a small couch facing a door opening directly into the director's private office. I was waiting to brief Casey on yet another upcoming appearance he would be making before the Senate Intelligence Committee on what the media was now calling the Iran-contra scandal.

Suddenly, the door from the seventh-floor hallway burst open, and in rushed the doctor in charge of the Agency's office of medical services, trailed by a couple of the director's security guards. They barreled directly past me and into the director's private office, slamming the door behind them. A few seconds later, the hallway door burst open again, bringing a couple of Agency nurses hauling a stretcher on wheels. They, too, disappeared into the director's office.

What the hell was happening? I was frozen in my chair, bewildered. Should I get out of there and do something, or should I stay there and do something?

No more than a minute after that, the door to Casey's office opened again and out came the stretcher, with Casey strapped on it, dressed in his familiar, expensive rumpled suit but without his trademark thick eyeglasses. I stole a furtive glance at his face as he was wheeled past me and out the door into the hallway. It was sheet-white and absolutely still.

Suddenly, oddly, I flashed back to the last time I saw my grandmother. I was about thirteen, and she was lying in her open casket. Casey had the same look. He looked dead. I sat there in the reception area, which was quiet and empty again, for about fifteen minutes, not sure where else to go.

But Casey wasn't dead, at least not then. He was rushed to Georgetown University Hospital, a few miles away from CIA Headquarters, where he was diagnosed as having suffered a seizure caused by a fast-growing brain tumor. He suffered another seizure at the hospital, underwent surgery to remove the tumor, and was subjected to radiation treatments. At first, his doctors issued optimistic statements about his recovery and return to work. No one back at the Agency ever really believed that, though, and six weeks later Casey signed a letter of resignation to the president from his hospital bed. It was said that his wife actually signed it for him.

The intelligence committees plowed forward with their investigations through the Christmas holidays. (This time I made sure to stay in town.) But it was clear that there was no way they could get the entire complex story together anytime soon, not without the testimony of Casey (who was incapacitated in the hospital) and North (who was lawyered up and not talking to anybody). But they were under pressure to produce something, so they hauled in some subordinate officials—for the Agency, it was George, Clarridge, and Fiers, among others. I attended as many of these sessions as I could, but some were happening simultaneously in the House and Senate. It was all very chaotic. Today it is largely a blur to me—just hustling our people in and out of committee rooms, trying to avoid the klieg lights and the hordes of reporters. Meanwhile, squadrons of committee staffers were furiously foraging through CIA operational files, and I had trouble keeping up with what they were looking at.

I spent the last fourteen hours of 1986 in an appropriately unexpected and pressure-filled setting. The Senate Intelligence Committee, which had vowed to complete its investigative report by year's end, had thrown together a document of about one hundred pages and sent word to the administration late on December 30 that it wanted it reviewed for declassification and that we had until the end of the year to do it. Which was about twenty-four hours away. And the committee refused to let the document out of its possession—it would have to be reviewed on the Senate premises. Finally, only ten representatives from the Executive Branch would be allowed access to it. It was a draconian set of ground rules, but the administration was not in any position to negotiate terms.

So the White House hastily assembled a team of representatives from its counsel's office, State, the DOD, the Justice Department, and the CIA. We had two slots, and I concluded, regretfully, that I should take one of them. For the other slot, I picked a very smart, very poised, but very junior DO classification-review specialist named Ken Johnson. Ken (who passed away several years later, far too young) proved to be a godsend. No higher in rank than a file clerk at the time, he bore the entire weight and responsibility for the DO in determining which of its secrets could be made public. Unlike much of his chain of command (who had basically "gone to the mattresses" by this point), Ken was unafraid to make the calls he was thrust into making on the spot. Half-jokingly, he told me he expected me to cover his ass. From my standpoint, I was not certain I could cover my own, much less his. I was already beginning to ponder the worst-case scenarios: Either I would miss some nugget of highly classified information contained in the draft report and let it become public to the detriment of national security, or I would insist on taking some critical, relevant nugget of such information out of the report and expose myself to charges of obstructing a congressional investigation. Either way, I would be screwed.

On the morning of New Year's Eve, Ken, I, and our not-so-merry band of brothers entered the sealed and guarded committee room at the Hart Senate Office Building, with the committee staff carefully handing out numbered copies of the report. On one central point the marching orders we had gotten from the White House and the committee were the same: Take as little out of the text (*redact* is the term of art) as absolutely necessary. Wisely, the Reagan administration's damage-control strategy was premised on two words: *full disclosure*. In retrospect, it appears likely the team around the president realized from the start that, whatever else he knew about the arms sales to Iran, there would be no proof that he knew about the proceeds being diverted to the contras (which, after all, was not mentioned in any of the Findings he had signed). And that was the biggest question of all. On everything else related to Iran-contra, the administration would be content to open the Executive Branch up wide and let people such as North, Poindexter, and, most of all, Casey take the hits.

All of which made Ken's and my job both easier and harder while we were cooped up inside that locked committee room. Easier because we were less likely to be second-guessed for declassifying lots of operational detail. Harder because we could expect no support from the White House if we felt we had to make a stand against letting particular details into the public domain. And while the draft report had lots of gaps, it was also crammed with details, with direct and lengthy quotes pulled out of CIA cables going back and forth from our stations around the world. Operational traffic like that has always been zealously guarded by the CIA. But Ken and I swallowed hard and let most of it stay in the report, saving our fights with the committee staff for those instances when the names of actual CIA sources were at stake.

The hours ticked on. A couple of times early in the day, when we were at loggerheads with the staff over a sentence or even a word, I was allowed to call back to headquarters to try to get some guidance. All I got back from Langley was, basically, "Do the best you can." I gave up trying for help around 3:00 p.m., when I heard that most of the senior Agency management had left early for the day. After all, it was New Year's Eve.

Right before the stroke of midnight, we were done. We beat the Senate committee's deadline by a few minutes. All of us had been in that room for fourteen hours, exhausted and increasingly feeling sorry for ourselves. But, for better or worse, the report was ready for the committee to release. I drove home in the dark to my home in Georgetown, maneuvering around revelers spilling out of the restaurants, wondering if the report was going to be publicly released with some astonishingly sensitive piece of classified information we had somehow missed.

Except that the report wasn't released.

In a strange and ironic twist to the Iran-contra saga—which presaged many more in the year to come—the Intelligence Committee narrowly voted not to make the report public, which we all thought was the whole objective of that New Year's Eve marathon. But the strangest part is that apparently it was the Republicans who voted to release the report, only to be thwarted by the Democrats. As best as any of us could surmise, the Republicans wanted the report out because there was nothing in it implicating Reagan personally in the diversion of funds to the contras, and the Democrats objected to its release for the same reason.

A week or so later, the report was leaked to the media. The top Democrat on the Intelligence Committee, Senator Pat Leahy, admitted to the incoming chairman, David Boren, that he showed the report to an NBC reporter and quietly resigned from the committee. He didn't publicly admit his role, however, until months after that, just before CBS was going to air a story about it. Up until then, most everyone supposedly in the know—including me—assumed it was a Republican who leaked it.

The roller-coaster ride that was Iran-contra had only just begun.

CHAPTER 6

Reality TV:
The Iran-Contra Hearings
(1987)

A week into 1987, the Senate and the House established a new, joint committee to investigate the Iran-contra affair. This was not unexpected—this was a new Congress following the midterm elections, and the House and Senate intelligence committees simply hadn't the time, the resources, or the access to key witnesses during the previous six weeks to piece together a comprehensive story.

The committee was large and ungainly. There were fifteen members on the House side, eleven on the Senate side. Those twenty-six were each supported by a couple of staffers, sometimes more. With the administrative employees, security officers, investigators, press assistants, and other cats and dogs thrown in, the committee staff approached two hundred. Since Democrats controlled both the House and Senate following the 1986 midterm elections, the balance of the members and staff tipped the Democrats' way.

On the Agency's side, those responsible for dealing with the committee numbered just four: me, plus the three OGC lawyers assigned to the OCA working under my supervision. That was partly by design. I thought from the outset that it was critical to keep the "choke point" interfacing with the committee small, focused, and coordinated. But keeping the CIA team small also reflected a new reality facing the Agency. For the first time, the CIA as an institution—and potentially dozens of its personnel—was the subject of a federal criminal investigation.

On December 19, 1986, a retired federal judge named Lawrence Walsh was named as special prosecutor to investigate the entire Iran-contra mess, and Walsh was now hiring a posse of aggressive, experienced criminal litigators. The CIA's Office of General Counsel was already struggling to cope with it. The OGC was now headed by a relative newcomer to the CIA, David Doherty. Most of his previous legal career had been spent at the Securities and Exchange Commission; he had joined his SEC boss, Stan Sporkin, shortly after Stan had been recruited by Casey to come to the CIA in early 1981. A few months before Iran-contra broke, Stan had left the CIA to join the federal bench as a district court judge (thanks in large part to Casey's strong backing). So poor Dave Doherty, a fine lawyer and a good and gentle soul, now found himself suddenly responsible for dealing with the rapidly expanding Walsh investigation, and he was already feeling overwhelmed. He needed all his lawyers on hand to deal with the special prosecutor. So Dave and I agreed that I would try to make do with the three attorneys I had to handle Congress. Neither of us knew whether the arrangement would work—the Agency was in uncharted territory.

I would get an unexpected, big break right at the outset, though at first it didn't seem like one. The leadership on the Senate side of the Iran-contra committee, Daniel Inouye of Hawaii, a Democrat, and Warren Rudman of New Hampshire, a Republican, brought in outside lawyers as their lead counsels, Arthur Liman and Paul Barbadoro, respectively. Meanwhile, the House committee chairman, Lee Hamilton, also brought in two attorneys, John Nields and Neil Eggleston. I knew nothing about any of these guys, except that they had zilch experience in the shadowy world of intelligence. What's more, three of them were Democrats, and the lone Republican, Barbadoro, was a young protégé of Rudman, a combative, independent sort who made no bones about being totally repelled by what went down in Iran-contra.

I quickly found all of them—especially Barbadoro and Eggleston, my primary interlocutors—to be eminently fair-minded and sensitive to the necessity of protecting true secrets. They insisted only on getting to the bottom of Iran-contra.

Liman, Nields, Barbadoro, and Eggleston agreed to one hugely important procedural arrangement a few weeks after they arrived on the scene. They would establish a small compartment of staffers to work with the Agency in obtaining interviews, testimony of CIA witnesses, and CIA documents. We wouldn't have to entertain random, ad hoc, out-of-nowhere queries/demands from the legions of other staffers (most of whom were total strangers to me). It wasn't just a theoretical concern; I was already starting to field them.

I remember one in particular. Sometime in late January, I took a phone call from one of these unfamiliar staffers from the Senate side. Saying he was calling "on behalf of the committee," he had a modest request: access to William Casey at Georgetown Hospital. At that point, I believe Casey either had just had surgery, or was about to have it. In any event, he clearly was in no shape to see anyone from the committee. Trying to stay calm, I responded as such.

"No, you don't understand," he replied evenly. "The committee needs to be satisfied that he is truly incapacitated."

That did it. "You mean you think he's faking?" I shouted into the phone, the memory of the comatose old man being strapped on the stretcher still fresh in my mind.

"Do I understand this to be an Agency refusal?" the voice said, this time with an edge to it.

"You're goddamn right it is!" I yelled, and then I hung up on him.

And then I stared at the phone. My emotions aside, did I just open the Agency up to a charge of obstructing a congressional investigation that was only now getting started? The Reagan administration had just trumpeted that it would give full cooperation to the committee, and here I was, on my own, preemptively stiffing it. Who did I think I was, anyway?

Bob Gates, who had succeeded John McMahon as CIA deputy director the year before, was now acting director in Casey's absence. There were increasing rumors that Casey was about to resign, and that the president would nominate Gates to succeed him. And Gates would surely have his own Iran-contra role to answer for. I decided I needed to get to Gates right away, to tell him about the call, and about what I did, before he got an irate phone call from Inouye or Rudman about a stonewalling, abusive functionary on his staff.

At that point in my career, I didn't know Gates well. He had spent his two decades in the CIA exclusively on the analytical side, and our paths seldom crossed. Only a few years older than I, he struck me as extremely smart but with a detached, almost chilly demeanor. With Casey gone and irreparably discredited, Gates was now minding the store. The Agency's future, and his, were hanging in the balance. The last thing Gates needed now was a public flap with the brand-new Iran-contra committee.

A few minutes later, I was ushered into his office. He was sitting behind his desk, looking impassively at me, as I nervously and hurriedly spilled out what had just happened. And then, for the first time I could remember, I saw Bob Gates smile. "I would welcome a call from the committee. I'll give them the same answer you did, except I'll be less diplomatic," he said.

Gates never got that call, and the issue of Casey's availability was never again raised by anyone on the Iran-contra committee. William Casey never did recover. In his final days, he was allowed to return to his home on Long Island, where he died in a local hospital on May 6, 1987. It was the day after the Iran-contra hearings began. When the news arrived at the CIA, Clair George, who loved Casey and shared his profane disdain for Capitol Hill, called it "Bill Casey's final fuck-you to Congress."

In late 1987, Bob Woodward published *Veil*, an account of Casey's tenure at the CIA. Like all of Woodward's books, it became a huge best seller and is in fact a gripping and (mostly) authoritative read, containing reams of accurate depictions of events that were then, and in some cases remain to this day, classified. But one passage has nagged at me for more than a quarter of a century.

The most sensational and controversial part of the book comes at the very end, when Woodward describes visiting Casey's hospital room (apparently at the beginning of February 1987, although Woodward is fuzzy about the date) and getting the old, dying man to admit, for the first time, that he knew all along about the diversion of the Iranian arms proceeds to the contras. In Woodward's telling, he then asked Casey why, and got a two-word, enigmatic response: "I believed."

The question of who in the administration knew about the diversion from the beginning was the biggest question of the Iran-contra affair. And next to the role of President Reagan, Casey's knowledge, or lack thereof, was the issue most deeply explored by the Iran-contra committee. Casey didn't live long enough to answer the question himself.

The hospital-room story caused a huge stir when the book came out. According to Woodward, he was in the room alone with Casey. With Casey dead, it became a question of believing Woodward or not. Many accepted his account, especially given Woodward's sterling reputation and unparalleled track record as an investigative reporter. Others did not—it was all too melodramatic, too pat a denouement to the book.

At the time, I don't believe anyone in the senior CIA ranks bought the Woodward story. I know I didn't. I still don't, and here's why.

First, however, a few caveats. I cannot prove—nobody can prove—the story is false. Also, there is no question that, over the last three years of his life, Casey had a number of offline, one-on-one conversations with Woodward as he was putting the book together. A number of us were aware at the time the conversations were taking place, and we were baffled about why Casey was having them. Finally, for many years I was convinced that "Deep Throat," Woodward's famous Watergate source, was not a single individual but rather a journalistic device Woodward had created, combining several different people who were providing him with inside information. But then, of course, a few years ago the former FBI official Mark Felt suddenly came forward and confirmed that he had in fact been Deep Throat.

On Watergate, I was just another news junkie with no particular special insights. On the Casey hospital-room story, I do have some insider perspective.

For starters, if Woodward is to be believed, he simply walked into Georgetown Hospital and marched unimpeded into Casey's room. I cannot fathom how that would have been possible. Casey was surrounded by a twenty-four-hour CIA security detail for his entire stay there—indeed, Woodward conceded in his book that when he attempted to gain access to Casey's room several days earlier, a CIA security officer stationed outside the door blocked him from entering. Security officers are required to report such incidents, and I remember word coming back to headquarters about Woodward's attempt. Woodward says nothing about how he managed to elude security on his second try, either about gaining access to the room or about getting out of it undetected, after supposedly talking to the bedridden Casey for at least several minutes. If Woodward had been seen, I guarantee that security would have reported his visit up through channels.

Is it possible that somebody in authority at the CIA somehow quietly permitted the second purported Woodward visit, without my knowing about it? Theoretically, yes, but I find it extremely unlikely under the circumstances in which we were operating. The only person with the power to do something extraordinary like that would have been Bob Gates. As acting director, he was the first senior official allowed to see Casey in the hospital. In his 1996 memoir, *From the Shadows*, Gates recounted his first visit, which occurred very close to the time Woodward claimed he got in to talk to Casey. Also at about the same time, Gates was beginning regular meetings with his senior team, including me, in order to be kept apprised of developments in the then-blossoming investigations, including media inquiries. Nothing was ever said about another Woodward visit. This would have been just about the time I told Gates about the disturbing call I had gotten from the Iran-contra staffer inquiring about the committee gaining access to Casey in the hospital.

Gates was an extremely cautious, careful man. I cannot believe that he would have countenanced allowing any reporter, but especially Woodward, access to Casey at a time when we were summarily rejecting access by the Iran-contra committee.

Finally, there is another passage in *From the Shadows* where Gates addressed the issue of whether or not Casey knew about the diversion all along. He was not only Casey's deputy, he was his closest confidant in Casey's last two years. Curiously, Gates made no reference to Woodward's claim of the bedside confession by Casey, which had attained mythic status by the time Gates was writing his memoir. What Gates did do, at considerable length, was to set out, in his dispassionately analytical way, all the reasons why he was "convinced" Casey did not know about the diversion of funds to the contras. How is one to interpret that, other than as an unmistakable, if implicit, repudiation of Woodward's story?

I believe Bob Gates, who would go on to become one of the most trusted and respected public servants in recent history. I don't believe Bob Woodward's breathless account of a Casey confession, made only to him and no one else. I didn't believe it in 1987, and I don't believe it now.

I was consumed during the first four months of 1987 with leading the Agency's efforts to respond to the Iran-contra committee's demands for documents and for interviews with CIA officers. The committee publicly promised that it would start its hearings in early May, so the pressure was on. The committee staff was working sixteen-hour days, and my small staff was swamped but displaying tremendous grace under pressure.

I attended the interviews and depositions of senior CIA officials whom the committee seemed to view with the most suspicion— Clarridge, George, and Fiers. In retrospect, it is surprising to me that the committee had no problem with our sitting in. After all, we made it clear both to the committee staff and our witnesses that we were there representing the CIA as an institution, not the individual officers. In subsequent years, when an all-too-frequent controversy about the CIA would erupt, the congressional committee investigating the flap almost always barred CIA lawyers from attending its interviews with our employees.

It was at this juncture during Iran-contra that I confronted for the first time a question that would bedevil me for years to come: When, if ever, is it appropriate to recommend to an Agency employee that he retain outside, private counsel? Until Iran-contra broke, never in my career had it ever risen as even a potential issue, because never before in my career did CIA personnel come under public, high-intensity scrutiny, not just by Congress, but by an outside special prosecutor.

And so when Clarridge, George, Fiers, and others asked me whether they should hire counsel, I tried to tread carefully through another new minefield. Privately, it seemed to me a prudent step for these guys to take; Iran-contra was going nuclear, and who knew where this thing was heading? At the same time, I recognized that they were reluctant to take that step, both because of the perceived stigma—"Why do I need a lawyer? I haven't done anything wrong"—and fears about how much it would cost them out of their relatively modest government salaries.

I agonized over what to tell them, but ultimately decided to offer the following calibrated (and somewhat self-serving) guidance. Look, I told them, I can't tell you what to do one way or the other. You have to decide if you want or need private counsel. I can't play that role. But I will tell you this: Regardless of what you decide, whenever you talk to government investigators, for God's sake, tell the truth.

Only Fiers eventually decided he should get a lawyer, and when he asked for a suggestion I put him in touch with Tony Lapham, the first CIA GC I worked for in the mid-'70s. Tony was the guy I would have hired if I ever thought I needed to hire private counsel. The others chose not to get their own lawyers, at least not until it was way too late. In his 1996 memoir, *A Spy for All Seasons*, Dewey Clarridge was defiant and unapologetic about many things, but he allowed that his major regret about Iran-contra was the fact that he did not hire a lawyer much sooner than he did. Dewey was right about that.

While all of this was happening in early 1987, another CIA drama was playing out publicly on Capitol Hill. As expected, President Reagan in early February nominated Bob Gates to succeed Casey as CIA director. Initially, the word from Congress and the media pundits was that Gates was a shoo-in—after all, in contrast to the freewheeling Casey, Gates was a nonpartisan intelligence professional. But soon the cresting wave of Iran-contra swept over him. As Casey's second in command, what did he know and when did he know it? The Gates nomination was doomed, and he eventually, reluctantly, recognized that. At Gates's request, the White House withdrew his nomination.

I watched as it unfolded, feeling profoundly sorry for Gates. I had come to know him a lot better in those months after Casey's exit, and I saw that beneath his formal exterior was a man of warmth and a whimsical sense of humor. I remember him standing in his office, as the drumbeat of criticism was getting ever louder and he was confronting the inevitable, quietly talking about the toll the whole ordeal of his nomination was taking on his wife and two young children.

Gee, I recall thinking, it's a hell of a wringer for a career CIA guy to go through, getting caught in such a political firestorm. I couldn't imagine ever going through something like that, and I was relieved that I would never have to.

It was exactly twenty years before my own confirmation meltdown.

The Iran-contra hearings began on May 6, 1987. By that time, the media hype had reached a fever pitch, and both PBS and CNN (this was in the nascent years of cable TV) televised the proceedings live, gavel to gavel. I believe it was the first time this had been done since the Senate Watergate hearings fourteen years earlier. This time, I was the man in the middle, between the CIA and the Iran-contra committee. Nonetheless, I decided that the best approach was to watch the proceedings on TV. So that's what I did, for every minute of all forty days of the hearings. Not merely as a spectator, but as an interactive participant of sorts, long before that term entered into the popular lexicon.

Reality TV: The Iran-Contra Hearings (1987)

This approach was unorthodox, but it proved to be effective and efficient. At the same time, it was an extraordinarily stressful experience.

The committee, created from scratch only a few months before, had established a very ambitious timeline for the completion of its work. In addition, the media kept the pressure on the committee to start the public hearings—parts of the entire tangled story were dribbling out piecemeal, but the key protagonists, such as Poindexter and especially North, had yet to be heard from. As a result, the hearings began before the committee had done a lot of its homework. The staffers were still slogging through massive amounts of highly classified documents, not sure which they wanted declassified so they could be waved around on television. The list of witnesses, and in which order they would appear, were in a constant state of flux. From the first day the TV cameras were turned on, the committee was pretty much winging it. Nonetheless, the committee was determined that the show must go on. And so, back at the Agency, I had to wing it as well.

For forty days, stretching over a period of three months, I was holed up in my office, staring at the TV for anywhere from four to ten hours a day as witness after witness, from the famous to the obscure, was interrogated by the twenty-six committee members and, more frequently, the chief lawyers, Nields and Liman. Their questions were frequently ad hoc, sometimes off-the-wall, and always unpredictable. Chain-smoking cigars, I turned my cramped office into something akin to a smoky fight club.

One of my primary tasks was simply to keep track in real time of everything every witness was saying about the Agency, and to provide comprehensive, daily feedback to senior CIA management. To that end, I prepared memos at the end of every day's testimony, consisting of bullet points recounting each instance the witness referred to CIA activities or personnel. Every night, I would forward the memos to Gates and others in key management positions, including George, Clarridge, and Fiers, the three Agency officials whose names seemed to come up regularly. If any of them had already left for home, or if they were out of town, I would have a courier deliver the memo to them. I thought it was important for these guys to see this stuff right away, rather than seeing it for the first time in the next morning's newspapers. The memos would run anywhere from two to five pages, and I produced forty of them—one for each day of the televised hearings. At the end of each day's installment, I would

123

append a paragraph or two of commentary (which I archly headed with the title "Analysis") in which I would sum up what I considered new and significant that had come up that day, as well as my two cents on how the witness, or Nields and Liman, or some committee member generally, came off in front of the cameras.

What I didn't realize at the time was that my daily reports on the hearings would later complicate the parallel criminal investigations being pursued by Lawrence Walsh. The testimony of some of the key witnesses, including North, was obtained under a grant of immunity that basically meant it could not be used in any later prosecutions of North and others. And here I was, spoon-feeding it to many of the people who would later become prosecution witnesses. Maybe I should have taken that possibility into account, but it honestly did not occur to me. If it had occurred to me, however, I doubt it would have made any difference. I saw it as my responsibility to keep everyone in the building up to date, on a real-time basis, on what was transpiring at the hearings. It was not to make the prosecutors' jobs easier.

I wasn't just a note-taker, though, as I peered at the screen in a constant state of expectation and dread. I would watch as one of the committee inquisitors would pause midquestion and whisper to one of the array of aides spread out behind them on the sprawling, two-tier dais. Uh-oh, I would think, blanching, as the aide scurried offscreen. Only then would I know what was coming, and I would instinctively put my hand on my phone. Seconds later, it would ring, and there was the aide's panic-stricken voice: Can my boss ask the witness about this CIA activity? Can he use this CIA spy's real name? Can he talk about CIA information in this particular document?

Every day of the hearings, every few minutes, it seemed, the phone calls would come, always different in substance, but with the same urgency: We are on live TV. We need a decision from the CIA. Now.

I would cringe. There's nobody else around, and no opportunity to talk to anybody in the building.

There I was, thrust into making instant judgments on what CIA classified information could be suddenly declassified and broadcast to the world. Everything from a CIA office's location in the organizational chart to a CIA agent's machinations in a foreign country. I really had no business making these on-the-spot decisions; they were way above my pay grade and sometimes well beyond my expertise. But they had to be made, and there was no time for anyone else to make them. Holding the phone, I would just take a breath, close my eyes, and make the judgment call. Heads, and I would agree to the disclosure of some sensitive secret. Tails, and I risked having the Agency accused of obstructing a congressional investigation, and the public's right to know.

For the first time in my career, I was alone on a high wire without a net.

Realizing career suicide was at risk, I occasionally would make an after-the-fact effort to cover my ass with my superiors. I recall one such incident that unexpectedly popped up during National Security Advisor John Poindexter's testimony. Arthur Liman started quoting to Poindexter the transcript of a critical phone conversation between Poindexter and Casey as Iran-contra was coming unstuck. Poindexter was taken aback, saying he had no idea the call had been recorded. A hubbub immediately ensued—had the secretive and wily Casey been wiretapping all his conversations without the other party's knowledge? Were there any more recordings? It all sounded so sinister, so Nixonian.

The truth was more banal, but it required disclosing a secret. Casey had been in Central America at the time of his conversation with Poindexter and was speaking on a secure phone in a CIA station, a device installed in all CIA facilities around the world. As a matter of protocol, the CIA Ops Center recorded all such calls it handled—not just those involving the CIA director, but any communications between Washington and the field. The system, which was sophisticated for its time, was called PRT-250. Its existence, and its capabilities, were fairly well known inside the CIA, but it was a zealously guarded secret kept from anyone in the outside world. Even from someone like Poindexter.

The hearing had recessed shortly after Poindexter's expression of surprise, and Liman rang me up immediately. He knew about the system, what it was intended for, and understood that the whole thing was a tempest in a teapot. But the teapot was boiling, and Liman implored me to help him turn the heat off. He wanted to make a public statement when the hearing resumed, explaining the PRT-250 along the lines I have described above. Given about thirty seconds to ponder, I told Liman to go ahead. Five minutes later, I watched on TV as Liman read the statement.

As it happened, the Liman statement came near the end of the day's hearing, and I was called down to Bob Gates's office. Here comes the shit storm, I figured, as I trudged down the hall and entered the office, where Gates was surrounded by a number of senior officials. However, the meeting was about something else entirely. As it broke up, Gates asked whether anything of interest had come out in Poindexter's testimony that day. And then it hit me: Nobody there had seen it yet.

"Nothing much," I responded with feigned casualness. I paused, and then murmured quietly, "Except that I declassified the PRT-250 system."

Everybody there shrugged.

And so it came to pass that neither this decision nor any of the other off-the-cuff decisions I made during the course of the Iran-contra hearings ever came back to haunt me. No repercussions either from the Agency for having declassified information, nor from the committee when I would take it upon myself to reject its more extreme demands, like descending on the terminally ill Casey in his hospital room.

There was one other cliff-hanging element to the Iran-contra hearings that I had to contend with throughout the proceedings: the testimony of Agency witnesses from the Directorate of Operations. These were covert CIA employees, people whose faces were unknown to the general public. Early on, the committee had three particular senior DO officials in its crosshairs: Clair George, Dewey Clarridge, and Alan Fiers. There was a fourth DO operative also in the mix, the Costa Rica station chief, Joe Fernandez. He certainly was deeply and wrongly involved in North's off-the-book machinations in helping the contras at a time when the Agency was prohibited from doing so. But he was a relatively small fish in the scheme of things, so a month or so into the hearings, the committee agreed to let Joe testify in a "closed" session, meaning no cameras, no media, and no one from the public. I attended that session, and Joe, who was a large and emotional man, broke down a couple of times during his testimony. The committee seemed sympathetic toward him, sensing— correctly—that he had gotten in over his head largely because of North's bravado. The testimony came off without incident, so I fully expected the same drill would be followed when the time would come for Joe's superiors to testify.

I was wrong. The Democrats on the committee, and their staffers, considered George, Clarridge, and Fiers to be the main CIA villains in the Iran-contra saga. They thought that those three had been disingenuous, or even deceptive, in their previous interviews and depositions with committee staff. Casey was dead and thus beyond their reach, but these guys weren't. And so the committee wanted to put them in front of the cameras. To take them apart.

I decided to push back hard. For one thing, having them testify on TV in real time would have been a security nightmare. It was hard enough to keep non-Agency witnesses from inadvertently blurting out some stray piece of unrelated classified information. But these CIA guys' heads were stuffed with all sorts of information accumulated from decades in the intelligence world. The questioning style of many members tended to be haphazard, so there was no way of prepping our guys in advance about the areas they couldn't get into publicly. I had nightmare visions of having to sit there behind them, constantly jumping up on live TV to object and plead with the committee to go into closed session.

But my worries extended beyond that. These were active-duty, career veterans of the spy service. The thought of them being paraded and pummeled on national television just seemed unfair and unseemly. To that, the committee staff had a rejoinder: Well, we can have them appear in disguises, or behind screens. Great, I thought. Just like they were Mafia stool pigeons. It was then that I truly realized that what the committee was after was not testimony, but theater.

And then Dick Cheney came to the rescue.

Cheney was the ranking House Republican on the committee. He had kept his own counsel during much of the proceedings, but he was no blind apologist for what the Reagan administration had done. Still, he was a serious-minded guy, and he despised theatrics. Fearing we were about to lose the fight, I went first to Cheney's key aides on the committee, David Addington and Dick Leon. Addington had worked for me as a young CIA lawyer a few years before, and it would be another fifteen years before he would gain notoriety as Cheney's hard-line alter ego in the George W. Bush administration. But at the time he was just a quiet, anonymous staffer. Even back then, Cheney trusted him completely, and David got Cheney on the case. Cheney raised a ruckus behind the scenes, and the committee Democrats quietly backed off.

George, Clarridge, and Fiers were allowed to testify in early August, in closed session, as the final witnesses at the Iran-contra hearings. I sat behind each of them as they testified separately over three days. Each was true to form. George was alternately jocular and sincere, trying to win over the committee with his case officer's charm. Fiers was earnest and tightly wound, tearing up at points about the "nutcracker" he found himself in. Clarridge was, well, Clarridge. He was straightforward, unapologetic, and barely able to control his contempt for his inquisitors. I remember once looking up and catching a glance from Arthur Liman up on the dais. Listening to Dewey, Liman looked down at me, shaking his head slowly with a small smile.

And with that, the Iran-contra hearings officially ended.

The implications of Iran-contra and its aftermath would have a profound impact on the Agency. It was also a turning point in my career, a time that I truly came of age as a CIA lawyer and executive. Operating for the first time on my own in a highly charged political environment, I learned the importance of staying calm and focused, and trusting my instincts to make a decision—any decision—rather than equivocating or obfuscating.

In addition, it confirmed to me that my Agency career was blessed by astonishingly good luck. If I had still been the DO's lawyer in 1985, I have no doubt that I would have been brought into the loop when the disastrous Findings were being drafted. Perhaps things might have turned out differently if I had been given a say—for a time I was pleased to believe that—but the truth is they probably wouldn't have. The arms-for-hostages initiative was conceived and approved at the highest levels of our government, including the CIA director. In all likelihood I would have gone along, whatever my private misgivings might have been. And then I would have been sucked in, tainted, and my career would have never been the same.

CHAPTER 7

The Iran-Contra Hangover
(1988–1992)

In November 1987, the Iran-contra committee issued its final report. It was the size of a big-city telephone directory—nearly seven hundred oversized pages of dense print. Just as it had for the ill-fated Senate Intelligence Committee report on the last day of 1986, the White House counsel's office organized an interagency group to conduct a classification review of the report prior to its public release. Unlike the New Year's Eve debacle, this was a more studied, deliberative process. The White House team was headed by two very capable and unflappable officials, Alan Raul from the counsel's office and Brenda Reger from the NSC staff. And the Iran-contra committee did not dump its entire report on the White House doorstep and impose a ridiculously short deadline on the Executive Branch to complete its review. Instead, the committee staff, as it completed a chapter, would send it over to the interagency group for comment, not just on classification issues but also for any possible factual inaccuracies. The committee staff encouraged the input of the Executive Branch, and made numerous adjustments to the text. The Iran-contra committee's approach was consistent with the way it had mostly operated throughout the investigation—professional, nonpartisan, and courteous.

The interagency group was made up of representatives from six agencies—the DOD, State, Justice, Treasury, the CIA, and the National Security Agency. The White House limited each agency to two representatives and mandated that these officials have the authority to make final decisions on classification. I could have let someone else represent the CIA, but at that point, having lived and breathed the investigation for nearly a year to the exclusion of everything else, I wanted to personally see it

129

through to the end. So I nominated myself and Ken Johnson, the DO's declassification expert, to represent the Agency. For two weeks straight in late October, we and other representatives were cooped up in a conference room in the Old Executive Office Building adjacent to the White House, slogging line by line through the report, fed to us in bite-size chunks by the committee. Personally, I found the process liberating— after a yearlong investigation, virtually the entire Iran-contra saga was now untangled and out in the open. There were not many secrets left, making the declassification process relatively straightforward. And going through the committee's report chapter by chapter, with all of its exhaustive detail, was an oddly cathartic way to decompress from the maelstrom I had been through.

Not that I'm complaining about any of it. The fact is, the Iran-contra scandal was the best thing that happened to me in my career. That might sound perverse, given that it wrecked the careers of a number of my friends and severely damaged the CIA as an institution, but it's true. I was a key player in the biggest and most dramatic Washington investigation since Watergate. The scandal put me on the map inside the Agency, giving me a visibility I did not have before. Lord help me for saying this, but the Iran-contra experience was fun as hell for me.

Now all I had to do was figure out what to do next.

After Bob Gates's nomination for DCI imploded back in February 1987, the White House moved quickly to come up with a new nominee. The choice was William Webster, a onetime federal appeals court judge who was wrapping up a nine-year tenure as FBI director. Judge Webster (as he preferred to be addressed) was a respected pillar of the Washington establishment, a dignified, nonpartisan figure. He was sworn in on May 26, in the midst of the Iran-contra hearings, with a mandate from Congress to clean up the mess at Langley.

Webster's stint at the Agency, which would last four years, has received decidedly mixed reviews from Agency alumni in the years since. Bob Gates, in his 1996 memoir, called Webster a "godsend" to the CIA. On the other hand, Dewey Clarridge, in his memoir published the next year, directed withering criticism at Webster. With his typical rhetorical flourish, Dewey presented Webster as an effete, social-climbing, empty Brooks Brothers suit. In Dewey's eyes, Webster's greatest fault was that he was a lawyer, a profession Dewey asserted was antithetical to heading up a spy service (never mind that his mentor Bill Casey was also a lawyer).

Notwithstanding my affection and respect for Dewey, I think he gave Webster a bum rap. True, Webster had no prior discernible experience or interest in intelligence, was not exactly a workaholic during his tenure at Langley, and never had much clout with the White House. In short, he was not at all like Casey. But that was the point—at that traumatic juncture in the Agency's history, he was precisely what we needed. What I respected most about him is the fact that he agreed to come to the CIA at all; as Bob Gates correctly observed, stepping in to take over the CIA at a time when it was being consumed by the fires of Iran-contra "was a job no one else seemed to want." Webster certainly didn't need the job—his career and reputation were unblemished, and he was winding down his long tenure at the FBI, with a quiet and doubtless lucrative career in the private sector awaiting him, when the call from the White House came. I did not know Webster before he came to the CIA, but I came to like him immensely. He restored stability and credibility to a badly shaken institution.

Webster's first order of business when he took over was to initiate an internal review of the CIA's conduct during the course of the Iran-contra affair, and in particular whether individual Agency officers should be disciplined for their actions. He enlisted Russ Bruemmer, a partner in a prominent D.C. law firm, to lead it. Several years younger than I, Russ was a protégé of Webster's, having served some years before as his law clerk. Affable and low-key, he had an unpleasant task to perform. For one thing, the Iran-contra hearings were then still unfolding, with revelations about the Agency spilling out every day on TV. Meanwhile, the criminal investigation under Lawrence Walsh was gearing up, with his hard-charging prosecutors churning out subpoenas for reams of CIA documents. The Agency felt under siege from all directions. The last thing anyone wanted or needed was still another probe by an unknown outsider viewed, fairly or not, as the new DCI's grim reaper.

Yet Russ and I hit it off right away, and I agreed to help him to the extent that I could. One major obstacle he had was that two of the chief Iran-contra figures—Dewey Clarridge and Clair George—refused to talk to him. Since I was friends with both of them, Russ asked me to intervene on his behalf to get them to change their minds. I declined—these were proud, stubborn men who probably couldn't be swayed, and besides, I knew deep down that, careerwise, their gooses were cooked anyway and anything they might say would be subject to attack, and possible criminal exposure, by the congressional and Walsh investigators.

The Bruemmer review ground forward as 1987 was coming to an end, with the final report and recommendations for disciplinary actions going to Webster a few weeks before Christmas. Russ shared the report in advance with me, on the condition that I divulge his findings to no one else. So I knew that Clarridge, George, Alan Fiers, and a few other officials were being singled out for tough criticism and disciplinary sanctions. Knowing the fate in store for them, I found it extremely hard to continue to interact with these people—guys who had devoted decades of brave and dedicated service to the Agency—as if nothing were amiss. But Christmas was around the corner, and I figured they would find out soon enough, once the holidays were out of the way.

I figured wrong. The day the office Christmas parties throughout the CIA were designated to take place, Russ told me that Webster was ready to call the employees in to mete out their punishments.

"Webster is going to do it today, when these guys are supposed to be celebrating with their staffs?" I asked incredulously.

"I know," Russ replied, "but it is a hard thing for him to do, so he wants to get it over with so it won't be hanging over him during the holidays."

What about the employees? I wondered to myself. What about their holidays?

I happened to be at the Counterterrorist Center Christmas party, having a drink with Dewey Clarridge and a couple of his deputies, when the call came from the seventh floor, summoning him to the DCI's office. "What do you suppose this is about?" Dewey asked.

"Dewey," I said, "if there is anything you need to say to defend yourself, now is the time to go upstairs and say it."

By the end of the day, the careers of Dewey Clarridge, Clair George, and several lower-ranking officers were effectively over. For years afterward, the day would be referred to inside the CIA as the Holiday Party Massacre.

From the day Russ Bruemmer arrived on the scene, rumors became increasingly rampant that Webster was grooming him to replace Dave

Doherty as CIA general counsel. Russ himself was studiously mum on the subject, but it made things a bit awkward between him and Dave. With Casey dead and Sporkin off to the federal bench, Dave had lost his base of support. It was unfortunate, but inevitable, that Webster would want his own person in place. And, sure enough, early in 1988, he named Russ to the job.

Shortly thereafter, Russ asked me to return to the OGC fold. He wanted to create a new position, deputy general counsel for operations, and he wanted me to fill it. Only a decade before, I had been the only lawyer assigned to physically reside in the offices of the Directorate of Operations. Now there were close to ten, scattered in the Counterterrorist Center, the Central America Task Force, and elsewhere. The idea would be for me to oversee and supervise them.

For a number of reasons, I decided to take the job. First, I liked and respected Russ, and I knew that he would give me a lot of autonomy. I knew far more about the culture and innards of the notoriously secretive DO than Russ ever would, and Russ was smart and secure enough to recognize that. Second, I thought the time was right to leave the Office of Congressional Affairs. I had been there for two years, one of which was consumed with handling the Iran-contra investigation, an exhausting but exhilarating, once-in-a-lifetime experience. Anything else I could possibly do in the OCA would pale by comparison. Finally, and perhaps most important, Webster had wisely decided to relocate the general counsel's office back to headquarters from its Casey-imposed exile. I would not have returned to the OGC as long as it was mired in a building several miles away. Once the OGC came back, I decided to come back as well.

The Webster years (mid-1987 through 1991) were shadowed by the aftermath of Iran-contra; the Walsh investigation was relentlessly expanding, consuming an enormous amount of Agency time and resources (the OGC alone had four lawyers working on the case full-time) and having a debilitating effect on CIA morale. But gradually, the CIA saw light at the end of the tunnel. In January 1989, George H. W. Bush became president, the first DCI ever to ascend to the Oval Office. He loved the Agency as much as it loved him. And when he took office, he took Bob Gates with him, making Gates deputy national security advisor and giving him a broad portfolio. Thus, the CIA suddenly had two powerful patrons in the White House.

The Agency was turning a page in other ways as well. In early 1988, clearly reacting to all the bad blood caused by Iran-contra, Congress cut off all paramilitary assistance to the Nicaraguan contras, effectively ending CIA involvement. It marked the close of a tumultuous, painful chapter in the CIA's history, but two years later, there was a surprisingly positive coda: In democratic elections there, the Nicaraguan people ousted the Sandinista regime. And across the world, in early 1989, the Soviets threw in a very bloody towel in Afghanistan, withdrawing the last of their troops and ending their decade-long occupation. The Afghan resistance had vanquished the invaders, and even the Agency's strongest detractors conceded that the victory would not have been possible without the CIA's massive financial and operational support. All in all, with respect to the Agency's two largest covert-action programs of the '80s, not a bad bottom line.

And all the while, of course, the Soviet Union was crumbling. In 1991, it finally fell apart. The Cold War, the raison d'être for the CIA's creation, was over. There have been many debates about the extent to which the Agency's covert efforts on so many fronts around the world, spanning nearly half a century, played a role in the Soviet Union's ultimate collapse. But there can be no argument that the CIA did play a role.

Nonetheless, despite all the reasons the Agency should have been able to feel good about itself again, I remember no real sense of happiness or pride in the hallways at Langley. Partly, this could be attributed to the hangover from Iran-contra—Walsh now was clearly aiming his sights beyond just the usual suspects such as Dewey Clarridge and Clair George, as high as Bob Gates. Moreover, with the programs in Nicaragua and Afghanistan shut down and the Cold War over, the Agency was facing significant cuts in funding and personnel. It was also increasingly obvious that Webster, for all his laudable qualities, simply had little clout with the White House, and clout with the White House is the CIA's coin of the realm.

Overall, the atmosphere at the CIA from 1988 through 1991 wasn't awful. It just wasn't what it was before, during the Reagan years.

In May 1991, President Bush nominated Bob Gates to succeed the retiring Bill Webster as DCI. We at the Agency were pleased with the announcement that Gates would be returning to Langley. He had two huge attributes that Webster never had—more than two decades of experience as a career officer at the Agency, and a close relationship with the president. Many of us also felt he deserved a second chance at the top job after his brutal, drawn-out confirmation ordeal of four years before, when his nomination for DCI tanked over unresolved questions about his role in the then-exploding Iran-contra scandal. I had seen that debacle close up and the toll it had taken on him, and I was convinced that Gates had been an honorable, decent man who simply was in the wrong place at the wrong time.

What none of us anticipated, apparently including Gates, was the brutal, drawn-out confirmation ordeal he would face the second time around. Lingering Iran-contra questions played only a relatively small role; instead, Gates had to endure withering attacks—including from some of his longtime friends and subordinates at the CIA—about his alleged failure over the years to accurately gauge the capabilities and ultimate deterioration of the Soviet Union. For a proud man like Gates, who had built his career and reputation as a Soviet specialist, it must have been an even more humiliating experience than what he had gone through four years before.

Gates persevered, however, and was ultimately confirmed by the Senate in November 1991. The nomination process had taken seven months, and his tenure as DCI would last only about a year. When President Bush was defeated by Bill Clinton in November 1992, Bob Gates was out of a job that he had just barely begun. His departure marked the end of the Reagan-Bush era at the CIA. It had been an eventful, turbulent twelve years, a period that began with the Agency reenergized and ascendant and ended with it being largely adrift and leaderless.

Alas, the next few years would be even worse.

CHAPTER 8

Dealing with Devils
(1993–1996)

The arrival of the Clinton administration in January 1993 marked the third time in my Agency career that there had been a "hostile takeover" of the U.S. Government, by which I mean that an incumbent president had been defeated for reelection by the candidate of the opposition party. In 1976 and 1980, however, the Agency knew pretty well in advance how the new president felt about the CIA: Carter was a wary skeptic, and Reagan was an unabashed cheerleader. And their choices for CIA director reflected these views.

Clinton was different. With his almost exclusive focus on the domestic economy during the 1992 campaign, Clinton hardly talked about national security in general, or the CIA in particular. But after the election, and even before taking office, he began sending unmistakable signals. He wasn't interested in, didn't care about, the Agency at all. For an organization whose relevance and impact is so utterly dependent on its relationship with the commander in chief, being ignored is even worse than being mistrusted.

Clinton waited until right before Christmas before getting around to announcing, seemingly as an afterthought, his choice of R. James Woolsey, a man he barely knew, as CIA director. Jim Woolsey was no lightweight. About fifty at the time, he was a successful lawyer who during the Carter administration had served as an arms negotiator and undersecretary of the navy. Although he could be charming and wryly humorous in private settings, Woolsey by nature was an acerbic, blunt-talking guy. Unlike a lot of Washington players I met and observed over the years, Woolsey didn't engage in self-puffery, boasting of his insider connections. Notably, he never pretended to anyone inside the Agency that he and Clinton were close; indeed, he seemed to be perversely proud of the fact that he was a White House outsider. In some ways, I found that to be a refreshing and admirable trait. The problem was, telling anyone at the Agency who would listen that you have no standing with the White House is no way for a DCI to build in-house morale. On top of that, Woolsey's pugnacious persona caused him in no time to achieve the considerable feat of alienating the Agency's congressional overseers on a bipartisan basis. Compared with him, Bill Casey was an unctuous diplomat.

That said, Jim Woolsey was not the problem. Bill Clinton was. Less than a week after his inauguration—and two weeks before Woolsey took the helm—Clinton gave the Agency the most hurtful presidential snub I witnessed in my entire career.

On the morning of January 25, 1993, I was on my way into work as usual.

When I was driving alone, my route to the CIA was to go north on Route 123 into McLean and take a right at an exit leading to the headquarters front gate. However, when my son, James, was staying with me at my Georgetown home, I would have to drive a short distance farther and take a left onto a road leading to his school. After dropping him off, I would take a right back onto Route 123, going south, and get into one of the two left lanes leading to the CIA exit, which was controlled by a traffic light.

As I sat waiting, about two hundred yards from the traffic light, a squadron of police cars raced past me on the median, their sirens screaming. I assumed it was some sort of vehicle accident.

It wasn't. It was the first and only terrorist attack ever launched on CIA Headquarters. A young Pakistani immigrant named Mir Aimal Kansi had emerged on foot out of nowhere, armed with an AK-47 assault rifle, and begun shooting indiscriminately into the cars of CIA workers waiting for the light to change to enter the compound. He murdered two people and grievously wounded three others. One of the victims, a kindly, bookish sixty-year-old analyst named Nick Starr, was a good friend. If I had dropped my son off at school a few minutes earlier, I could have been a victim too.

The Agency went into a collective state of shock. It was shaken in a way

I had never experienced before, and wouldn't be again until the morning of 9/11, nearly a decade later. The CIA is a family, and members of the family had been randomly slaughtered, just for trying to get to work on a sunny Virginia morning. We had all considered the headquarters to be an impregnable, inviolate fortress where we were safe and protected. It was understood and accepted that CIA personnel and facilities abroad could be vulnerable and targeted; that was the nature of the intelligence world. But not here, not sitting in commuter passenger lanes in a leafy Washington suburb.

The Agency scrambled to organize a memorial ceremony in tribute to our fallen colleagues. Former and current dignitaries from the U.S. Government and from foreign governments attended, coming from far and wide. One person was conspicuously absent, however. Bill Clinton, our new president, couldn't find the time to make the ten-minute trip from the White House to the CIA to pay his respects. He sent his wife instead. It was an unforgivable slight from a man who had famously told the American people during his just-completed campaign, "I feel your pain."

The atmosphere at the Agency had turned profoundly sad and dispirited in those early months of 1993. But, at least for me, it wasn't just because of the lingering trauma from the CIA shootings, or because it was increasingly apparent that President Clinton couldn't care less about the Agency or the rest of the intelligence community. What I first learned during that period, and what only a handful of people inside the building knew, was that there was a new disaster on the horizon, something that would shake the institution to its core: A longtime, murderous traitor was walking freely in the halls of Langley. And he was one of us.

Sometime in the winter of 1992–1993—I don't remember the precise date—an officer from the CIA Counterintelligence Center came to see me in my office. The officer was part of a small, cloistered group of analysts that had been formed a few years earlier to try to solve a haunting mystery that dated back to the Casey era: Who or what was responsible for the relentless and unexplained disappearances and deaths of the U.S. Government's most valuable human sources inside the Soviet Union?

The officer, a friend of long standing, came in and closed the door. In a quiet and grave voice, she led off with a volley of specific questions. How can the Agency go about getting lawful access to the records residing in the Northwest Federal Credit Union, the in-house financial institution for current and former CIA employees and their families? Furthermore, the officer asked, who would have to know why we want them, or which records we want? How much would we have to put in writing?

I knew the officer well enough to know that she was not the alarmist, melodramatic type. I was caught flat-footed by her questions, but I stumbled my way through a reasonably accurate explanation of the laws on financial privacy, an area in which I was no expert. The officer nodded, but remained seated, like she expected me to ask my own questions. I took the opening.

"How serious is this?"

"We think we've found the reason our Soviet assets have been disappearing. Do you know an employee named Rick Ames?"

I knew Rick Ames only vaguely. He was the sort of bland, anonymous, mid-level functionary that populates any large federal bureaucracy, and the CIA, for all its legend and mystique, is at bottom a large federal bureaucracy. He and I had had a few interactions, and to the extent I gave any thought to him at all, he didn't seem all that smart or all that dumb. In the weeks and months ahead, I would learn far more about him. Namely, that he was an irredeemable drunken lout who for years had been pocketing millions from the Soviets in return for reams of highly classified information. That his boorish and brazen behavior, his absurdly lavish lifestyle, had long been either tolerated or systematically overlooked by his various superiors. That he had the blood of at least nine CIA sources on his hands.

By early 1993, I had been in the Agency long enough to have witnessed more than my share of the CIA's mistakes, missteps, and follies. But Rick Ames represented the ultimate nightmare—a turncoat imbedded for years in the ranks.

After that visit by the officer from the Counterintelligence Center, I was brought into the very small loop of people who were privy to the investigation. The loop had to be kept small. Rick Ames was still walking the halls, unaware of the noose tightening around his neck. Meanwhile, the FBI bugged his office, his home, his Jaguar sedan.

During the course of my long Agency career, it usually wasn't very hard to keep a secret. It's part of the compact you make when you enter the organization. You can't tell secrets to your family, your friends, anyone who doesn't hold the necessary security clearances, and, even if someone has the clearances, you don't unless they need to know a particular secret. It doesn't matter how exciting the secret is (and there were thousands of that category I came to know), or how much you trust the person to whom you might tell the secret. You just don't do it.

The secret about Rick Ames and his treachery was the most difficult one I ever had to keep. I had to do so for a year, until the day he was arrested outside his home, on his way to work, on February 4, 1994. (A handful of people who were in on the investigation from the beginning had to keep the secret even longer. The Ames case, like most espionage investigations, required several years of discreet, painstaking work before there was enough evidence to make an arrest.) The reason it was so hard was that after the day the Counterintelligence Center officer came to see me, after not having seen Rick Ames for years, I suddenly could not seem to avoid the SOB's dull, clueless presence. I went to several meetings where Ames mysteriously and unaccountably appeared. I couldn't bear to look at him, but I didn't dare look away. On most of those occasions, the other Agency people attending knew nothing about the investigation, so it was easy for them to act as normal. Once in a while, however, there would be a meeting where Ames would be sitting there along with his boss at the time, the chief of the Counternarcotics Center. I knew that the chief knew about the investigation, and I knew that he also knew that I knew. A longtime officer in the clandestine service, he was well schooled in keeping up a false front, effortlessly engaging in friendly banter with me and the unsuspecting Ames. He seemed so much more at ease than I was about carrying on the charade.

And then there would be the times I would spot Ames chatting up other Agency employees in casual settings. His office was on the ground floor of what is referred to inside the CIA as the New Headquarters Office Building (NHB), a six-story structure erected in the late '80s adjacent to the Original Headquarters Office Building (OHB). The two buildings are separated by a courtyard, and employees can go from one building to the other via a glassed-in walkway that looks out on the courtyard. In the months after I first learned about the Ames investigation, I would go through the walkway, on my way from one meeting to another, and frequently observe Ames standing in the courtyard, taking a cigarette break, and schmoozing with fellow employees who, of course, had no idea they were talking to a Russian mole. What is he asking them? I would wonder to myself. What are they telling him? I remember one time in particular when I spotted Ames in the courtyard having an animated, one-on-one conversation with a guy who was in charge of one of the Agency's most massive, successful, and sensitive technical intelligence-collection programs. It was an appalling thing to behold, and I felt an overwhelming urge to sprint into the courtyard and pull the guy away from Ames, to stop him from perhaps innocently mentioning something in passing—something significant—that Ames could pass back to his Russian handlers. But I was powerless to do anything but keep on walking.

My most excruciating moment of all came one day in January 1994 when I had a chance encounter with Ames on an NHB elevator. As fate would have it, I had just come from a briefing in the OHB in which the latest developments in the investigation were being discussed. I learned that his arrest was finally near and the apparent jaw-dropping extent of his treachery: the millions he had gotten from the Russians, the thousands of secrets he had likely passed to them over the previous decade, the deaths of Russian sources—at least nine, maybe more. My head was still spinning as I walked back to my office, which was located on the top floor of the NHB. As I arrived at the first-floor elevator, I was still trying to absorb the enormity of his betrayal. Standing there at the elevator, all by himself, was Rick Ames.

Still oblivious to everything, he grunted a perfunctory hello as we waited for the elevator to arrive. And waited—I didn't think the damn thing would ever get there. As the seconds ticked by, he finally engaged me in some small talk. I have no recollection of what either of us said to each other; all I remember is that my heart was pounding so hard I thought my head was about to explode. Finally, mercifully, the elevator doors opened. The elevator was empty. Ames stepped in, but I didn't. I couldn't bear to spend another single second in his presence. I muttered something to him about forgetting something back in the OHB. As I turned away, and as the elevator doors closed, I stole one last glance at the most evil, destructive traitor in CIA history.

Ames was arrested a couple of weeks later. The ensuing public firestorm was predictable and devastating. The CIA was justly excoriated by Congress and ridiculed in the media for letting such an amoral, drunken slacker as Rick Ames operate with impunity, and cause so much damage, for so long a period of time. The luckless Jim Woolsey, who had inherited a looming debacle he had nothing to do with, was attacked for allegedly not being tough enough in meting out punishment to those who had been in Ames's chain of command during his decade of perfidy. True to form, Woolsey turned combative with his critics. His relations with Congress, already rancid, became toxic.

Meanwhile, the FBI was enjoying itself immensely. It took bows, at the Agency's expense, for finally uncovering Ames, while subtly—and sometimes not so subtly—putting out the word that a traitor such as Ames could never exist in its ranks. (The Bureau's smugness was premature. At the very moment of the Ames arrest, one of its own trusted veterans, Robert Hanssen, was freely selling secrets to the Russians that were at least as extensive and deadly as those passed by Ames. Hanssen would not be caught for another seven years.)

The Ames case was an unmitigated, humiliating disaster for the Agency's reputation and standing. The fact that it deserved all of the opprobrium it got made the episode even more searing, and the damage more lasting.

The '90s were going from bad to worse. And things would continue to go downhill. The heady days of the early '80s, when the Agency was flush with money and full of power and influence, seemed a distant memory. But then, in a way, the '80s returned. Only not in a good way.

In the aftermath of the Ames debacle, Jim Woolsey's days at the CIA were numbered. That was apparent to everyone in the building, doubtless including Woolsey—a savvy realist. Perhaps he would have been more successful if he had served at a different time, under a different president. He relinquished his position as director at the end of 1994 in the same way he came to the job less than two years earlier—with little notice and no fanfare.

Given the Agency's lowly status and battered reputation at the time, it was not surprising that there were few takers eager to become Woolsey's successor. As the Clinton administration spent weeks casting around for candidates, that became embarrassingly obvious. Finally, John Deutch, the deputy secretary of defense, was announced as the nominee. Deutch, a brilliant scientist formerly at the Massachusetts Institute of Technology, was by all accounts—including his own—a very reluctant candidate. No one could blame him, I suppose, but for a demoralized organization, the last thing we needed to hear was that we had a new leader who had to be virtually shanghaied into the job.

At the time and in the years since, the common perception advanced in the media and by CIA alumni was that Deutch was extraordinarily unpopular within the ranks of career Agency personnel. That is undoubtedly true, but I may be one of the only exceptions. I came to greatly like and respect John Deutch. I found him to be a sympathetic, fascinating figure. He could come off as being arrogant, dismissive, and out of touch in large settings or with people he didn't know, but among those he felt comfortable with, he was caring, witty, and unpretentious. At six feet three, he had an imposing physical presence with a somewhat imperious air, but at the same time had an endearing tendency in small groups to reach out and touch a person—man or woman—he was talking to, up to and including dispensing awkward hugs if he wanted to convey his congratulations or happiness about something.

Early on, Deutch made some remarkably tone-deaf public comments about the inferiority of CIA personnel vis-à-vis the U.S. military. That was not what the battered but proud Agency workforce needed to hear from its new leader. In particular, the closed society that makes up the Directorate of Operations collectively decided that he was not on their side, and Deutch was simply too stubborn—and perhaps too proud—to curry their favor. I spent my entire career working with succeeding generations of DO officers, and I yield to no one in my enduring admiration for them and for the difficult, thankless, and often dangerous work they do for our country. Deutch, I am convinced, came to feel the same way, except that he somehow was never able to outwardly convey it.

A few years after Deutch left the Agency (we remain friends to this day), we had lunch one day near his office at MIT, and he told me something that has stuck with me ever since. "You know," he recalled, "when I took over the CIA job, Bob Gates warned me that the DO would try to make nice with me but would never tell me anything. What I discovered, once I got there, was that the DO didn't like me and never would. But they always told me everything, no matter what." In that one offhand comment, Deutch made the most perceptive observation I ever heard from a CIA director about the unique, inscrutable culture of the DO.

Another overlooked, praiseworthy aspect of Deutch's controversial tenure at the CIA is the quality of the people he brought with him to the Agency. Virtually all of them were both knowledgeable about the Agency and staunchly supportive of its people and mission. Jeff Smith (the new general counsel), Mike O'Neil, John Moseman, Gina Genton, Britt Snider, and John Nelson all became not just trusted colleagues, but good friends. Also, Deutch's handpicked choice as deputy director was already well known and liked by many of us CIA lifers—a burly, gregarious Greek American and former staff director of the Senate Intelligence Committee named George Tenet.

Nonetheless, even with all of that horsepower behind him, Deutch immediately ran into a withering barrage of criticism from inside and outside the Agency.

Walking in the door, Deutch had to wrestle with what I consider to be the most enduring and vexing policy and legal conundrum the CIA has faced in its modern history: its use of "dirty assets." In a 1996 report, the President's Intelligence Oversight Board concisely framed the issue in just one deceptively simple sentence: "[A]lthough the conduct of clandestine intelligence collection at times requires dealing with unsavory individuals and organizations, the value of what we hope to gain in terms of our national interests must outweigh the costs of such unseemly relationships and be worth the risks always inherent in clandestine activity." Dealing with a devil, in other words, lies in the details.

In the '80s the Agency had cultivated relationships with dictatorships in foreign countries that successive U.S. administrations deemed strategically important to America's foreign policy and national security interests. Deutch was confronted with a species lower down in the pecking order of unsavory characters: functionaries in foreign governments or groups that have a track record of human rights abuses. As part of its portfolio, the CIA needs to secretly recruit individual members of these governments and groups to find out what their superiors have done or plan to do, especially if Americans are imperiled. And that's where it gets tricky. The best people to recruit are those who are closest to the "action," which means they, too, have been complicit in human-rights abuses. At what point does the blood—particularly when the blood belongs to a U.S. citizen—get stuck to the Agency's hands? In the morally ambiguous role that a spy agency plays in a democratic society dedicated to the preservation of human rights, where is the line to be drawn?

These are questions that have always bedeviled the CIA, where the recruitment of well-placed "assets"—Agency vernacular for human sources of intelligence—is one of its most fundamental missions. Twice they have burst into public view. The second time was in the wake of 9/11, when the Agency was pummeled on Capitol Hill and in the media for its alleged reluctance—the term bandied about was *risk averse*—to recruit individual terrorist members of the Al Qaeda network during the years leading up the 9/11 attacks. The first time was in those early weeks of Deutch's tenure, but the attacks from outside critics about the use of "dirty assets" was strikingly different: The Agency, they charged, had become too closely associated with, too protective of, too many unsavory thugs possibly with American blood on their hands. A *New York Times* editorial intoned, on the eve of Deutch's confirmation, that he needed to "cleanse" the CIA.

So that's what Deutch set out to do. He inherited a roaring controversy over the Agency's past relationships with right-wing military dictatorships in Central America, in large part a legacy of Bill Casey's crusades against the Sandinistas in the 1980s. A particular focus was Guatemala, where the CIA was being charged with hiring as paid informants military officers suspected of political killings, kidnappings, and torture, most notably the murders in the early '90s of a U.S. citizen living in Guatemala named Michael DeVine and a rebel insurgent named Efrain Bámaca. As it happened, a media-savvy American lawyer and human rights activist named Jennifer Harbury was married to Bámaca, and she successfully enlisted members of Congress and the media in spotlighting the Bámaca and DeVine cases—and to alleged CIA connections to the perpetrators of the murders inside the right-wing military regime. This soon metastasized into charges that the Agency had since the 1980s actively consorted with an organized ring of killers dispatched by the regime to eliminate its leftist internal opposition and its perceived sympathizers, a group the media dubbed "the Guatemalan death squads." All of this spurred a two-year investigation by the CIA inspector general into the allegations, the final report of which hit Deutch's desk shortly after his 1995 arrival. The report harshly criticized a number of Agency officers, many of them longtime, well-known DO figures.

Deutch was in an impossible position. The IG did not conclude that our people were actually complicit in the human rights abuses—there was no evidence they were—but rather, that they lied to their superiors and, most damaging of all, to Congress about the nature of their association with the "death squads" and with their "dirty" Guatemalan assets. So Deutch, who came into office publicly vowing to be less "tolerant" of CIA misdeeds, felt compelled to act. He chose the ultimate sanction, firing two senior DO officers, Terry Ward and Fred Brugger. They previously had spotless records in decades of service, and they were both enormously popular figures inside the Agency. I had always been tremendously fond of both of them—I had known them for years and considered them honorable, self-effacing professionals. Suddenly, they were gone. The reaction inside the building was the most hostile I ever saw directed at a CIA director in my career. The workforce, almost as one, saw it as a craven surrender by Deutch to shifting political winds. In my heart, I felt the same way. In my head, I knew Deutch had no choice.

The Guatemala mess, and the attendant pressure from Congress, prompted Deutch to order a comprehensive internal review and assessment of the entire roster of CIA-recruited foreign operatives around the world. This "asset scrub," as the project came to be called, was led by Jeff Smith, Deutch's new, handpicked general counsel. Jeff was a longtime friend of mine dating back to the late '70s, when I was the lawyer for the DO and he was an attorney at the State Department responsible for its intelligence account. Knowing of my long experience with the DO, Jeff asked me to assist him on the "asset scrub" effort. There were two objectives: 1) working with the DO and its files to identify any assets with any history of engaging in human rights abuses (murder, kidnapping, torture, and so on) and to determine, on a case-by-case basis, whether the asset's current value as an intelligence source was significant enough to outweigh his violent past; and 2) to create a formal procedure going forward to ensure that before any new asset could be recruited in the field, that individual's background would be thoroughly explored and senior officials at CIA Headquarters would make the final call on the recruitment of any asset with human rights "baggage."

During its review of its existing stable of assets, the Counterterrorist Center pulled out the multivolume file it had compiled over the years on its most valuable and well-placed asset inside an international terrorist organization. Recruited in the late '80s, the asset was so well placed because of his impeccable terrorist credentials: He personally had the blood of innocent victims on his hands. Including, the CTC belatedly discovered when it reviewed his file, the blood of innocent Americans.

Within days, the case became a cause célèbre among a small, select pocket of people inside the Agency. Within weeks, it would play out on the front page of the country's most prominent and influential newspaper in what I consider to this day to be the most egregious and unforgettable leak I witnessed in the course of my entire career. I say that because it is the only leak I can remember that indisputably caused the death of a CIA source.

I don't believe I ever knew the guy's true name. The fact is, human assets are never identified by their true names in any documents generated by the CIA—not to anyone on the outside, and not even in internal communications, including the raw, highly classified cable traffic between headquarters and the field discussing the asset and reporting the intelligence the asset is providing. Instead, an assigned code name is always employed, not just in documents but in any conversations among CIA officers at headquarters about that person. I had long since grown accustomed to that practice, which is premised on one of the most bedrock principles in the intelligence business: The identity of a human asset is something to be protected like the crown jewels.

Still, there was plenty of information available in the asset's file to get a feel for him. He was relatively young, with European blood, sleek in appearance, and quiet in manner. Based on the physical description the CTC provided, I pictured Al Pacino in his signature movie role as Michael Corleone. In the early '80s, full of youthful hate and fury at Western democratic values, he had joined a terrorist organization just in time to participate in that group's wave of hijackings and bombings across Western Europe. But by the late '80s, something in his psyche changed. He became ashamed and repelled by the chaos he had caused, the innocent people he had killed and injured. He wanted to make amends, and hence he began cooperating with the CIA. He would tell us all he knew, and he would stay on the inside of the terrorist network to do it. The information he provided was incalculable in value, and he asked for little or nothing in return. Agency experts had vetted him from all angles, and everyone agreed: This was a stone-cold killer who had somehow acquired a conscience. It was as simple and astonishing as that.

When the CTC reviewed his extensive file as part of the "asset scrub" exercise, it found a piece of information he had told his CIA handlers at the beginning, back when he was laying bare all of his past sins, probably in part to establish his bona fides and in part as an act of expiation. One of his bombings, he volunteered, was at a location in Europe where he knew Americans would be. And Americans were indeed there when the blast went off. Several were wounded. His intent had been to kill them.

That piece of explosive information sat buried in the asset's file for years, either overlooked or ignored, until the "scrub." Should it have flatly disqualified him from ever being recruited? Not necessarily—the guy was a once-in-a-lifetime find, uniquely positioned to save more lives in the future than he had destroyed in the past. But Jeff Smith and I knew that wasn't the point. The point was, the guy had freely admitted to taking part in an attempted mass murder of U.S. citizens abroad. That is a crime under U.S. law, and the Agency had a legal obligation to immediately report it to the Justice Department. Would he have been prosecuted? In the end, probably not—his extraordinary value as an intelligence source was simply too great. But, again, that wasn't the point. By sitting on the information, and by then going ahead and establishing a secret relationship with him, the Agency had for all practical purposes immunized him from U.S. prosecution. In the sometimes ambiguous interplay between intelligence operations and the law, there are nonetheless certain absolutes. One of them is that the CIA has no authority—ever—to grant anyone immunity from U.S. prosecution. Only the Justice Department can do that.

So there we were in mid-1995, in the midst of all the controversy publicly churning over the wisdom and morality of the CIA's use of "dirty assets," suddenly confronted with the quintessential case: a guy who had acknowledged to us years ago that he had American blood on his hands. And, thanks to our screwup, no one outside the CIA knew anything about it. There was only one thing to do: Go to the Justice Department and go to our committees on the Hill and tell all.

Typically, when the Agency learns about a possible violation of U.S. law by one of its employees or assets, or even by someone not affiliated with the CIA, the Office of General Counsel prepares a "crimes report" letter to the head of the DOJ criminal division, setting forth the bare facts of the case. However, when the facts are too sensitive, or if time is of the essence, the OGC instead seeks an urgent meeting with our intelligence focal point in the criminal division. This matter clearly qualified, so I made an appointment to visit the criminal division a day or two later. During my career, I initiated dozens of such meetings, and typically they consisted of a lot of eye-rolling by our DOJ counterparts as they would listen to me spin out some bizarre, tangled tale of crime and intrigue. Over time, I had learned to ignore the eye-rolling and just plow ahead with what I had to say, never sugarcoating anything. I always knew and trusted that the small, select cadre of Justice lawyers with whom we shared our information would treat anything I told them with the utmost professionalism and discretion. I cannot recall a single instance in my career where the criminal division leaked or otherwise compromised any information from a "crimes report" we made, and believe me, we made thousands of them. This occasion would be no exception.

A few days later, the chief of the CIA Counterterrorist Center traveled to Capitol Hill to perform the thankless task of telling the whole messy story surrounding this "dirty asset" to the staffs of the House and Senate intelligence committees. I didn't attend the briefing, but the chief reported back that the staffers asked all sorts of detailed questions and that he had left behind a "fact sheet" on the case.

Less than twenty-four hours after the staffers had been briefed, the CIA Office of Public Affairs got a phone call from Tim Weiner, the national security correspondent for the *New York Times*. Weiner reeled off virtually every detail of the CTC chief's presentation. Weiner said he was going to write a story about it. Did the Agency have any comment to make about the case? he asked.

Who leaked the information to Weiner? The timing strongly suggested it came from someone on the Hill, but an ensuing FBI investigation was inconclusive. The Agency, given its failure to inform law enforcement about the asset on a timely basis, was in no position to push the issue.

In any case, whenever a reporter calls the Agency to ask for an official comment about a CIA story he or she is about to publish, the Agency mostly reacts in one of two ways: It either denies that the story is accurate (and that is done only when it is in fact false) or simply declines to comment.

This time, however, the Agency reacted by imploring Weiner not to run the story. It took a step it takes rarely—it brought Weiner out to Langley for a personal plea from the Counterterrorist Center chief, who told Weiner, in a series of long and tense discussions, why this was literally a matter of life and death. A story "burning" the asset would not only undermine the Agency's best counterterrorist source, it could get him killed—a gang of ruthless terrorists is the most unforgiving of groups when it comes to an informer in their midst.

A "bug-eyed" Weiner, as the CTC chief later described him, listened to all the pleas. In a desperate effort to appease Weiner and his editors, the Agency agreed to let Jeff Smith be quoted on the record with some general comments about the "asset scrub" and the complexities surrounding the use of intelligence sources with human rights baggage. The idea was to steer the story away from any details about this particular asset. Despite all our entreaties, the *Times* ran the story on page 1 on August 21, 1995. Some identifying details were omitted, but way too many weren't.

The case officer handling the asset tracked him down overseas for an emergency meeting. To warn him about the story, to offer him protection and safe haven. The asset, stunned and betrayed, refused. He would have nothing more to do with us, he told the case officer. He promptly went underground and disappeared. No one ever saw him again. No one.

In 2007, Tim Weiner's book *Legacy of Ashes* was published. Running almost eight hundred pages, it was an exhaustively researched chronicle of the sixty-year history of the Agency. It earned rapturous reviews from the critics and became a best seller and National Book Award winner. It was also a relentlessly scathing portrayal of virtually everything the Agency had done in its history, recounting virtually every controversy, every episode, in a way that portrayed the institution as incompetent, untrustworthy, and irresponsible. Nowhere in his massive tome, however, did Weiner mention the front-page article he wrote, more than a decade before, outing our most irreplaceable "dirty" asset.

At the time the Weiner piece was published in the *Times*, it was one more log on the political fires then burning in Washington, D.C., over the morality of the CIA's historical practice of enlisting the services of individuals with unsavory, violent pasts. After the Guatemala revelations and the resulting opprobrium directed at the DO officials caught up in them, the Agency's clandestine service officers in the trenches were quietly deriving what would be a lasting, fateful lesson: It's too dangerous to recruit nasty characters crawling in the back alleys of the world. To do so meant not only risking your career, but getting your source compromised and killed. Sure, this was probably an overreaction, but under the circumstances, it was an understandable one.

A few years later, in the wake of 9/11, Congress and the media would famously, and derisively, call this "risk aversion." As Exhibit A, they cited the regulations that John Deutch, under intense congressional and media pressure, had directed Jeff Smith, with my help, to put in place in late 1995 in an effort to bring some degree of clarity and order to the complex, no-win dilemma of whether, and how, to use "dirty assets." The "Deutch Guidelines," the post-9/11 critics charged without a trace of self-awareness, were all Deutch's fault.

By then, Deutch was long gone from the Agency. He had lasted less than two years as CIA director, leaving at the end of 1996. Shortly thereafter, he was caught up in an ugly personal scandal of his own making, when it was discovered that he had recklessly used his personal computer at home to write and store classified information. It was an egregious breach of security on his part, and it served to cement his standing as the most maligned CIA director in modern history.

Except with me.

All in all, the years 1993 through 1996 were depressing times for the Agency. From a professional standpoint, I look back at the period as one in which I had to cope with one debacle after another. From a personal standpoint, however, it was a happy juncture, because I became a newly married—remarried, actually—man.

On October 16, 1993, after a whirlwind (?) six-year courtship, I married the former Sharon Breed. The wedding ceremony took place at the stately Jefferson Hotel in downtown Washington, and my former boss Stan Sporkin, now a federal court judge, presided over the vows. Sharon and I, both divorced single parents, first met in the fall of 1987 during a picnic at the Potomac School, a private elementary school just up the road from CIA headquarters. Our respective nine-year-old kids—my son, James, and her daughter, Stephanie—happened to be in the same fourth-grade class together. It was your typical elementary school picnic, a scene of organized chaos with masses of little kids darting between the paper-plate-and-cup-strewn tables. As the festivities were mercifully winding down, Sharon and I struck up a conversation when we found ourselves alone in the parking lot, both attempting to locate and corral our separate offspring among all the tykes careering around the premises. A chance encounter—pure serendipity and, I suppose, fate. We went out on our first date a few days later. I was immediately smitten.

As I write this, we are happily closing in on our twentieth year of marriage. To this day, whenever someone at a cocktail party or other social occasion who doesn't know us asks how we first met, Sharon has a favorite response. "We met in the fourth grade," she says with a mischievous smile.

CHAPTER 9

Bin Laden Bursts Out
(1997–2001)

After Deutch's departure at the end of 1996, his number two man, George Tenet, became acting CIA director. Clinton had nominated his national security advisor, Anthony Lake, for the CIA director position, but the nomination foundered in the face of obdurate opposition by Republicans on the Senate Intelligence Committee, led by its incoming chairman, Richard Shelby. Clinton then turned to Tenet. In his 2007 memoir, *At the Center of the Storm*, Tenet admitted that Clinton scarcely interviewed him before offering him the job, which Tenet said he found "odd." When I read that, I actually didn't think it odd, at all; Clinton by then had clearly demonstrated monumental indifference toward the Agency's work and its people.

With the exception of Bob Gates (who had been a career CIA official), George Tenet was the first and only nominee for CIA director that I personally knew before he was tapped for the position. He was also the first and last nominee younger than I was at the time of nomination, something that I remember as finding vaguely disconcerting. I first met Tenet in 1987, when Senator David Boren, the Intelligence Committee chairman at that time, plucked him out of nowhere to be the committee's staff director. George was only in his early thirties at the time, and other committee staffers openly grumbled to us at the Agency, for he was considerably younger and less experienced in intelligence issues than most of his staff colleagues.

George and I hit it off right away. His personality in the mid-'80s was the same as it would always be—open, informal, friendly, and utterly without pretension or any sense of self-importance (the latter two traits uncharacteristic among Hill staffers). He also had a charming, playful side in the way he carried out his serious responsibilities for intelligence oversight.

For example, I recall an episode in the late '80s when I was sent down to the intelligence committees to deliver some bad news that we had discovered only days before: One of the leaders of the Nicaraguan contras, Adolfo Calero, was implicated in the possible misuse of Agency (and thus U.S. taxpayer) funds. I spilled out the whole story in all its embarrassing and gory detail in a closed briefing at the Senate Intelligence Committee as the phalanx of committee Democrats sitting there listening to me got more and more incensed. At one point, the normally genial and supportive Boren demanded to know who in the Agency was going to be punished for allowing Calero's transgression to happen.

"Well," I responded wanly, "so far the only person being punished is me, because I'm the guy who was sent down to tell you this story."

A few of the Democrats managed a sympathetic laugh, but not Boren. He then ordered that I be placed under oath, which was an unusual and hostile step for the committee to take. Typically, it's an indication that the committee doesn't necessarily believe what the witness is saying. (Which I thought was odd—if I were going to make something up, it would have been a hell of a less incriminating story than the one I was telling.) But in any event, as I dutifully rose to take the oath, I spotted George Tenet, sitting in his usual place against the wall behind his boss, Boren. There he was, unseen by Boren but in my direct line of sight, grinning broadly and aping me raising my arm taking the oath, only in his pantomime he kept tugging his arm up and down. With Boren staring balefully down at me from the dais, I had to stifle my own grin, which wasn't easy. But George did effectively convey an implicit, welcome message: This is theater, Rizzo, so just relax and go with it.

Damn, I thought as I drove back to the Agency after finally escaping the briefing, this guy Tenet is a piece of work. Looking back now, if there was one day that sealed my enduring affection for him in the years to come, it was that day at the Senate Intelligence Committee.

Our paths would continue to cross when George joined the Clinton administration in 1993 to serve as Lake's focal point with the Agency at the NSC. In the weeks leading up to the arrest of Rick Ames in 1994,

George eagerly played a role in a ruse intended to get Ames out of his office so that investigators could do another search of it. Under a pretext, Ames's boss told him and a couple of his Agency colleagues that they needed to brief Tenet on a matter in Tenet's NSC office. Details of the Ames investigation were then still known to very few people inside the government, so George was told about the case but was not told which of the three CIA guys he would be meeting with was the Russian mole. The sham meeting came off without a hitch, and I was told that George played his part convincingly. Later, after the arrest finally went down, I asked Tenet if he had any inkling during the meeting about which of the Agency guys he met with was the traitor.

"Sure," he replied jovially. "I knew it had to be Ames. He was the only one of the three of them who was wearing expensive Italian shoes."

And so, for all sorts of reasons, I was happy when John Deutch picked George to be his deputy in 1995, and I was even happier when George was confirmed as CIA director on July 11, 1997. He knew and loved the Agency, and, unlike Deutch, actually wanted the job and made it clear that he hoped to stay in office for a long time. For a workforce that had seen three CIA directors come and go in the previous five years, hearing that was music to our ears.

From the start, he fit right in. In terms of personal demeanor, George was the most "regular guy" DCI I ever worked for. Only in his midforties when he took office, George was a contemporary of much of the CIA's population and bonded easily with everyone he met, whether in meetings or waiting in the cashier's line in the employee cafeteria. He often shambled into meetings in the hallowed director's conference room with tie askew, sometimes in his stocking feet, gnawing away on an unlit Cuban cigar from the stash he had accumulated courtesy of visiting heads of foreign intelligence services. (Forbidden from smoking after having suffered a heart attack, he had a habit of reducing these primo cigars to a lumpen, saliva-soaked mass, which always drove me—a devoted cigar smoker dating back to college—quietly nuts.) Whether the meetings were small or large, George also displayed a virtuoso skill in managing to drop the "f-bomb" liberally into the conversation, variously employing it as a noun, adjective, verb, and occasional prepositional phrase (in my experience with DCIs, only Leon Panetta years later would rival George in f-bomb dexterity).

With George, somehow none of these habits ever came off as vulgar or offensive. Rather, they seemed genuine coming from a first-generation Greek American from Queens who exuded an earthy, Zorba-like warmth. For me, it was crystallized best in the way he dealt with his ever-present security detail. In my observations over the years, other DCIs treated their personal CIA bodyguards as either invisible furniture or intrusive nuisances. George, by contrast, seemed to view his bodyguards as hale companions; sometimes I would spot him striding around the building with his arms draped around their shoulders, like they were all a bunch of carefree fraternity buddies on their way to a party.

I know of no one at the CIA who ever dealt with George who did not like him. It was impossible not to like him.

George's ascension to the DCI job gave the Agency a jolt of energy and optimism that had been largely absent in the decade that had passed since Iran-contra. And, relatively speaking, he seemed to have Clinton's trust and confidence; while Deutch's deputy, he had been assigned delicate (and unusual) duties as a presidential diplomatic emissary in the thorny Israeli-Palestinian peace negotiations. Plus, like Deutch, he was given cabinet status. Nevertheless, Clinton was Clinton, after all, so he kept his DCI at arm's length. George was not allowed to attend the morning intelligence briefing Clinton received each day from his national security aides. In his 2007 memoir, George described his face-to-face meetings with Clinton as "sporadic" and wistfully remarked that "[b]eing in regular, direct contact with the president is an incredible boon to a CIA director's ability to do his job." With Clinton, George admitted in his memoir, if he had an important message to deliver or plea to make—such as for significant increases for the CIA counterterrorism budget—he would sit down and write the commander in chief a letter. Those letters in which he rattled a tin cup had scant effect: "For the most part I succeeded in annoying the administration for which I worked but did not loosen any significant purse strings."

And all the while during the late '90s, the threat posed by a Saudi-born man named Osama bin Laden and his Al Qaeda network was inexorably growing. Correspondingly, my focus and responsibilities on legal issues related to bin Laden were also growing. They would dominate, and eventually consume, the balance of my CIA career.

Bin Laden Bursts Out (1997–2001)

• • •

By 1997, the Office of General Counsel had grown to about eighty lawyers, and I had become second in command, which was historically the highest position a career CIA lawyer could hope to attain. When he became DCI, George arranged for the White House to tap Bob McNamara (no relation to the former secretary of defense) for the general counsel position. Congress had recently passed a law mandating that the GC be a presidential appointment subject to Senate confirmation (one of the leftover "reforms" recommended by the Iran-contra committee). McNamara was the first GC candidate to come under this new statutory regime, and only in retrospect does it seem astonishing that the Senate quickly confirmed him without bothering with the formality of a confirmation hearing. As it happened, McNamara and I had been friends for a long time, dating back to his years as a senior lawyer in the Treasury Department. Bob could be intense and uptight at times, but overall he was a smart, honorable guy I knew I could get along with. I also knew that he trusted me enough to give me considerable sway in handling the "covert operations" account, which is all that really mattered to me at that point.

The first World Trade Center (WTC) bombing had occurred in early 1993, but the CIA had not been a major player in the government's reaction afterward. For one thing, the new Clinton administration, partly out of wariness and partly out of apathy, had no inclination to plunge head-first into the murky waters of covert action in the counterterrorist arena. Moreover, in early 1993, Al Qaeda was still largely an unknown entity inside the intelligence community, and its connection to the 1993 bombing was not discovered until much later.

The unanimous view inside the government in the wake of the 1993 WTC attack was that the law-enforcement community would have the lead for combating terrorists: They were to be indicted, arrested, and prosecuted in U.S. courts, which in effect meant after an attack had been carried out. If the CIA could provide leads on where these criminals might have fled or be hiding overseas, great, but that was it in terms of our role. I may be oversimplifying a bit here—the Agency also was responsible for trying to discover possible plots against the homeland coming from abroad—but I believe my essential point is valid: the CIA in the early '90s was assigned a third-fiddle role, behind the Justice Department and FBI criminal investigators, in dealing with the global terrorist threat.

And no one at the CIA, including me, saw anything wrong about that approach. Certainly, it never crossed our minds to suggest that hey, these rabid, martyr-wannabe jihadists are not going to be exactly cowed by the threat of a criminal prosecution, especially when the hammer would most likely come down after they achieved their goal of killing as many people as they could. In 1993, I spent months as the CIA's focal point on a high-level intergovernmental task force convened in the wake of the first WTC attack. Our assigned objective was to identify new, out-of-the-box ways for the intelligence community to "support" law-enforcement efforts. It never occurred to me to question the premise. Or to even muse to myself that maybe the government should be focused on killing terrorists, not indicting them.

By the end of 1998, however, the White House was handing the baton, albeit tentatively, to the CIA. Like Jimmy Carter, the last Democratic president before him, Clinton belatedly turned to the Agency and its covert-action capabilities to deal with a burgeoning threat to national security. For Carter, it had been the Soviet invasion of Afghanistan and Soviet- and Cuban-sponsored subversion in Central America. For Clinton, it was bin Laden and Al Qaeda. Also like the Carter administration, the Clinton White House ordered up a rapid-fire series of MONs from the Agency over a period of several months. I took the lead in drafting these documents, and as always I did my best to reflect in the clearest possible language what sorts of actions the president wanted us to carry out. Which would prove to be a difficult task indeed.

I had first heard the names Osama bin Laden and Al Qaeda around 1993, a time when bin Laden was operating out of Sudan. I don't recall knowing many details back then about bin Laden or what he was up to, much beyond his being a charismatic terrorist financier who would occasionally surface to deliver anti-U.S. diatribes. As the 9/11 Commission would later note, for all his vitriol and veiled threats against "the far enemy," there were no concrete links that could be established between bin Laden and the most prominent terrorist attacks that took place during the early and mid-'90s, such as the 1993 WTC bombing, the 1995 Manila plot to blow up a dozen U.S. airliners over the Pacific, and the 1996 truck bomb detonation at the Khobar Towers complex in Saudi Arabia housing U.S. Air Force personnel.

By 1998, however, bin Laden had made his intentions crystal clear. In February 1998, he issued his infamous public "fatwa" calling for the murder of any American, anywhere on earth, as the "individual duty for every Muslim who can do it in any country in which it is possible to do it." Six months later, in August 1998, bin Laden's words turned into tragic, spectacular, chillingly coordinated action: The U.S. embassies in Kenya and Tanzania were bombed, almost simultaneously, killing 240 people, including a number of Americans, and wounding more than 4,000. The evidence, although not conclusive for prosecution purposes, pointed to bin Laden and Al Qaeda as being behind the attacks.

During the months before the embassy attacks, the Agency was already developing contingency plans for the capture of bin Laden and his delivery to the United States for prosecution. Our analysts were certain that he was in hiding somewhere in Afghanistan, perhaps in the vast no-man's-land along the Afghanistan-Pakistan border. But there was one major hitch: There was no indictment pending against him. Nonetheless, at White House direction, I drafted an MON in May 1998 authorizing a specific plan that involved having some Afghan tribal groups, with CIA support and funding, capture bin Laden and deliver him to justice, either in the United States or elsewhere. There was an old Presidential Finding on worldwide terrorism that was still on the books, issued by President Reagan in 1986, that contained language that was probably broad enough to cover the sort of "snatch" contemplated against bin Laden. I knew that, because I was the guy who had drafted the Reagan Finding and, among all the officials who had been involved in the Finding back then, I was the only one still around in 1998. But I didn't want the Agency to act simply on the basis of that Finding: I wrote it in another era, to deal with terrorists from another era, long before there was anyone comparable to bin Laden. Besides, the more I learned about the plan, the more iffy it sounded to me; among other things, bin Laden was not facing criminal charges in the United States (federal prosecutors would not secure a sealed indictment until that June), and there was no other country yet willing to take him off our hands. To top it off, even if the Afghan tribals were to get to him, our people were telling us that bin Laden was unlikely to come along quietly. There would be a shoot-out, and bin Laden—and maybe women and children around him—could be killed. And the Clinton White House was only talking about capturing bin Laden, not knocking him off.

And so, with Bob McNamara's support, I told George Tenet we needed new, specific presidential authority, via an MON, before directing our Afghan tribal surrogates to attempt a "snatch." I suppose one could call that "risk aversion." So be it. In any case, the plan was called off in mid-May, and the MON I drafted was shelved. To this day, I don't know for certain who actually made that call. The 9/11 Commission, in its meticulous reconstruction of events in the years leading up to 9/11, couldn't definitively pin that down, either.

Following the embassy bombings in August, however, the Clinton White House decided to up the ante. Only it would prove very hard to discern how much.

At first, the MON authorizing a "snatch" of bin Laden by our Afghan tribals was dusted off. This time around, I was instructed to add language authorizing the tribals to use force only for "self-defense." It was a phrase I did not remember ever including in a Finding or MON before and one more suited for a judge's jury instructions in a criminal trial than as a covert-action directive. But we did as we were told, and Clinton signed the document in late August.

As the summer of 1998 turned into fall and early winter, and as vaguely sourced but chilling intelligence reports filtered in, hinting at possible Al Qaeda attacks on other U.S. embassies and even U.S. aircraft, the Clinton White House gingerly inched forward. It was becoming abundantly apparent that any chance for the tribals to pull off a successful "snatch" would require them to employ force well beyond any reasonable definition of "self-defense"; in other words, they would need to go in to get bin Laden with guns blazing. I recommended to George Tenet that, in order to protect the CIA and to reflect the cold reality, any new MON needed to include blunt language in which the president would acknowledge the likelihood that bin Laden would be killed in any effort to capture him. I had never drafted a Finding or MON before that contained such stark language, but I didn't see any other way to say it.

And yet somewhere along the way up the chain in the NSC structure, another turn of phrase was inserted in the MON that Clinton would ultimately sign in December: The CIA could authorize the Afghan tribals to kill bin Laden only if capture was "not feasible." It was another term I didn't remember ever seeing before in a presidential covert-action authorization, and it was disconcertingly opaque. Who would decide if capture wasn't feasible? The tribals, or their Agency handlers? When would the call be made? Before any capture plan was launched, or in the middle of the fray, with bullets flying?

Or, in the worst-case scenario, would the call be made well after the firefight, with bin Laden shot dead, and some Monday-morning quarterback behind a desk in the Executive Branch or Congress concluding that it would have been "feasible" to take him alive?

I had been in the business of drafting Findings and MONs for twenty years, and my guiding principle had always been to write language that established bright lines about what a president was authorizing the Agency to do in terms of covert action. This one was fuzzy in the most legally and morally hazardous area of all: when, and under what circumstances, the Agency could sanction the killing of a particular individual.

Fortunately (albeit unfortunately for the country, as history would show), my worries were unwarranted. The Afghan tribals soon proved supremely incapable of mounting any sort of operation against bin Laden, capture or otherwise. As a result, with the drumbeat of intelligence growing louder about Al Qaeda plans to strike the United States, the Agency frantically cast about for some other Afghan indigenous group that had the methods and the motivation to find where bin Laden was hiding, and get to him.

The CIA turned to a group called the Northern Alliance, led by a man named Ahmed Shah Massoud, a fearless, legendary hero of the Afghan resistance to the Soviet occupation of the '80s. (Massoud also had a well-deserved reputation as being a brutal warlord possibly mixed up in the flourishing Afghan drug trade. But hey, nobody's perfect.) Massoud certainly had the chops to go after bin Laden. So, in early February 1999, I was directed to draft yet another MON to unleash Massoud and his Northern Alliance. And then things got even more confusing.

The language I used mirrored wording of the MON covering the Afghan tribals that Clinton had signed just a few weeks before: capture if possible, kill if capture isn't feasible. As noted above, I didn't like that formulation, but I figured it was important to keep the marching orders consistent, no matter which Afghan group the Agency was dealing with. No sense in muddying the waters even further, especially when the ground rules involved potentially lethal actions.

The language was vetted and approved by everyone involved and got all the way to the Oval Office, but before signing the MON, Clinton did something that I never saw any other president do, before or since: he scribbled his own handwritten changes to the text. As best I can recall, he scratched out what I thought was the most important passage of the previous MON, which was an acknowledgment that in all likelihood bin Laden would be killed in any effort to capture him. Clinton instead inserted a few, new qualifying words that, to my mind, appeared to revert to the more restrictive standard he had set in his original MON governing the Afghan tribals in August 1998, in the wake of the embassy bombings: Lethal action could be taken against bin Laden only in self-defense.

I found Clinton's seeming equivocation on such a fundamental national security policy decision baffling, to say the least. Five years later, I would be even more baffled when I read his testimony before the 9/11 Commission, in which this indisputably brilliant, details-oriented man claimed not to have any recollection as to why he made his handwritten changes.

And so, in February 1999, with Clinton having signed three MONs authorizing capture operations against bin Laden in the space of five months, I thought the Agency was being left out on a precarious limb. In effect, the president had given the CIA more leeway to approve lethal actions by one group (the Afghan tribals) that had no capability or stomach for taking them than by another (Massoud and his Northern Alliance) that had every means and motive to do so. It took the concept of "mixed presidential signals" to a new and perilous level.

Janet Reno, Clinton's attorney general, was a problem for the Agency as well during this period. The AG, then and now, is in the loop on all proposed new Findings and MONs. I was present at a number of covert-action briefings CIA personnel gave Reno during her nearly eight years in office, and she was always a courteous and interested listener. When it came to the MONs regarding bin Laden, however, she acted in ways that were often erratic and alarming. When each proposed MON was sent to her for review, she or her staff would agonize over and flyspeck every word, no matter how bland it was. For at least two of the three MONs regarding bin Laden, her legal approval, when it finally came, was accompanied by a separate memo she sent to Clinton in which she expressed her opposition on "policy" grounds.

Now, as one of the cabinet principals taking part in national security decision-making processes, it was certainly her prerogative to do that—over the years, I had seen various secretaries of state and defense express policy objections to their president about specific covert-action proposals. But for an attorney general, the nation's chief law-enforcement officer, to go on record against a Finding or MON sends an implicitly intimidating message to those carrying out the president's directive: If things go awry, you're on the legal hook, not me.

And Reno went further. Once during this period when the various MONs shifting the ground rules on bin Laden "capture" operations were churning, a shaken George Tenet reported back to Bob McNamara and me about a session he had just had with Reno. The AG, he said, had just informed him that she would consider as "illegal" any CIA operation intended solely to kill bin Laden. George heard the nation's chief law-enforcement officer say the word *illegal* and immediately translated it to *murder*. As far as I know, she never expressed that position in writing, but it hardly encouraged us at the Agency to push the lethal envelope against bin Laden.

In the aftermath of the 9/11 attacks, Bill Clinton insisted that while in office he had issued direct, unambiguous orders to the CIA to kill bin Laden. Perhaps he sincerely believed that. I wonder if he had checked with his former attorney general.

All that said, Clinton and the people around him can't be entirely faulted for this tangled state of affairs, and they certainly weren't the reason bin Laden escaped capture or death during Clinton's last years in office. I never saw any CIA covert-action proposal during that period that, at least to me, seemed to have any real prospect for success. Reliable intelligence about bin Laden's whereabouts was hard to come by, and the stuff that did come in had mostly to do with where bin Laden had previously been, not where he currently was or where he was going. Further, even if the Agency had gotten any "smoking gun" intelligence about bin Laden's location, from what I read and heard inside our building I had no confidence that the groups the CIA was supporting in Afghanistan had anywhere near the wherewithal to carry out the job. So, looking back now, the Clinton administration's inconsistent and unsettling operational mandate to the Agency proved, as a practical matter, to be irrelevant.

Apart from the spate of MONs on bin Laden, the Agency was conducting other, less-high-risk/high-reward covert-action activities against

Al Qaeda during '98 and '99. At Tenet's direction, the entire intelligence community was going all out in targeting Al Qaeda from an intelligence-collection standpoint. However, Clinton issued no new Findings or MONs on counterterrorism from mid-'99 through the end of his administration, not even in the wake of the Al Qaeda bombing of the USS *Cole* in October 2000. In the 9/11 postmortems, Clinton took some heat for that, but I think it's unfair criticism. Clinton was a lame-duck incumbent wrapping up his second term, and outgoing presidents historically have been reluctant to saddle their successors with last-gasp, high-stakes covert-action initiatives. Ronald Reagan, the last two-term president before Clinton, similarly refrained from signing any new Findings and MONs during his last year in office. Besides, as I indicated above, it wasn't as if bin Laden and his closest cohorts were low-hanging fruit from an intelligence standpoint; even if Clinton, say, had issued clear, unconditional orders after the *Cole* bombing for the CIA to kill those guys, the Agency didn't know where they were, and even if we had, we didn't have the means to get to them. And that's the inconvenient truth.

I voted for Al Gore in the 2000 presidential election. It was consistent with a simple—and probably overly simplistic—pattern I had followed up to then and would continue to follow throughout my CIA career. Every four years, I would vote for the incumbent president, or his successor from the same party. Thus, I voted for Ford in '76, Carter in '80, Reagan in '84, Bush in '88, Bush in '92, Clinton in '96, Gore in 2000, and Bush in '04. (It was only in 2008—in the waning months of my career—that I deviated from this pattern. What I had heard and personally observed about John McCain gave me serious pause about his temperament.)

I always thought it was best, both for the CIA as an institution and for me personally, to have continuity in the Agency's leadership and in the White House people it was dealing with. Every time a new administration from a different political party arrived, there inevitably was a "learning curve" involved for the Agency's career workforce—we had a different set of players in the top ranks of the Executive Branch to educate and work with, and they in turn had to become familiar and comfortable with us and the shadowy, somewhat intimidating organization of which we were a part. It was always a time-consuming, and often disruptive and frustrating, process to have to go through.

In particular, by 2000 I was mindful of the fact that over my career up to that time every incoming president from a party different from that of his predecessor—Carter, Reagan, and Clinton—had replaced the sitting CIA director. It thus seemed certain that if George W. Bush won, then George Tenet would be gone, too. And I didn't want that to happen. I thought Tenet was a great fit for the Agency, and, just as important, I knew he wanted to stay. Unlike Clinton, Al Gore had always seemed to be a sophisticated, engaged, and supportive patron of the CIA. Plus, I had met him a few times by then, and while the encounters were brief, he struck me as a very capable and likable guy. George W. Bush, on the other hand, was a governor with zero experience in intelligence matters.

But I had a more parochial reason for wanting George Tenet to stay in place. A new CIA director almost certainly would mean there would be a new general counsel. As a deputy, I had broken in four new GCs—Elizabeth Rindskopf Parker, Jeff Smith, Mike O'Neil, and Bob McNamara—in the space of the previous ten years, and the prospect of having to show someone the ropes yet again was distinctly unappealing to me. I was firmly rooted in the second-in-command position in the office, and I had no expectation of going any higher—no career CIA lawyer had been tapped for the top job since I joined the CIA nearly a quarter century before. In short, I had nothing left to prove, and nothing left to shoot for, in the OGC. I had even started to informally explore the possibility of leaving the office for another senior assignment elsewhere in the organization—there was one posting, to a place I had always wanted to live, that was particularly intriguing. I was quite comfortable with Bob McNamara at the helm as GC and assumed that if George stayed in a Gore administration, Bob would stick around as well, at least for a year or two. After that, I figured, I would make a move to do something else. Something different in the intelligence field, something fun.

Political prognostication and career planning were never my strong points.

As everyone knows, George Bush, with assistance from the Supreme Court, belatedly won the 2000 presidential election. Then Bush did what very few of us in the Agency expected: He asked George Tenet to continue serving as director. Not only that, but he immediately showed an avid interest in intelligence matters and welcomed Tenet back into the intelligence briefings held in the Oval Office every morning. Those of us in the senior Agency career ranks were delighted—not only did that mean there would be continuity at the top of the CIA, but we knew that a director with daily, direct access to the president was paramount in our business. We hadn't had that since Bob Gates was DCI and the new president's father was in the Oval Office.

I, for one, thought this happily surprising turn of events was partly due to the quiet influence of Bush's father, and partly because George Tenet's affable, frat-boy bonhomie meshed nicely with that of the new president. Mostly, however, I think that Bush's decision at the outset to keep George and the Agency close by was prompted by the waves of intelligence reporting he was getting from the moment he took office, reports all pointing at an inevitable, likely spectacular, and bloody Al Qaeda attack on American citizens somewhere in the world. The intelligence drumbeat that began in the final two years of the Clinton administration was getting ever more loud, and George Tenet was the drum major.

Within a month or so of the arrival of the new Bush team, George ordered up a new, more comprehensive and aggressive draft MON against the Al Qaeda target that would supersede the confusing welter of MONs left over from the final Clinton years. The Counterterrorist Center put together a list of covert-action options that went well beyond anything the CIA had been granted previously, including uncovering bin Laden's massive financial network. With respect to lethal action against bin Laden, I contributed language to the draft MON that was as direct and unambiguous as I could make it: We would be given authority to either capture or kill bin Laden, period. In other words, dead or alive. I thought the Agency might as well tee up the issue right off the bat with the new president and the new attorney general.

George shipped the MON off to Condoleezza Rice, the incoming national security advisor, and used it as a vehicle for trying to prod the Bush White House to focus on the ever-growing and increasingly dire threat posed by Al Qaeda. I don't know if he realistically expected that Bush would approve such a dramatic, precedent-shattering expansion of our counterterrorism authorities in his first several months in office. I know that I did not. Again, I drew on the lessons learned from my twenty years of observing how presidents approached covert action. Just as presidents whose terms are winding down are reluctant to launch major new covert-action initiatives, so too are presidents who are just newly arrived in office. I always found this initial reluctance on the part of new presidents totally understandable—covert action is a tempting but potentially scary incendiary device in the government's national security arsenal, and a new Oval Office occupant (and his advisors around him) rightly tends to approach it warily. Perhaps they all remember that President Kennedy gave his final okay for the Bay of Pigs invasion less than three months after he was sworn in.

So I don't share the view expressed by some post-9/11 critics that the Bush White House in its first months in office was either too cavalier or too obtuse to address the growing evidence of Al Qaeda threats against the homeland. A new balls-out MON signed by Bush would have been nice, I suppose, but I doubt it would have changed history. The covert-action authorizations Clinton left behind may have been inconsistent and equivocal, but they were more than sufficient to grant the Agency all the legal authority it would have needed to detect and prevent the 9/11 attacks.

Despite the best efforts of everyone from George Tenet on down, we just didn't do it.

CHAPTER 10

The Attacks and the Response
(September 2001–January 2002)

When the news first broke on that sunny Tuesday morning of September 11, 2001, I and thousands of other employees at the CIA's Langley headquarters were just settling in for another day at the office. Like the rest of the country, we watched our office TVs with unbelieving shock and horror as the World Trade Center towers collapsed. Many of us were aware of the increasingly ominous intelligence reports during the previous two years about a possible attack, but no one had envisioned this particular nightmare scenario. Yet everyone in the building who had been privy to those reports, myself included, immediately realized that this had to be an Al Qaeda operation.

And then came the news that another passenger jet had hit the Pentagon, just a few miles away from the Agency. Shortly after that, word came that yet another hijacked plane was still in the air, perhaps headed for the Washington metropolitan area. We watched as TV reporters, just as shaken and bewildered as everyone else, began excitedly speculating about its potential target. Perhaps the White House, they said. Perhaps the Capitol. Or perhaps CIA Headquarters.

It is an indelible memory, yet impossible to describe adequately, what it was like for us at Langley as we stared out our office windows—in my case, on the top floor of the original headquarters building—toward the skies. From my perch, I could look across the courtyard toward the new headquarters building and see dozens of my colleagues at their windows, looking out.

A few minutes later, an urgent message appeared on every office computer screen at the Agency: "Immediate Evacuation." There would be exceptions to that edict, of course. Everyone involved on the counter-terrorist account stayed at his post. George Tenet took a handful of his top aides to a separate, small building—the CIA's printing plant—on the headquarters campus. General Counsel Bob McNamara was included in that small group, but I was not. Still, I decided to stay where I was. It was a decision made on strictly practical grounds. I could see from my office window, and from the windows in the Office of Public Affairs across the hall, that the roads to the main exit gates were already grid-locked. I could also see hundreds of employees spilling out of the two buildings and heading—most walking, some running—toward their cars in the vast parking lots encircling the buildings. It would take me hours to get off the compound and home, I figured. So I decided the hell with it. I closed the door to my office suite, ignored the blaring recorded voice on the hallway intercom repeating the evacuation order, and hunkered down at my desk. I wanted to do something, anything, that might be productive. My first move was to follow any lawyer's natural instinct. I took out a blank yellow legal pad. Focus, I told myself. Focus.

I knew that two things were bound to happen to the Agency in the immediate postmortems (for once, in the literal sense of that term) of this catastrophe. There would be investigations and recriminations directed at the CIA, demanding answers on how we could have let this happen. All the previous controversies I had been involved in during my Agency career would pale by comparison. But there was nothing to be done about that. Besides, for now, that was totally beside the point.

The other thing was that the White House would order the Agency to develop and undertake a full-scale assault on Al Qaeda, to employ all means necessary to prevent any further attacks on the homeland. So I poised my pen on the legal pad and began scribbling a laundry list of potential covert actions the CIA could undertake in the weeks and months ahead. Things we had never done before in my career. On that unimaginable morning, I let my imagination run wild.

I didn't keep any personal files on covert-action programs in my office, so I had to rely on memory to establish a baseline on what authority we already had to act against Al Qaeda. The spate of Clinton MONs in 1998 and 1999—which were still on the books—were confusing and contra-dictory, and in any case were woefully insufficient now. They permitted us to kill bin Laden and his close associates, maybe, but the authorities were honeycombed with conditions and caveats. I tried to remember the terms of the proposed MON that Tenet had ordered up and presented to the new Bush administration in the early months of 2001. It was more aggressive and less ambiguous than the Clinton MONs, giving clear direction to the CIA to take lethal action against bin Laden. Yet even that seemed not to go far enough. Not on the morning of 9/11.

I scribbled down a new formulation: "Lethal action against members of Al Qaeda and any affiliated groups," or words to that effect. We would hunt down and kill anyone in Al Qaeda, or acting under its direction or influence, involved in the 9/11 attacks or actively planning attacks on the homeland or on U.S. citizens anywhere.

But then I wondered, was that all that we could do? Covert-action programs were never conceived to be primarily instruments of national vengeance, at least during my long career. They are supposed to be forward-looking documents, combating ongoing or future threats to the United States. Killing Al Qaeda leaders or operatives was one thing, but a dead man can't give you his intentions or plans. Even if we had the capacity and capability to kill them all—which I doubted—was that smart? Was that enough? Maybe, I thought, we should retain the option to take terrorists alive, not just to take them out of circulation but to get them to tell us about what their confederates still at large might be plotting.

I scribbled down the phrase "capture, detain and question" on my legal pad. I was totally winging it now. The CIA, in my experience, never had a program to hold people against their will. I had no idea where we might hold them (although it surely would not be anywhere inside the United States) or what sort of facility they would be held in. The manner in which we would question them did not cross my mind.

I made a few other notes to myself about what to include in any new program—language authorizing the CIA to call upon the services and personnel of all other federal agencies as well as foreign governments, things like that. It was early afternoon by then, and I decided it was time to go home to be with my wife and family. The unaccounted-for plane, United Flight 93, had just been reported as having crashed in a field in Shanksville, Pennsylvania. The carnage, at least for that day, seemed to be over. My trip home to Georgetown didn't take very long, but it seemed to last forever.

Over the next few days, John Bellinger, the legal advisor to the National

Security Council staff, convened a series of marathon sessions, attended by senior lawyers from the White House and the national security community, to hash out the terms of the new MON. Bob McNamara went to some of the sessions, and I went to others. Less than a week after the 9/11 attacks, President Bush signed off on the final version. Multiple pages in length, it was the most comprehensive, most ambitious, most aggressive, and most risky Finding or MON I was ever involved in. One short paragraph authorized the capture and detention of Al Qaeda terrorists, another authorized taking lethal action against them. The language was simple and stark.

When the MON was delivered to the intelligence committees a day later, Republicans and Democrats alike had the same reaction: Is this enough? Is this everything you guys need to protect the country? As far as I was concerned, there was nothing else we possibly could have included; we had filled the entire covert-action tool kit, including tools we had never before used.

As far as I know, the MON remains in effect to this day.

In mid-October, Bob McNamara told me he was stepping down from his position as general counsel to accept a position in the private sector. It was not entirely a surprise to me, since Bob had been signaling for several months that he was exploring outside opportunities. Once 9/11 happened, however, I assumed he would postpone his plans for a while. Still, I understood Bob's decision—he had been in office for nearly four grueling years, and the pace and pressure were surely going to become even more relentless for years to come.

And so, when Bob departed in mid-November 2001, I became acting general counsel. It was not an unfamiliar position for me, having filled in for a few weeks at a time during the previous several years when the incumbent GC was out of town or in the interregnum between outgoing and incoming GCs. This would be no ordinary interregnum, of course. Workers were still sifting through rubble at Ground Zero and the Pentagon. The attempted "Shoe Bomber" attack on another U.S. passenger jet, as well as the murderous, unsolved "anthrax letter" incidents in D.C. and Florida, were keeping the nation in the grip of dread and fear. Meanwhile, the most high-stakes, high-risk covert-action program in CIA history was just getting under way. So, yes, I had been "acting" on previous occasions, but never in circumstances remotely resembling these. To be the chief legal advisor at the CIA at that point of history was at once intoxicating and frightening.

What's more, I had the distinct impression that this time I could be in the hot seat for a while. In the months before 9/11, when Bob McNamara was making no secret of his plans to leave, I discerned no move by the White House to identify a replacement. Once Bob was gone, I still didn't. One day early on, I asked John Moseman, Tenet's chief of staff and by now my close friend, if he knew of any talk about a new general counsel. Based on past experience, I knew that the process could take months—a candidate would have to be interviewed by the director, cleared by the White House political office, undergo a thorough background security investigation, be formally nominated by the president, and confirmed by the Senate.

"The White House hasn't said anything about it to George, and George hasn't said anything about it to the White House," John replied. "So just sit tight. No one's in any hurry."

"Have fun," he added with a mordant chuckle.

In 1996, shortly after he became deputy CIA director, George Tenet had begun convening biweekly meetings with the CTC so that he could be kept personally abreast of world terrorism developments. In the wake of the 1998 African embassy bombings, George had started holding these sessions on a weekly basis. A few days after 9/11, they morphed into a daily ritual that was officially called "the CTC Update" but soon came to be known around the building as "the five o'clock." It was no longer a mere briefing forum—it became the command bunker in the CIA's war on Al Qaeda, with George wielding the marshal's baton.

Each day at the appointed hour, a group of about thirty-five of us would gather around the oblong polished oak table in the director's conference room to review and discuss the daily developments in the Agency's full-throttle campaign against Al Qaeda. On one side of the table sat George, along with his deputy, John McLaughlin, Executive Director Buzzy Krongard (a spectacularly successful and colorful investment banker whom George had recruited a couple of years before), Deputy Director for Operations Jim Pavitt, and Deputy Director of Intelligence Jami Miscik. Several other senior officials—the directors of public and congressional affairs, the CIA comptroller, the acting general counsel, and a few other high-level straphangers—filled out that side of the table.

Across the table were arrayed the CIA's true warriors in this new, post-9/11 war. Each day about twenty officers from the Counterterrorist Center (CTC) and the Near East (NE) and Special Activities (SAD) divisions would troop in, sit down, and, for about an hour or so, basically scare the bejesus out of the rest of us with up-to-the-minute updates on the latest intelligence coming in on Al Qaeda plans, capabilities, and threats. Their presentation also included descriptions of what our people were doing, or proposed to do, in response.

The maestro of the group was the CTC chief, Cofer Black. An imposing presence with the physique of a retired NFL tight end, Cofer had a face and slicked-back, receding hairline that together reminded some of us of a late-career Jack Nicholson. Also, like most of Nicholson's screen characters, he spoke in a staccato, world-weary cadence liberally sprinkled with dark, cynical humor. But the dramatic image he presented was not an affectation—Cofer was a bona fide, hard-bitten product of the CIA's clandestine world, having spent years in hotspots and hellholes where he consistently performed with bravery and verve. In 1994, for instance, he had been the key CIA operative in orchestrating the capture in Sudan and rendition to France of the legendary terrorist fugitive Carlos the Jackal. In the post-9/11 literature, Cofer has been famously cited as having supposedly exhorted his troops to bring him "bin Laden's head in a box." I never heard him say that, either at the five o'clock meeting or elsewhere, but having gotten to know him well over the years, it rings true to me as the quintessential Cofer quote.

Cofer typically would lead off the meeting with the intelligence "headlines," then turn things over to the working-level operatives and analysts lined up in a row down the table from him. One would describe the most recent reports on threats to the homeland. The next would update Al Qaeda efforts to acquire biological and chemical weapons (which reliably elicited the most head-shaking and muttering from the rest of us). After that, a CTC analyst tracking intelligence on the possible location of bin Laden and his top commanders would give the latest update. The next two guys, from the CTC and the SAD, would describe the progress of the paramilitary war in Afghanistan. At the end of the row, the CTC's financial operations whiz, a thin, pale figure always wearing an impeccably tailored black suit, would quietly and methodically catalogue all the unprecedented ways in which he was detecting and disrupting Al Qaeda's international money flow.

One by one, these officers would crisply make their presentations. Some of them were only in their twenties; few were older than fifty. Their preternatural calm and the thoroughness with which these rank-and file employees delivered their daily digests of danger and derring-do were a constant source of wonder to me. Watching them perform, I would think to myself: If the American people could only see this, they would be so proud and reassured.

Shirt-sleeved, tie askew, and chomping an unlit cigar beyond recognition, George Tenet would lean forward and listen eagerly, alternately cross-examining and encouraging the briefers at every turn. Occasionally, he would interrupt and bark out terse orders: That piece of new threat information you just gave me? Get it to the FBI pronto. That foot-dragging you're getting from the Pakistanis (or the Yemenis, the Saudis, and so on)? I'll get on the phone tonight and ream them out personally. George was hands-on all the way in those daily sessions.

As the months went on, these daily meetings acquired a certain cachet. Other than a couple of FBI and NSA employees who were on detail to the CTC, no one from outside the Agency was allowed to regularly attend. High-level officials from around the Executive Branch would quietly lobby to get into them, convinced that it meant entrée to some shadowy inner sanctum. In most cases, the Agency would resist those blandishments from outsiders (there was a blanket ban on anyone from a foreign intelligence service getting in, for instance), but on occasion George would allow a visiting U.S. government colleague to attend—I remember the NSA director, Mike Hayden, and the White House homeland security advisor, Fran Townsend, sitting in a few times in those early years.

Ironically, however, the really sexy, sensitive stuff was not bandied about at the five o'clock meetings. For something that was extraordinarily closely held, there would be a "rump" session of sorts scheduled immediately after the five o'clock meeting. These would be held in George's office, with only a handful of people in attendance. I had an open invitation to sit in on all of them.

One such "rump" session, in those frantic first months after 9/11, sticks out in my mind. The subject was a nascent CTC plan for CIA officers with weaponized, unmanned aerial vehicles (UAVs) targeting the prey, from thousands of feet up, in their lairs on the Afghan frontier. But in late 2001, drone technology was still a work in progress; it was not yet certain that it would be lethally effective. True, I was fully aware that the MON that I helped prepare clearly sanctioned lethal actions against the Al Qaeda network. But those were only lawyers' antiseptic words on a page.

Instead, as the fateful year of 2001 turned into 2002, my energies and priorities were being directed to a separate and what proved to be a far more legally perilous area: the CIA's detention and interrogation of high-value Al Qaeda operatives.

From the outset, the top two names of the Agency's post-9/11 "most wanted" list were Osama bin Laden and his alter ego, Ayman al-Zawahiri. Technically, I suppose, they were wanted dead or alive, but I remember no one in the know at the CIA who seriously thought that either of them, if ever cornered, would allow himself to be taken into custody. Nonetheless, the Agency's preferred strategy for the next rung of high-value Al Qaeda targets (HVTs) was to capture them, not blow them away. It was these guys who were the most knowledgeable about the ongoing plots, about who was going to carry out the next wave of attacks, and about exactly where and when they would take place. And in late 2001 and on into 2002, there was every reason to believe Al Qaeda was planning more attacks. The experts at the CIA were convinced of that, and most of the still shell-shocked American public expected it. That same public, and their elected representatives, demanded that the government prevent it from happening, whatever that took.

To the CIA, that meant not only taking bin Laden's key henchmen out of circulation, but getting them to talk.

The first task for the Agency, accordingly, was to figure out where to put these HVTs, if and when we captured them (at which point, in the strange, new post-9/11 alphabet-soup terminology, they would morph into high-value detainees—HVDs). Defense Secretary Donald Rumsfeld put down a marker early on to George Tenet: The DOD wouldn't play the role of jailer for the CIA. No one was sure exactly why Rumsfeld felt that way—the DOD was busily turning the Guantánamo Bay Naval Base into a detention facility, after all—but Rumsfeld was obdurate and implacable.

The CTC told George, at one of the earliest "five o'clocks," that this was just as well: For the big fish we're after, we didn't want them mixing with the Al Qaeda foot soldiers who were rapidly filling up Gitmo. They needed to be held somewhere where no one but we could get access to them, the CTC said, where no one but we knew where they were. And foreign governments couldn't be relied on to hold them for us either, the CTC advised—who knew what might happen to them then? They could get killed, they could be let go. If we were going to get into this, the CTC recommended to George, the CIA needed absolute control over these HVDs.

And so, with George's go-ahead, the Agency began casting about for its own incarceration site. I soon found myself sitting in George's office, where terms like "deserted island" and "mystery ship" were being thrown around. Only in retrospect is it remarkable to me that such a fateful decision was made with so little hesitation. In those days, hesitation simply was not an option, not with some senior Al Qaeda operative about to fall into our lap any minute, and not with another attack on the homeland possibly just around the corner. Still, I do remember feeling a vague, inchoate sense of trepidation at the time. Jeez, I thought to myself, the CIA has never in my experience built and run a prison. Before long, another new term was thus introduced into the Agency dialogue: "black site."

By early 2002, the first such black site was in place. Just in time, because its first guest was about to arrive.

My first CIA-badge photograph when I entered on duty in January 1976. Note the dark hair and bewildered expression.

Aerial view of CIA headquarters "campus." My home away from home for thirty-four years.
(Photographs in the Carol M. Highsmith Archive, Library of Congress, Prints and Photographs Division)

William Colby and George H. W. Bush, the first two CIA directors I served under. I went on to work for ten more. (AP Photo/John Duricka)

Ankle deep in mud in the Dead Sea in 1981. The photographer was from a foreign intelligence service; the bottle of beer was from Egypt.

Duane (Dewey) Clarridge. The most colorful, controversial CIA operative I ever dealt with. Iran-contra destroyed his career. (*The New York Times*)

With director Bob Gates at his farewell ceremony in late 1992. He was a CIA "lifer" like me, and I came to like and respect him immensely.

Aldrich Ames after his arrest in 1994. The most evil, destructive CIA traitor in history. I couldn't seem to avoid him after he first came under suspicion. (AP Photo/Wilfredo Lee)

A surreptitious photo of me taken by a foreign intelligence service while I was traveling abroad circa 1985. That night, the photo was slipped under my hotel door, apparently just to let me know that my movements were being watched.

Oliver North testifying before the Iran-contra committee in July 1987. I first met Ollie several years earlier, before he became famous. (AP Photo/Lana Harris)

President Bush with director George Tenet at CIA headquarters in March 2001. I was surprised and delighted when the new president kept George at the helm. (AP Photo/Pablo Martinez)

Getting an award from director George Tenet in late 2002 after my first stint as acting general counsel. My wife, Sharon, is in the middle. George's inscription on the photo: "Well, you kept me out of the slammer." George was the most "regular guy" director I ever worked for.

With my CIA colleague Jennifer Millerwise at the U.S. military airport in Kabul, Afghanistan, in 2005. Two Washington desk jockeys in Kevlar jackets.

Today

Confirmation Hearing for CIA General Counsel

C-SPAN

Me testifying at my Senate confirmation hearing in June 2007. At first, I thought it went okay. It turned out to be a disaster.

At an outdoor ceremony at CIA headquarters commemorating its sixtieth anniversary in September 2007, three days before the withdrawal of my nomination for general counsel.

Director Leon Panetta presenting me with the Distinguished Career Intelligence Medal at my retirement ceremony in December 2009. He was my last director, and in my opinion the most successful.

With Jose Rodriguez, former head of the CIA clandestine service, at my retirement ceremony in December 2009. Even though Jose's decision in November 2005 to destroy videotapes of terrorist interrogations had caused me considerable grief, I invited him to the ceremony to show there were no hard feelings.

With Sharon at the CIA Wall of Honor during my retirement ceremony.

CHAPTER 11

The Birth of the Enhanced Interrogation Program (2002)

I first heard the name Abu Zubaydah about six months before 9/11, when alarming intelligence reports were building toward a fever pitch about a possibly imminent Al Qaeda attack against U.S. targets somewhere in the world. One report identified him as planning suicide car-bomb attacks against U.S. military targets in Saudi Arabia. Another came from the FBI, based on its interrogation of Ahmed Ressam, the so-called millennium bomber, who had been arrested at the Canadian border in the closing days of 1999 as he tried to enter the United States in a car laden with nitroglycerine and explosive devices apparently intended to be used for an attack at Los Angeles International Airport. Ressam had told the FBI that this Zubaydah guy was somehow engaged in plans for a wave of attacks against major U.S. cities.

In the weeks after 9/11, his name seemed to pop up nearly every day at the five o'clock meeting, with shards of information about him turning up in all sorts of independent, separate source reporting. It was becoming apparent that Zubaydah was an essential, ubiquitous cog in the Al Qaeda logistical structure, especially when it came to organizing future attacks against the United States, smuggling Al Qaeda operatives across borders, procuring forged documents, and arranging safe haven for terrorist fugitives and trainees.

In those early days following 9/11, Zubaydah's name was the one coming most consistently and urgently out of the mouths of all the CTC briefers at the five o'clock. The talk reminded me of *Where's Waldo?*—he seemed to be everywhere, and nowhere. Apart from bin Laden and al-Zawahiri, he was considered the biggest, and most elusive, fish out there at that time. I remember his photograph being passed around the table at one of those meetings and being struck not only by his boyish appearance but also by how ordinary and unprepossessing—almost nerdy—he looked. It caused me to recall the famous title of Hannah Arendt's 1963 book on the trial of Adolph Eichmann: *The Banality of Evil.*

At the beginning of 2002, the CIA's equivalent of an APB was sent to stations around the world. The order was to take Zubaydah alive, if at all possible—the intelligence specifically tying him to the 9/11 attacks may not have been there, but our CTC experts were convinced that if there were more attacks on the Al Qaeda agenda, Zubaydah was the guy who would know about them. And dead men can't talk.

Then, suddenly, a new, promising lead about Zubaydah's possible location in Pakistan appeared on the screen in February. The CTC sprang into action, with George Tenet cracking the whip every night. In the wee hours of March 28, 2002, owing to the CTC's meticulous planning and a dose of good luck, the Agency hit the jackpot. A team of Pakistani commandos stormed into a house in Faisalabad, where they encountered both Zubaydah and a furious gunfight. In the process, Zubaydah was shot up badly, but taken into custody alive.

So now we had him. It was the best—actually the first—piece of good news coming the Agency's way since 9/11, and I remember the atmosphere at the five o'clock the following day as one of quiet pride and satisfaction. The head of the CTC HVT Task Force, a fortyish, boyish-looking type with an unassuming and diffident manner, gave the group a step-by-step account of how the Zubaydah takedown unfolded. It was a dramatic story, which he told in a remarkably undramatic way. There was no macho posturing, no gloating. Not from him, nor, for that matter, from anyone else around the table. Almost immediately, the talk turned to the next priorities with Zubaydah: Keep him from dying, get him to our detention facility, and find out what he knew.

In the following days, Zubaydah's physical condition, and what he was telling his CIA and FBI inquisitors at the CIA facility, became the headline item at the five o'clock. At first, the news was good on both fronts: He was out of medical danger, and he was talking. But the more he became convinced he was not going to die, the more confident, the more arrogant, he was becoming. He kept talking, all right, but now Zubaydah, feeling his oats, took to taunting our people. He was proving to be a twisted, smug little creep, offering up little tidbits that were either old news or outright lies, all the while taking care to torment his questioners by making clear that lies were his specialty and that he knew far more about ongoing Al Qaeda plots than he was ever going to tell us.

The Agency shrinks, working with the CTC experts, were busily putting together a psychological profile of Zubaydah. This guy is a cold-blooded psychopath, they concluded. They told George at one of the five o'clock sessions in early March that the Agency needed to do something to change the equation with Zubaydah, shift the dynamics of the interrogation. The "Joe Friday" approach was never going to work. Come up with something, and come up with it fast, George instructed them. As they were dispatched, no one in the room, including me, had any inkling what they were going to come back with.

I found out about a week later, when a couple of our lawyers assigned to the CTC (our contingent there had tripled from three to nine since 9/11) came to my office with a couple of their clients. They told me about a different approach the CTC had just devised to deal with Zubaydah. It had a deceptively bland name: "Enhanced Interrogation Techniques," or EITs for short. During my previous twenty-five years as an Agency lawyer, I had never heard of anything remotely like this.

Evidently aware of the distinct possibility that what they were proposing would scare the hell out of me, the CTC contingent prefaced their presentation with a number of assurances: The EITs they were proposing to employ on Zubaydah were not techniques the CTC had just dreamed up; with a couple of exceptions, the U.S. military has used them for years in training exercises (called SERE, for Survival, Evasion, Resistance, and Escape) on thousands of soldiers to prepare them in case they were captured and subjected to such methods by the enemy. Further, CTC analysts, psychologists, and a couple of outside consultants had carefully culled only those EITs from the SERE menu that they believed best suited, and most likely, to break Zubaydah's resistance. Finally, the EITs would be judiciously applied, beginning with the ones that were least coercive, for a limited period of time, and would end as soon as Zubaydah demonstrated that he was no longer resisting and was ready to cooperate. They had no interest, and no intent, to employ EITs any longer or any more harshly than was absolutely necessary. While I don't remember them saying it exactly, their message was implicit: We want no part of torture.

I suppose I was somewhat reassured by all of that, although I still had no idea what they specifically had in mind. It must be something extraordinary, I thought, if the CTC thought it had to lay that sort of groundwork with me first. It was consistent with a trait I had seen in CIA clandestine service officers for as long as I had dealt with them: When they are about to ask you for permission to do something really hairy, they begin by taking pains to show that they have thought through the implications and are not just compulsive, crazy cowboys.

"Okay," I said, bracing myself. "Describe everything you'd like to do. In the order you'd do them. In detail, and take your time."

And so they began. One at a time, the proposed EITs were spelled out. The following is my best recollection of the way the CTC guys described them to me at that time. As I will describe later, there would be subsequent written documents prepared, describing them in more detail, and a couple of additional and relatively noncoercive EITs would be added as time went on (as, indeed, would a few of the harshest techniques listed below be dropped in time). But at the very beginning, on this day in my office in early April 2002, this is what I recall being told about the proposed EITs. It's not easy to forget.

- *Attention grasp.* The interrogator would grab Zubaydah by the collar with both hands, pulling him closer to the interrogator.
- *Walling.* The interrogator would shove Zubaydah backward shoulder blades first, into a flexible false wall, which would be designed to produce a loud noise. Zubaydah would have a protective collar placed on him to protect against whiplash.
- *Facial hold.* The interrogator, holding Zubaydah's head immobile, would put one open palm on each side of his face, keeping fingertips away from Zubaydah's eyes.
- *Insult slap.* The interrogator would slap Zubaydah in the face, taking care to keep his fingers spread and to strike between the chin and the earlobe. The idea would be to startle/humiliate Zubaydah and disabuse him of the notion that he wouldn't be physically hit.

- *Cramped confinement.* The interrogator would put Zubaydah in a box—either a "big" one (allowing him to stand) for up to eighteen hours, or a "small" one (where he would have to curl up) for up to two hours. For the small box, the interrogator would have the option to place a harmless insect inside. (At this point, I couldn't resist interjecting: "Why an insect?" The response: "Zubaydah hates bugs. It'll be something harmless, but he won't know that." The bug gambit, apparently, was not something ever done by the U.S. military in its SERE training.)
- *Wall standing.* The interrogator would have Zubaydah stand facing a wall from about four feet away, have him stretch his arms straight out in front of him, so that his fingers were touching the wall and could support his weight. He would be made to hold that position indefinitely, so as to induce discomfort or fatigue.
- *Stress positions.* The interrogator would have Zubaydah either sit on the floor with his legs extended in front of him and his arms raised over his head, or kneel on the floor while leaning back at a 45-degree angle. Again, the intent would be to cause discomfort or fatigue.
- *Sleep deprivation.* Self-explanatory. Zubaydah would be made to stay awake for up to eleven days at a time.
- *Waterboarding.* The interrogator would strap Zubaydah to an inclined bench, with his feet slightly elevated. A cloth would be placed over his forehead and eyes, and water would be applied to the cloth in a controlled manner—for twenty to forty seconds from a height of twelve to twenty-four inches.

There was another technique so gruesome that the Justice Department later stopped short of approving it. After about an hour, the CTC was finished with its presentation. It wasn't all just talk—the briefers supplemented their verbal descriptions with demonstrations (on each other) of some of the more relatively benign proposed EITs. I have to admit that I didn't ask a lot of questions, mostly because a lot of what they were telling me was so alien to anything I had ever thought about before then that I was left largely speechless. Some of the techniques they described sounded like something out of a Three Stooges slapstick routine. Others sounded sadistic and terrifying.

After the briefers left, I took a long walk around the headquarters compound, smoking a cigar and trying to process what I had just heard and to figure out what the hell to do next. What I had to think about—bugs in boxes and simulated drowning—would have been unthinkable to me only an hour before. I had never before been confronted with a CIA proposal that even potentially transgressed the federal antitorture statute, but parts of what the CTC was contemplating certainly seemed at least close to whatever the legal line was. My first reaction was to tell the CTC, at a minimum, to forget waterboarding. It just seemed so frightening, like a plot line out of Edgar Allan Poe. Besides, I had been around the CIA long enough, had been through enough of its misadventures and controversies, to develop a gut instinct about what could get the Agency—and its people—into trouble down the road. And this had huge, unprecedented trouble written all over it.

I was confident that I could squelch at least the more aggressive proposed EITs, then and there, if I wanted to. Besides being the Agency's chief legal officer, I had the experience, credibility, and influence to have made that call, and to have made it stick with the DDO, Jim Pavitt, and George Tenet. At that point, no one outside the Agency was aware that these sorts of tactics were even being contemplated—the Bush MON issued days after 9/11 authorized the capture, detention, and questioning of Al Qaeda leaders, but was silent about the means by which any of it could be carried out. I have no doubt that if I had said the word, much if not all of the EIT initiative would have quietly died before it was born. It would have been a relatively easy thing to do, actually.

But over the next day or two, as I turned things over and over in my mind, I concluded that the issue was anything but easy. We were less than six months removed from 9/11, the nation was still in the throes of fear and dread about another catastrophic attack, intelligence reports were cascading in indicating the possible imminence of such an attack, and the CIA had in its custody and control the one guy who would likely know when, where, and by whom the next attack would be carried out. And he was taunting and mocking us about it. The Agency's singular objective, for the sake both of the country and of its own institutional existence, was to do anything and everything in its lawful power to prevent another attack from happening. At the same time, the CIA was being pilloried in Congress and the media for having been "risk averse" in the years leading up to 9/11—too unimaginative, too timid about dealing with the evil forces in the world.

With all of that churning in my head, I couldn't shake the ultimate nightmare scenario: Another attack happens, and Zubaydah gleefully tells his CIA handlers he knew all about it and boasts that we never got him to tell us about it in time. All because at the moment of reckoning, the Agency had shied away from doing what it knew was unavoidable, what was essential, to extract that information from him. And with hundreds and perhaps thousands of Americans again lying dead on the streets or in rubble somewhere, I would know, deep down, that I was at least in part responsible. In the final analysis, I could not countenance the thought of having to live with that.

Less than a week after the CTC gave me the EIT briefing, I attended one of those "rump" sessions in George Tenet's office after the daily five o'clock meeting. The topic was whether or not to move forward with the EIT proposal (because of its sensitivity, it was something that was never discussed at the larger meeting in those early days). I cannot remember now if George knew all the details about the proposal beforehand, but in any case the CTC went over everything again. George asked me if I thought the EITs were legal. My staff had done some hurried research on the torture statute, a federal law making it a criminal offense for "any person outside the United States acting under the color of law, to commit torture." Thus, it covered anyone overseas affiliated with the CIA or acting on its behalf. The research didn't provide much in the way of guidance; the definition of torture was vaguely worded (phrases like "severe mental and physical pain and suffering"), and there had never been a prosecution under the statute, even though it had been on the books for many years.

This was the moment I knew was coming. "Well," I responded, "some of the techniques seem okay, but others are very harsh, even brutal. What I can't do is sit here and tell you now if it legally constitutes torture. And if it does meet the torture threshold, it doesn't matter what the justification is, even it's being done to prevent another nine-eleven." Everybody just looked at me. Understandably, nobody in the room found that response satisfying. Finally, someone—I believe it was the CTC chief, Jose Rodriguez—broke the silence and declared, "Our people won't do anything that involves torture."

"You're damn right," George interjected. I couldn't tell if their reaction was based on the law or their moral dictates, but it was exactly the right response.

But by then I had decided not to just end things there. "Look," I said, "let me take this to the Justice Department, to get something definitive, something in writing. We tell them everything we want to do, every detail about how we would conduct the EITs. And let them make the final legal call. And not just settle for a simple yes or no—we make them go on the record for every single one of the techniques, especially if it's a yes."

I was punting, of course, but it was a strategic punt. The Justice Department—specifically, its Office of Legal Counsel (OLC)—has always served as the final, binding arbiter inside the Executive Branch for legal interpretation of all federal statutes and the U.S. Constitution. Over the course of my career, the CIA referred proposed operational activities to the OLC dozens of times, so while dumping the EIT proposal in the OLC's lap would dwarf all the others in terms of scope and sensitivity, it would not be a new departure for us to bring the OLC into the loop.

Above all, I wanted a written OLC memo in order to give the Agency—for lack of a better term—legal cover. Something that we could keep, and wave around if necessary, in the months and years to come, when memories would fade or be conveniently altered to tack with the shifting political winds. I didn't know how the OLC was going to come down on the proposed EITs. What I did know was that, either way, there would be eventual fallout, somehow and someday. If the OLC were to rule out their use, and there was another attack, then at least the CIA wouldn't have to bear the brunt of a renewed fusillade of "risk averse" accusations. If the OLC did authorize the use of EITs, and there was no second 9/11 attack, then I knew that eventually and inevitably, there would be those in some parts of the government—maybe in the Bush administration, more likely in a different administration—who would charge that the EITs were not only barbaric but lapsed into criminality. An OLC legal memorandum—the Executive Branch's functional equivalent of a Supreme Court opinion—would protect the Agency and its people forevermore. It would be as good as gold, I figured confidently. Too confidently, as things would turn out.

Before the "rump session" broke up, George gave me the go-ahead to approach the Justice Department. Get all the lawyers involved who you think need to be involved, he instructed, but no more than absolutely necessary. Meanwhile, he said, he would let the White House know what we were up to, beginning with National Security Advisor Condi Rice.

The EITs were leaving the building. It was early April 2002. Zubaydah at that point had been in custody for two months, and the CTC was more convinced than ever that he was holding out. Time was becoming of the essence.

Right away, I called John Bellinger, legal advisor to the NSC, to broker the first discussion with the OLC. I had first met John in 1988 when he was a very young attorney whom DCI Bill Webster brought in to serve as his executive assistant. I had kept in touch with him, and I was pleased when Condi Rice named him to be her chief counsel at the beginning of the George W. Bush administration. I liked and trusted John. By now he was in his early forties and an experienced Washington lawyer, but he still retained the boyish good looks and earnestness that he had in his Webster years.

I wanted John in the loop from the beginning on the EITs for several reasons. First, since George Tenet had indicated he was going to let his boss, Condi Rice, know about the issue, I thought that as a professional courtesy John should know as well. Second, I knew that he was hurt and frustrated that the White House had cut him out of internal legal deliberations in the early days after 9/11, possibly because of tensions between him and Vice President Cheney's chief legal advisor, David Addington (another guy I had met when he was a young lawyer at the CIA in the 1980s, and for whom I also had great respect and affection). Finally, and most important, I wanted as many lawyers as possible in the government's national security establishment to be aware of the EITs from the get-go, to the extent that the extreme sensitivity of the matter would allow. DOJ involvement was essential to protect the Agency, but I wanted White House lawyers in the boat, too. And I knew John Bellinger, both for his own protection and because he was a good soldier, would be sure to bring Addington and the White House counsel, Al Gonzales, along as well. We would all be in this together, for better or worse.

After I gave him a brief overview of the impasse with Zubaydah and the proposed interrogation techniques the CIA was considering, John quickly set up a meeting in his office on April 16 with John Yoo, the number two guy in the OLC, and Mike Chertoff, head of the Justice Department's Criminal Division. I had known Mike for about ten years, dating back to his service in the first Bush administration. Mike was an enormously impressive guy, a brilliant legal intellect combined with an easygoing, imperturbable personality. I had met John Yoo only a couple of months before, when he was the OLC rep at White House meetings (the ones where John Bellinger had been excluded) to discuss legal issues in the immediate 9/11 aftermath. A courteous, soft-spoken Korean American in his early thirties (who looked like he could pass for half that age), Yoo had been so quietly authoritative in those earlier meetings that I mistakenly assumed he was the new chief of the OLC. Turns out he wasn't, but he was clearly the Bush administration's designated go-to guy in the OLC for the most important and sensitive post-9/11 legal issues.

I arrived at the meeting with two of our lawyers from the CTC. I decided not to bring the CTC officials who actually came up with the EITs, because I had no idea how the outside lawyers would react to the proposal and I didn't want our guys getting grilled at that point. We took Bellinger, Chertoff, and Yoo down the list of EITs, as well as what our preliminary, hurried legal research had yielded. The idea was to give them—Yoo, especially—enough detail to either get the formal legal review under way or to tell us we had lost our senses and that a lot of this stuff clearly constituted torture. Which, if they had, would have been perfectly okay with me—provided the "no way" was put in writing.

Mostly, however, they just sat there, taking it all in. They asked a few follow-up questions about why the CIA had concluded such measures were necessary for Zubaydah and how a few of the techniques would actually be applied and monitored—not surprisingly, the bug in the box and the waterboarding elicited the bulk of their questions. John Yoo's overall reaction was that he didn't think the EITs crossed the line into torture but stressed this was only his preliminary view, pending a more thorough analysis. John Bellinger said very little; I felt sorry for him, knowing that he was by nature a very straight arrow and that this stuff must have sounded pretty gnarly to him. Mike Chertoff was courteous and collected as always, but by observing his body language as the meeting went on, I sensed he was wishing he could be somewhere—anywhere—else.

The meeting broke up with Yoo agreeing to start work on a memo.

He said he would need more details about Zubaydah's background and about the precise means by which each of the EITs would be carried out to include in his memo. That was fine with me; as far as I was concerned, the more the OLC was immersed in these often unsavory details, the better. I emphasized that we didn't have the luxury of time to await an answer from the OLC—Zubaydah was sitting in his cell with knowledge of another imminent attack potentially in his head, and basically he was giving his interrogators the finger. That was as close as I got to advocating the EITs. I returned to the Agency and told our people that this initial meeting went about as well for the CIA as could be expected: We had not been summarily dismissed as lunatics or aspiring criminals.

Three months later, on July 13, the group assembled in Bellinger's office again. Other than responding to OLC requests for additional, specific factual information, the Agency did not play a role in any of the OLC's internal deliberations. Still, I didn't have to be a CIA spy to figure out by that time that the OLC was going to conclude that most, if not all, of the proposed EITs did not violate the torture statute. The purpose of the meeting was to go through all the proposed techniques again (the CTC by then had a much more comprehensive, nuanced plan on how they would be administered) and for Yoo to give the group a status report of where the OLC was in its analysis.

There was one new face at this second meeting: Dan Levin, chief of staff to Director Bob Mueller of the FBI. The Bureau, which had participated in the initial questioning of Zubaydah in the first few weeks after his capture, had pulled its people out when it learned that the CIA interrogators were recommending a new, harsher interrogation regimen. Going into the meeting, I didn't know how much Dan knew about the proposed EITs. But he must have known enough, because at the beginning of the meeting he calmly announced that the FBI as a matter of policy was not going to be part of any questioning of Zubaydah that did not conform to established Bureau guidelines (basically, how it treats suspects in criminal investigations). I was not surprised by Dan's position; it was a legitimate and understandable one for the FBI to take. However, I was a bit surprised that Dan, after making that announcement, remained in the meeting, listening intently as all of the EITs were being discussed in explicit, excruciating detail.

I did take the opportunity to raise a new issue at this second meeting. I asked whether, in addition to an OLC memorandum legally authorizing the EITs, the Justice Department would be prepared to issue an advance declination of prosecution for any CIA employee involved in the EIT program whose participation was in good faith and within the terms and conditions of the memorandum. It was my idea alone, and I floated it because of my determination to secure the maximum possible legal protection for our people. At the time, I thought that the need for additional legal cover beyond the OLC memo was unlikely; little did I anticipate that less than two years later, John Yoo's successors at the OLC would start moonwalking furiously away from a number of Yoo-authored national security legal opinions.

Anyway, when I floated that trial balloon at the meeting, the DOJ Criminal Division chief, Mike Chertoff, shot it down before it got off the ground. "Out of the question," he said flatly. "The Justice Department doesn't decline criminal prosecutions in advance. Period." And that was that, as far as I was concerned. I felt a little grubby about putting Mike, who was and is a good friend to me and the Agency, on the spot like that. A few minutes later, he announced that he had to leave; it was a Saturday afternoon, and Mike said he had tickets to a Sheryl Crow outdoor concert. I am certain that was true. Still, I speculated to myself at the time that Mike would have happily accepted tickets to a Tiny Tim ukulele concert if that's what it took to get the hell out of there.

By the end of the meeting, I knew that the OLC was going to write a memorandum giving a bright green light to the EITs. John Yoo, in his low-key way, sounded utterly convinced in the strength of his conclusions—no equivocation, no obfuscation, no loopholes. That was exactly what I thought the Agency needed in order to proceed. I spent the last two weeks in July fielding John's final few questions as he completed work on his memo. First, he called me about one proposed EIT. "How important is that to the program?" he asked politely. "If you absolutely need to have it, the memo will take a while longer to finish because I'm not sure we can get there on that one." I was quietly relieved—this was the EIT that I thought was the most chilling, even more than the waterboarding. I consulted with CTC management, and since getting a definitive OLC memorandum as soon as possible was the first priority, CTC management agreed not to hold things up just to try to get OLC blessing for that one.

A day or two later, John Yoo had another question. The memo he was drafting, he said, would be signed by his boss, Jay Bybee, the head of the OLC. John wanted to know whom I wanted as the CIA addressee. Honestly, I hadn't given it any thought before then. Historically, OLC memoranda to the Agency were addressed either to the director or the general counsel. Given those alternatives, it took me only a couple of seconds to decide. I didn't think it was necessary, and certainly not desirable, for George Tenet's name to be on a document that was going to have hairy stuff like EITs in it. That's what his lawyer was for. "Address it to me," I told John.

On August 1, 2002, the eighteen-page OLC memo arrived. It was stamped TOP SECRET, and it was circulated only to a handful of people outside the DOJ and the CIA. Save for the one abandoned option, the OLC concluded that none of the EITs that the CTC originally proposed violated the torture statute. The memo painstakingly laid out the specifics of each EIT and gave each of them explicit legal approval, taking care to lay out all terms and procedures we told the OLC the Agency would follow in administering them. As agreed, on top of the first page, in bold print, it read: "Memorandum for John Rizzo, Acting General Counsel, Central Intelligence Agency."

The Agency quickly converted the OLC memo into a detailed "guidance" cable to the black site where Zubaydah was being held, and the EITs started, with the least coercive going first. The site soon reported back that Zubaydah was still being resistant; accordingly, pursuant to the protocols that had been set up, headquarters approved use of waterboarding. Over a period of several days, the technique was applied eighty-three times (meaning each occasion where water was poured onto the cloth covering his face—not, as some critics would later charge, the number of times Zubaydah was actually strapped up for a session). Just days after the EITs began, they ended. They ended as soon as Zubaydah's resistance ended—he had reached the stage of what our outside consultants called "learned helplessness." He began to talk. A lot. The site reported that Zubaydah was becoming downright loquacious, in fact.

Among other revelations, Zubaydah provided information that soon led to the capture of two other Al Qaeda "big fish." One was Ramzi bin al-Shibh, a member of Al Qaeda's "Hamburg cell" and a close associate of several of the 9/11 hijackers, including their leader, Mohamed Atta. The other was Abd al-Rahim al-Nashiri, a key figure in the October 2000 Al Qaeda bombing of the navy warship USS *Cole* in the Gulf of Aden, which killed seventeen U.S. sailors. Bin al-Shibh and al-Nashiri were hardened, cold-blooded lieutenants in the Al Qaeda chain of command, the type of tough nuts not only eager to kill more Americans but also potentially knowledgeable about ongoing plots to do so.

Since the OLC memo we had gotten a couple of months before was specifically addressed to the EITs being applied only to Zubaydah, I quickly got confirmation from the DOJ that the conclusions reached by the OLC on its August 1 memo pertaining to Zubaydah would also cover similarly high-value—and resistant—Al Qaeda prisoners. And so the EITs began with al-Nashiri and bin al-Shibh. But it's important to note here that the EITs were never intended to be applied in a cookie-cutter, "one size fits all" way. For example, Agency psychologists and interrogators at the site assessed that the ultimate EIT—waterboarding—was necessary for al-Nashiri, but not for bin al-Shibh. And even with al-Nashiri, the waterboarding was stopped almost as soon as it started—for all his thug bravado, al-Nashiri's resistance to cooperation ended after only a few doses, in marked contrast to the more academically inclined psychopath Zubaydah. (By the way, the "bug in the box" EIT was never actually employed on any of the CIA detainees.)

A few months later, in March 2003, the biggest Al Qaeda fish of all— with the exception of bin Laden himself or his second in command, Ayman al-Zawahiri—was caught in the CIA's net. It was Khalid Sheikh Mohammed (KSM), the undisputed (least of all by him) mastermind of the 9/11 attacks and proud personal butcher of the *Wall Street Journal* reporter Daniel Pearl. It had been less than a year since anyone in the intelligence community even knew he existed. Certainly, no other Al Qaeda detainee, before or since, came close to him in terms of cunning and cold-blooded evil. In the years since, I have sometimes wondered what would have happened if KSM, rather than Zubaydah, had been the CIA's first high-value prisoner. My guess is that the now-infamous EITs the Agency originally conceived would have been even more brutal and relentless.

As it happened, however, the CIA made do with what it already had in its kit bag. They were used on KSM, all doughy five feet three of him, again and again for weeks. Each night back at headquarters, I would hear the reports and cringe to myself—there was waterboarding and then more waterboarding. A CIA IG report would later put the number of times at 183, and while there would be heated debate in the succeeding years over how that number was arrived at, I knew that no matter how you cut it, this guy was withstanding simulated drowning longer than I would have ever imagined humanly sustainable. All the while, KSM was cryptically responding "Soon you will know" to demands for information about future attacks on the homeland. As the days dragged on, I increasingly became worried that one of two results was inevitable: 1) KSM was going to die before telling us about the next catastrophic attack, and when the attack happened blame would be laid at the Agency's feet for killing him before he could tell us; or 2) he would weather the EITs, not tell us about the next attack, and when the attack happened blame would be laid at the Agency's feet for not getting the information out of him. Either way, it was an unthinkable scenario.

Finally, his interrogators reported back that his resistance had been broken. He was prepared to talk, probably not entirely fully and honestly, but enough to justify stopping the EITs. What EIT ultimately brought him to "learned helplessness"? The interrogators seemed divided, but when I later talked to the one that I knew longest and best, a guy I knew to be a total straight shooter, he had no doubts. "It was the sleep deprivation," he told me as we smoked cigars during a lunchtime walk around headquarters one day. "We figured out KSM would rather die than not be able to sleep. Besides, he also figured out after a while that we weren't going to waterboard him to death."

KSM was the third detainee in CIA custody to be waterboarded. That was in the spring of 2003. Overall, the Agency kept a cumulative total of about one hundred prisoners in its black sites in the seven years the EITs were in existence, from 2002 until early 2009. KSM was the last one waterboarded. Again, in succeeding years outside groups would claim otherwise. If that were true, I am convinced I would have known about it. And I didn't.

Meanwhile, during these early months of the EIT program, a small, select group of senior government policymakers were being brought into the loop. On White House orders, the OLC had provided its August 1 memorandum only to the CIA and the White House. Nonetheless, the existence of the memo and the details of the EITs were soon briefed to the National Security Council Principals Committee, which, as the term implies, consists of the most senior of the president's national security and foreign policy advisors. Every administration has had such a group, although the official name and membership have sometimes varied over the years.

In the first term of the Bush administration, the Principals Committee was chaired by National Security Advisor Condi Rice. She would sit at the head of the table in the cramped White House Situation Room, with the seal of the president of the United States appearing over her head on the dark-paneled wall behind her. Arrayed on either side of the table would be the members: Secretary of State Colin Powell, Secretary of Defense Don Rumsfeld, Chairman of the Joint Chiefs of Staff Dick Myers (and later Pete Pace), Attorney General John Ashcroft, White House Chief of Staff Andy Card, White House Counsel Al Gonzales, and DCI Tenet. Vice President Cheney occasionally would sit in on the sessions in which the EITs were discussed (otherwise, his chief of staff, Scooter Libby, or his counsel, David Addington, would attend). Each member would be allowed to bring what was referred to as a "second," meaning an aide who would sit behind his boss, crunched into the small chairs along the walls of the Situation Room. As the designated briefer for the EITs, George Tenet was allowed to bring a couple of additional aides, which always included his deputy, John McLaughlin, and frequently included me and a senior CTC official.

As a backbencher, I found it fascinating to observe the body language and dynamics of the various principals at these sessions—held every month or so—as George would give his detailed updates on the specifics of the EITs and how they were being administered first to Zubaydah, then al-Nashiri and bin al-Shibh, and finally KSM. Some, such as Card and Myers, would sit there stoically. Ashcroft was mostly quiet except for emphasizing repeatedly that the EITs were lawful. Rumsfeld was notable more for his frequent, conspicuous absences during these sessions—he kept trying to get his chief intelligence deputy, Steve Cambone, to attend in his place but was always rebuffed by the White House. It was quickly apparent that Rumsfeld didn't want to get his fingerprints anywhere near the EITs. But the most interesting figure of all at these meetings was Colin Powell. Now, there was a man giving off an unmistakable vibe of being there out of a sense of duty but intensely uncomfortable about it. At the end of each EIT update session, Powell would bolt out of the Situation Room as fast as he could.

It was also interesting, and illuminating, to listen to how the various principals reacted to the descriptions of the various EITs. Understandably, George Tenet spent more time talking about waterboarding than anything else. Yet I don't recall there ever being much in the way of resistance from any of his colleagues around the table about waterboarding, or the way it had been used extensively on Zubaydah and KSM. What instead sticks in my mind is how Condi Rice, for instance, seemed troubled by the fact that the detainees were required to be nude when undergoing some of the EITs. Colin Powell, on the other hand, seemed to view sleep deprivation as the most grueling of all the techniques.

The one senior U.S. Government national security official during this time—from August 2002 through 2003—who I believe was not knowledgeable about the EITs was President Bush himself. He was not present at any of the Principals Committee meetings (in my experience over the years, it was rare for any president to attend such sessions), and none of the principals at any of the EIT sessions during this period ever alluded to the president knowing anything about them, or expressing the view that he needed to be told. I also never heard anything to that effect in the numerous other separate discussions on EITs we had with individual principals. As late as 2005, I relayed to Steve Hadley, who had succeeded Rice as national security advisor, a recommendation by the CIA inspector general that President Bush be briefed on what the EITs were. Hadley, an experienced foreign-policy hand and a careful, disciplined lawyer, responded evenly: "That recommendation will be taken under advisement." I did not hear anything further on the subject.

Therefore, I was startled, to say the least, when I read *Decision Points*, President Bush's 2010 memoir. In it, Bush not only forthrightly defended the use and effectiveness of EITs but put himself in the middle of their conception and employment on Zubaydah and KSM. On pages 168 through 171, he wrote the following:

[In late March 2002] CIA experts drew up a list of interrogation techniques that differed from those Zubaydah had successfully resisted. George [Tenet] assured me all interrogations would be performed by experienced intelli-

gence professionals who had undergone extensive training. Medical personnel would be on-site to guarantee that the detainee was not physically or
mentally harmed. . . .

I took a look at the list of techniques. There were two that I felt went too
far, even if they were legal. I directed the CIA not to use them. . . .

[On March 1, 2003,] George Tenet asked if he had permission to use
enhanced interrogation techniques, including waterboarding, on Khalid
Shaikh Mohammed. . . . "Damn right," I said.

All of this was news to me. And some of it didn't compute. The president reviewed the EITs to be used on Zubaydah in advance? When would
that have been? The Agency began them just a couple of days after we got
the go-ahead memo from the OLC. As for the two techniques he said he
vetoed, I have no idea what they could have been. Finally, there would
have been no need to consult with the president in advance before using
EITs on KSM—we had already gotten the okay from Justice that all the
EITs it had green-lit for use on Zubaydah could also be applied to KSM.

The president's narrative might have made more sense to me if he had
attributed it to conversations he had with one of his close White House
advisors—say, Condi Rice, Al Gonzales, even the vice president. After
all, we at the CIA necessarily would not have been made privy to private,
offline discussions inside the West Wing. But Bush didn't assert that in
his memoir—instead, he said he had the conversations in question with
George Tenet. And that's what I found most puzzling of all. I was in daily
contact with George in the run-up to the authorization to the EITs and
their use on Zubaydah and the other detainees in the 2002–2003 time
frame. All during that time, George had said nothing about any conversations he had with the president about EITs, much less any instructions
or approvals coming from Bush. It simply didn't seem conceivable that
George wouldn't have passed something like that on to those of us who
were running the program.

The EIT program in general, and the waterboarding in particular,
were—and continue to be—probably the most contentious issues growing out of the Bush administration's response to the 9/11 attacks. Moreover, EITs played a predominant role in the last seven years of my own
career and in many ways were most responsible for my suddenly becoming a public, controversial figure in those final few years. So I was simply

curious as hell—just what was President Bush talking about? Had I been missing something this important all along?

I decided to contact George Tenet after reading Bush's book. We have remained in touch over the years, and I consider him a close and trusted friend. In November 2010, I sent him an e-mail in which I posed the question as directly as I could: Were Bush's assertions accurate? George's response was just as direct: He did not recall ever briefing Bush on any of the specific EITs.

I am left baffled by all this. I view President Bush as a man of great integrity, and I will always be grateful to him for nominating me in 2006 for the position of CIA general counsel. Still, the account in his memoir about his conversations with George Tenet about EITs is specific and vivid, and yet George doesn't remember any of it. How could George—how could anyone, for that matter—ever forget having conversations with the president of the United States about something like that? It's impossible. And, as I indicated earlier, there are aspects of the Bush version of events that just don't add up. So, in the end, I have to conclude that the account in Bush's memoir simply is wrong.

In the final analysis, I find the episode perplexing but nonetheless admirable on Bush's part, odd as that sounds. My experience over the years is that a president, and those closest around him, instinctively try to put some distance between him and risky, politically controversial covert actions the CIA is carrying out, even when those actions are being conducted pursuant to a specific authorization by the president. This phenomenon is sometimes referred to as "plausible deniability." In his memoir, however, Bush does the exact opposite: He squarely puts himself up to his neck in the creation and implementation of the most contentious counterterrorist program in the post-9/11 era when, in fact, he wasn't.

Now, that's a stand-up guy.

And then there's the role of Congress in the EIT saga. The secret directive to the CIA that Bush issued a few days after 9/11 was provided promptly to the intelligence committees of the House and Senate as well as the defense subcommittees of the House and Senate appropriations committees. When the EIT program was created in 2002, the White House instructed the CIA to restrict knowledge of the program to the leaders of the House and Senate, plus the chair and ranking member of the two intelligence committees—the so-called Gang of 8. As always, the CIA dutifully followed White House orders, so for the next four years we told only those select members about the EIT program as it developed and expanded.

The Gang of 8 notification process is explicitly authorized in the congressional oversight provisions of the National Security Act for covert actions of "extraordinary sensitivity." Thus, it was an entirely lawful way to proceed. Nonetheless, I have come to believe that in retrospect, that approach would prove to be one of the biggest strategic blunders the Bush White House made in the post-9/11 era, and I and other Agency veterans also deserve blame for not pushing back at the White House orders much earlier and harder than we did.

The CTC chief, Jose Rodriguez, led the delegation that first briefed the Gang of 8 in early September 2002, shortly after use of EITs began on Zubaydah (the briefing would have been earlier had Congress not been away on summer recess). In his 2012 memoir *Hard Measures*, Jose recounted (and contemporaneous notes by the other CIA representatives, including one of our CTC lawyers, confirmed) how all of the approved EITs were described in detail and how no one on the congressional side expressed any objection to any of them, including waterboarding. Follow-up briefings were given in February 2003 and thereafter, still with not a word of opposition from the Gang of 8.

Flash forward six years—seemingly a lifetime away from the shock and fear spawned by 9/11—to when the newly inaugurated President Obama publicly rescinded and repudiated the EIT program, and for good measure declassified all the EITs. Several members of the erstwhile Gang of 8 seemed to have amnesia about having been briefed at the creation of the program. On the other hand, Nancy Pelosi (ranking minority member of HPSCI in 2002 and by now House Speaker) was anything but wishy-washy: She went before the cameras in May 2009 and insisted strenuously, with a tight grimace and darting eyes, that all the CIA had ever—ever—told her in previous years was that waterboarding had been "considered" as an interrogation tactic, not that it would ever be used.

On its face, her claim was preposterous (the CIA would brief the Hill leadership on something that it was *not* doing?), and even the new CIA director, Leon Panetta, a staunch Democrat and friend of Pelosi's, couldn't let that stand. He released the contemporaneous notes of the 2002–2003 briefings, and Pelosi had to back down. Sort of. Her story then evolved into, well, maybe she knew all along about waterboarding and the rest that were going on, but she had always opposed EITs and, alas, was powerless to do anything about them. All of which was also total, demonstrable bunk. And then, flustered and in full retreat, she refused to say any more about the subject publicly, except to blithely observe, without a hint of irony, that "the CIA lies all the time." A classy final touch, that, casually slandering an entire institution and workforce. (Not missing a beat, she would continue to receive the personal classified intelligence updates every House Speaker gets, always being gracious and complimentary to her CIA briefers.)

But my main point is this: Pelosi's prevarications, however reprehensible, in hindsight were hardly unforeseeable. We—meaning the White House and those of us in the CIA who had been around long enough to know better—were naïve to expect that a handful of politicians would remain stalwart forever after being forced to sit and listen to the dicey and disagreeable details of the EIT program in sporadic, off-the-record sessions. The decision in 2002 to limit congressional knowledge of the EITs to the Gang of 8 and to stick to that position for four long years—as the prevailing political winds were increasingly howling in the other direction—was foolish and feckless. For our part, we in the CIA leadership should have insisted at the outset that all members of the intelligence committees be apprised of all the gory details all along the way, on the record, in closed congressional proceedings. To allow all of our congressional overseers—to compel them, really—to take a stand and either endorse the program or stop it in its tracks.

Looking back, it is my biggest regret about the role I played in the EIT program.

But I am getting ahead of myself. By the end of 2002, the EIT program was newly up and running, and all of us involved in it at the CIA were convinced that it was the only way to go. With the August 1 OLC memo to me in hand, I thought that we had strong, enduring legal protection against any charges that the program amounted to torture. But even then, in those halcyon days when the public and the politicians were firmly on the side of protecting the country at all costs against a second wave of Al

Qaeda attacks, I couldn't entirely suppress a vague sense of foreboding about what starting down the EIT road might ultimately mean to the Agency and to me.

On November 21, 2002, the American Bar Association's Standing Committee on Law and National Security was holding its annual conference in the ballroom of a large Washington, D.C., hotel. With the 9/11 attacks still fresh in everyone's hearts and minds, the audience of four hundred or so was the largest ever for the event. As I had done in previous years and would continue to do in the years to follow, I agreed to serve on a panel, with my counterparts at State, the DOD, and the FBI, to give the audience the views of the Executive Branch.

The EITs were the elephant in the ballroom that only I could see. So when the time came for each panelist to offer parting comments, I allowed myself to say this: "We at CIA have to be careful what we wish for. The Agency has gotten all the authorities it has requested, but I wonder what will happen if something goes awry. The pendulum is bound to swing back, and today's era of political consensus for increased intelligence authorities will come to an end sometime in the future. It will be good for the country when the terrorist threat is perceived to be less, but it could be bad for CIA."

It was far from a Cassandra-like warning. But for 2002, it wasn't all that far off the mark, either.

CHAPTER 12

Trouble on the EIT Front, and the Valerie Plame Diversion (2003–2004)

My November 2002 appearance at the ABA conference was a milestone of sorts in my post-9/11 career. It coincided with turning over the reins of the OGC to Scott Muller, who had just been confirmed by the Senate as CIA general counsel. About fifty years old, he was an experienced and highly successful litigator who specialized in high-profile white-collar criminal defense cases. Sad to say, that was a highly desirable skill set for the top CIA lawyer at that point in the Agency's history.

I had first met Scott during the vetting process a few months earlier, when the White House sent his name, along with those of two other outside lawyers, over to the Agency for consideration. Director Tenet asked John Moseman, his chief of staff; Buzzy Krongard, the executive director; John Brennan, Tenet's close aide; and me to interview and rank the candidates. We met with each of the three and agreed Scott was clearly the best choice. He came across as a mature, nonideological, low-key guy with a sense of humor. I thought he was a perfect fit for the Agency. He volunteered to us that he considered his greatest strength was as a "crisis manager," and we all thought that neatly summarized the CIA's posture in the year since 9/11.

Tenet met Scott and agreed with our assessment. The White House then submitted Scott's name to the Senate. Scott's Senate confirmation hearing in October had gone smoothly and was largely uneventful, save for some remarks made at the outset of the hearing by the Intelligence Committee chairman, Bob Graham of Florida, a Democrat. The hearing was open to the public, so Graham's remarks were obviously meant to be a message not just for Scott, but for the Agency and the outside world. Here is what he said:

"I know from my work on this committee for the past ten years that lawyers at the CIA sometimes have displayed a risk aversion in the advice they give their clients. Unfortunately, we are not living in times in which lawyers can say no to an operation just to play it safe. We need excellent, aggressive lawyers who give sound, accurate legal advice, not lawyers who say no to an otherwise legal operation just because it is easier to put on the brakes. . . ."

I was not at the hearing, but when I read Graham's remarks the next day, I had a number of reactions. The "risk aversion" charges were not new—a bipartisan bevy of Congress members had been hurling them at the CIA ever since the 9/11 attacks. The only difference here was that the charges for the first time were being specifically leveled at Agency lawyers, and I have to admit that personally they stung. I imagined giving my own rebuttal to Graham: Hey, Senator, if we lawyers were risk-averse during the '90s, maybe it was because all during that decade your colleagues on the Hill and the media were loudly and mercilessly castigating and hounding our clients at the CIA for consorting with thugs and lowlifes, when all they were trying to do was perform their difficult and dangerous jobs. And we were supposed to counsel them to do risky and aggressive things in that sort of toxic environment?

But I belatedly realized that maybe I was missing the larger and more important message Graham was implicitly sending. Only a few weeks before, he had been one of only a small handful of members of Congress who were informed in detail about the new EIT program. I allowed myself to think that Graham was trying to signal to the Agency, and Agency lawyers, that risky and unprecedented tactics such as EITs would not only be tolerated, but also encouraged, in the post-9/11 world. It was okay, I thought the top Democrat on the Senate Intelligence Committee was trying to say. And as I entered 2003 with a new general counsel at the helm, that thought assuaged the vague sense of foreboding I had, at least for a while.

Instead, my predominant feeling was a profound sense of relief. I had been acting general counsel for an extraordinarily eventful and stressful year, but now I could step aside for the new guy. I figured Scott, who seemed excited to take the job, would stay for at least the remainder of Bush's first term, if not longer. Of course, I was prepared to stay by his side and help him in any way I could, just as I had done for his predecessor GCs. But I would no longer have to shoulder the burden—and the pressure—of making the final legal calls for the Agency. I knew that the tumultuous times at Langley would continue, but at least it wouldn't be me in the hot seat anymore. Not for a long time, if ever again. That's what I figured.

In March 2003, the war against the Saddam Hussein regime in Iraq began. Among many other things, it would consume a vast amount of the Agency's attention and resources for years to come. And, of course, it would embroil the CIA in a seemingly never-ending torrent of criticism, both from Congress and other quarters in the Bush administration. The CIA came in for relentless pounding over its abject failure—there is no other way to put it—to accurately assess whether or not Saddam possessed weapons of mass destruction. From my parochial perspective, the quixotic search for WMD, and for that matter the toppling of the Iraqi regime and the chaos that followed, was an anomaly. It was one of the very few major public controversies ensnaring the CIA during my career that did not heavily involve lawyers. Instead, it was largely about the expertise and integrity of the Agency's analytical side.

My most vivid recollection about any of these swirling controversies is a small vignette in which I was merely an observer. The single most supposedly authoritative human source about the existence of WMD was an Iraqi expatriate living in Germany, who was given the code name Curveball. Although Curveball was handled exclusively by the German intelligence service, the stream of information he provided was regularly passed to the Agency, which judged it to be highly credible. Accordingly, the CIA relied on it heavily in its written analytical assessments, which were passed on to the highest-level Bush administration policy makers, including Secretary of State Powell, who cited Curveball's reporting extensively in his dramatic presentation at the U.N. General Assembly in February 2003, making the case for the invasion of Iraq.

By early 2004, however, it was becoming increasingly apparent that a more apt code name for Curveball would be Foul Ball. His story and his supposed expertise as an insider to the Iraq WMD program were not holding up to scrutiny. He turned out to be a fake, and his story was a fabrication. It was an embarrassing, high-profile debacle for the Agency, and George Tenet felt it more than anyone: After all, Powell had insisted that George sit behind him, in full view of a world television audience, as Powell delivered his U.N. speech with its heavy reliance on Curveball's reporting. One day, as the Curveball story was collapsing, I looked up from my desk and unexpectedly saw George, coatless and with his tie askew, shuffling into my office. Without a word, he flopped onto my couch, sprawled on his back, and stared at the ceiling. After a few seconds, he finally said something, more to himself than to me.

"I am so fucked," George muttered quietly.

All that said, in the early months of the Iraq conflict I did manage to get sucked into one of its most baroque and longest-running sideshows: a July 2003 article by the syndicated columnist Robert Novak publicly "outing" the covert CIA employee Valerie Plame, wife of the former ambassador Joseph Wilson, a highly vocal critic of the Bush administration's policies on Iraq.

At the time this minidrama began, Plame was a midlevel officer in the Counterproliferation Division, which was part of the Directorate of Operations. Although she had been an Agency officer, she was so obscure that I didn't ever recall hearing her name, much less meeting her.

Nonetheless, "outing" an undercover officer is never a trivial thing, no matter where that officer is located in the hierarchy. Over the years, CIA covert personnel have been attacked and sometimes murdered as a result of being compromised like that. So, a few days after the Novak column appeared, I dutifully had our office send a "crimes report" to the Justice Department, notifying it of the leak. The OGC sends dozens of such letters to Justice every year, since hardly a day goes by without some piece of classified CIA information popping up somewhere in the media. (Contrary to media speculation at the time, Tenet did not instruct the OGC to make the crimes report. It is obligatory for the Agency to report a possible crime to the DOJ; a CIA director cannot dictate whether or not to file a report. As it happened, I told George after the fact that we had made the report.) And, on the scale of such things, the Plame leak, while deplorable, was negligible in terms of harm to the nation's security. I fully expected Justice to treat it the way it treated 99 percent of our crimes reports, which is to say, to do little or nothing.

Based on the assessment we made, the Plame leak appeared to be a most unlikely candidate for a full-blown Justice/FBI investigation. There was no evidence indicating that any CIA source or operation—or Plame herself, for that matter—was placed in jeopardy as a result of the "outing." And it appeared that dozens if not hundreds of people knew she was an Agency employee. (To be sure, that was not Plame's fault—indeed, the ensuing investigation would show that she was always remarkably careful and discreet about maintaining her "cover," even with her close friends on the outside. For that, she deserves considerable credit—being that disciplined is an arduous task for an undercover operative.)

Accordingly, I confidently predicted to Scott Muller and George Tenet at the time of the referral that there was no way Justice/FBI would devote time and resources to pursue an investigation. Not after having witnessed Justice over the years repeatedly take passes on truly damaging leaks that had far smaller pools of potential suspects.

Surely, I figured, a marginally harmful leak such as the Plame disclosure wouldn't be investigated and prosecuted simply because of the partisan political pressure being applied at the time by opponents of Bush administration policies in Iraq. The crimes reporting process had never been trivialized and distorted like that in all my years at the CIA. The entire episode would quickly fade away, I sagely concluded.

Well, nobody's perfect.

Patrick Fitzgerald, a noted crime buster who was a longtime friend of mine dating from his days as the lead prosecutor in pre-9/11 terrorism cases, was appointed by the DOJ as a special prosecutor with unfettered power. Pat carried out his mandate with his trademark thoroughness and zeal, doggedly pursuing an investigation that would last four years. It finally culminated in the conviction of Lewis "Scooter" Libby, chief aide to Vice President Cheney, for lying to the FBI and a grand jury. Mind you, Libby was not found guilty of leaking Plame's name—it turned out that Pat learned who those culprits were early on. For reasons that remain unclear to me, they never faced prosecution. In the end, therefore, the Plame case was hardly a compelling cautionary tale for future would-be leakers. And, at least insofar as we at the CIA were concerned, hardly worth the thousands of hours Agency personnel (including two of our lawyers working on the case full-time) had to devote to supporting the four-year investigation and trial of a guy who wasn't even the leaker.

To this day, I have not met Valerie Plame. Of those who knew and worked with her, the consensus was that she was a capable, dedicated officer who was involuntarily catapulted into a political maelstrom not of her own making and then manipulated and exploited by her publicity-seeking, preening blowhard of a husband. Suddenly robbed of her anonymity, she did her best for a couple of years to try to cope with balancing her dual loyalties to her job and to her husband.

But it was a struggle. I remember at one point Plame pleaded with the Agency to provide her with round-the-clock security protection, citing the potential threat her unwanted notoriety posed to her and her family. What I determined was that there was no credible information of any kind indicating she or anyone in her family was in any sort of danger. So I reluctantly concluded that the Agency could not lawfully expend the considerable amount of taxpayer money that would be required to shield her from a nonexistent threat. I was told that Plame was hurt and upset by that decision, and those were sentiments I fully understood. I hoped that for her part she understood that her case for needing protection was not helped by her husband's relentless pursuit of an ever-higher public profile, including, I am told, his inveigling her to pose with him in a ludicrous *Vanity Fair* photo shoot in which she wore Garbo-like sunglasses and a scarf.

Valerie Plame ultimately decided to resign from the CIA in 2007. In many ways, it was a sad ending to the saga, with Plame having to give up a productive career after being made a pawn by people who cared more about their own agendas than about her. Of course, in the process she also became a full-fledged celebrity and a fixture on the lecture circuit, with a best-selling memoir (over which I had to wrangle with her lawyer during the classification review process) that became a major, albeit somewhat fictionalized, motion picture. In the final analysis, then, it might be argued that her "outing" turned out to be the best thing that ever happened to Valerie Plame.

However, for those of us at the CIA who had to live with her case, the entire episode was little more than a seemingly interminable distraction and a colossal waste of time and money.

Meanwhile, the EIT program continued apace. But as 2003 turned into 2004, the shock and fear generated by the 9/11 attacks were becoming an ever more distant memory for the country. There had been no second wave of attacks against the homeland, which was of course a blessed thing. At the same time, inevitably, the passage of time and the absence of another attack resulted in the political pendulum starting to swing back, with the message to the CIA migrating from "protect us at all costs" to "what the hell have you guys been up to, anyway?"

As I write this, with all vestiges of the EIT program dead and buried for years courtesy of the Obama administration, the postmortem debate about its utility and morality rages on. Books devoted to both sides of the debate continue to be churned out, including "insider" accounts by former government officials such as the CIA's Jose Rodriguez and the FBI's Ali Soufan. In his 2012 memoir, Rodriguez, the former CTC chief and DDO in the immediate post-9/11 years, forcefully defends the necessity and value of the EITs, spelling out in detail the number of plots thwarted, the thousands of intelligence reports generated, and the fact that the universally praised, seminal 2004 report of the 9/11 Commission relied so heavily, and placed such credibility, on what CIA detainees such as the waterboarded Abu Zubaydah and KSM had to say about the 9/11 attacks and other plots. Soufan, a seasoned FBI interrogator who participated in the pre-EIT questioning of Abu Zubaydah in 2002, argues just as vehemently in his 2011 book, *The Black Banners*, that the EITs were unnecessary and feckless.

For my money, the best "outsider" perspective on the early years of the EIT program was Marc Thiessen's 2010 best-selling book, *Courting Disaster*. Thiessen, a conservative columnist and a former speechwriter in the Bush White House, obviously came at the subject from that ideological perspective, but his exhaustively researched book makes what I consider the most authoritative case yet presented on the necessity, morality, and effectiveness of the program.

Nevertheless, I suspect that the heated, emotional debate about the EIT program will continue indefinitely even as the program itself recedes into history, with both sides hurling charges—and statistics about intelligence reports produced and attacks averted—at each other. I will not rehash those same arguments in any great detail here. Instead, let me offer a somewhat different perspective on why I became convinced during those first couple of years of the program that it was the necessary and right thing to do. It comes down to something pretty basic: Every, and I mean every, career CIA employee who was involved in it believed in it wholeheartedly and unswervingly.

Why was that the most decisive factor for me? Because after twenty-five years at the Agency, I had a pretty good handle on the culture and psyche of the career CIA workforce. In the 2002–2004 time frame, it was what it always had been in my experience—a polyglot group of professionals from all walks of life and from all across the spectrum in terms of their political persuasions. Like me, many of the career employees who played a role in the EIT program had been around Langley long enough to understand that we were all going down a road paved with peril for us personally and professionally. At all the meetings I would attend with them about the program as it was developed and implemented—the hard-bitten DO operatives, the studious DI analysts, the earnest if sometimes nerdy scientists and psychologists—I would observe them closely, watching for any hint of doubt or skepticism about the wisdom of the EITs or the results they were achieving in terms of significant, reliable, otherwise unobtainable intelligence about Al Qaeda. I knew that some of them harbored views on the liberal side of the political spectrum and were not generally fond of the policies of the Bush administration. And, as I say, they were all savvy enough to recognize that being connected to the EIT program was not destined to be career-enhancing for them in the long run. Yet none of these career professionals ever wavered—it's not that they were rabid cheerleaders for the program, but they were staunchly, if stoically, convinced that EITs were proving to be an indispensable element to discovering and thwarting a reprise of the 9/11 attacks.

Nonetheless, beginning in 2004, outside factors were serving to erode the foundations of the EIT program. It, and everyone associated with it, would become vulnerable. Myself included.

Looking back, 2004 was a perfect storm for the EIT program.

Media leaks about the CIA secret prison system and the EITs had begun, drip by drip. On White House orders, all of it was still being kept from all but a handful of top congressional officials, so it was unlikely that the leaks were being sprung on Capitol Hill. Inside the Executive Branch, however, it was a different story. Technically, it was still a top-secret, compartmented program, meaning that information about it could be provided only to officials who had a demonstrable "need to know." But the reality is that every closely held secret seeps into an ever-widening audience inside the Executive Branch. Outside the CIA, senior national security political appointees come and go, and inside the CIA, career officers regularly rotate into and out of components conducting major covert-action programs. And no CIA covert-action program was ever bigger than the CTC's hydra-headed, post-9/11 offensive against Al Qaeda. In particular, the secret prison/EIT program was growing like Topsy, with more HVDs being captured and the number and location of the prisons changing as operational requirements dictated.

Leaks, in short, were bound to happen. And, as usually happens, some of the leaks were on the mark, while others were wildly off. Prisons were alleged to be located in countries where they never existed (as this is written, the exact location of the prisons is one of the very few remaining classified facts about the program) and nonexistent techniques were cited as part of the program. Still, the tidbits and sound bites were tantalizing and sinister—"black sites," "waterboarding," and the like. Let's face it, they made for great copy.

Meanwhile, in April 2004, the Abu Ghraib scandal burst into the public consciousness. The abuse of prisoners by military guards at the Iraqi prison, documented in a series of shocking, repulsive photos by the guards themselves, was in many ways the tipping point of the post-9/11 era for the CIA. The photos were horrifying—naked Iraqi prisoners posed in piles with grinning male and female guards looking on approvingly, a prisoner with electrical wires attached to every appendage, and on and on. None of the prisoners were part of the Agency's program, and the cruelty and sadism depicted in the photos made the EITs seem almost benign by comparison. Of course that wasn't apparent, and couldn't be forcefully pointed out at the time, because of the veil of secrecy over the EIT program. So the public and the majority of Congress could be forgiven for conflating what had happened in Abu Ghraib with what the Agency was doing in its black sites, whatever that was. The images in those photos were absolutely devastating, and I don't believe the EIT program ever was viewed, even by non-CIA people inside the government who were present at its creation, in quite the same way as before.

Most notably, it looked like the Justice Department was starting to wobble. John Yoo (along with his elusive boss, Jay Bybee) was long gone from the OLC. In late 2003, a former Harvard law professor named Jack Goldsmith took over the reins at the OLC, and he proceeded to review the national security legal opinions Yoo had prodigiously churned out during his tenure. And Jack Goldsmith didn't like what he was reading. I consider Jack Goldsmith not only a man of immense intellectual firepower and integrity, but also one of the best and most lasting friends I have ever made inside the government. But back in 2004, Jack was scaring the hell out of me.

For starters, he repudiated the Yoo-authored legal opinion authorizing the NSA's unprecedented, far-reaching post-9/11 terrorist surveillance program. The CIA played only a supporting, relatively minor role in that program, and I didn't even see the Yoo opinion until David Addington pulled it out of his office safe one morning in early 2002 to let me read it for the first time (and I will readily admit that it was so long and so technically detailed that I didn't understand much of it). But then Jack turned his attention to a Yoo opinion that struck closer to the EIT program. On August 1, 2002—the same date of the top-secret eighteen-page OLC memo to me legally authorizing waterboarding and the other EITs—Yoo sent a separate, unclassified fifty-page memorandum to the White House counsel, Al Gonzales. It was clearly crafted as an OLC analogue to what he had sent to me on the same day, and it basically was a lengthy, bone-dry law-review-type article on the standards of conduct under the torture statute in the area of interrogations. It was, not to put too fine a point on it, a very aggressive interpretation of the Executive Branch's powers and prerogatives under the statute.

I never entirely understood why the OLC decided to turn my request for guidance on EITs into two opinions—the classified memo to me, the unclassified memo to Gonzales—on the same day on the same topic. And, honestly, I didn't pay the Gonzales memo all that much attention at the time; after all, the memo to me stood on its own and gave the Agency what we needed, which was detailed, definitive legal authorization to conduct the EITs. I only truly focused on the Gonzales memo nearly two years later, when Jack Goldsmith decided it was fundamentally, fatally flawed. In June 2004, he recommended, and Attorney General Ashcroft agreed, to rescind ("withdraw" is the formal term) the Gonzales memo. True, Jack took pains to emphasize to Scott Muller and me that the OLC would continue to stand behind its classified memo to me on the EITs,

but I was only partially mollified. In my experience, OLC memos almost always stood the test of time, and on those rare occasions where one was rescinded, it was done by a succeeding administration. Here, a Bush appointee was dumping a memo prepared less than two years earlier by a previous Bush appointee. It was a disconcerting, alarming turn of events. Was it a precursor to a subsequent OLC moonwalk on the classified memo? Were the leaks about the program or the Abu Ghraib scandal starting to rattle the Justice Department? Was the EIT program—was the CIA, for that matter—destined to be left in the lurch?

I didn't realize it at the time, but it was all starting to get to Scott Muller. Dropped from private practice into the cauldron of the new EIT program scarcely eighteen months earlier, he couldn't have anticipated the nature and extent of the pressure he would face or the stakes that would be involved. No one from the outside, no one new to the intelligence world, could be expected to. By mid-2004, he was wrangling, at various times, with the CIA IG, John Helgerson, Al Gonzales and David Addington at the White House, even the ineffable Jack Goldsmith at the OLC (who himself, worn down by the relentless stress of duels with the Bush White House, tendered his resignation in June 2004, less than a year after he took the job). In mid-July, Scott privately told me he didn't think he could be an effective advocate for the Agency too much longer. Totally oblivious, I assumed he meant he would probably be stepping down in a few months.

Not so. "I'm submitting my resignation to the White House today," he said. "I intend to be gone in a couple of weeks." That meant the end of July 2004. I can't remember now if Scott also told me that he had already informed George Tenet of his decision. But a few days earlier, George had suddenly announced his own personal life decision: He was resigning as CIA director, effective July 11. George had valiantly served for seven tumultuous years, the second-longest DCI tenure in the Agency's history. He was burned out, exhausted by his straddling of the pre- and post-9/11 era, and dispirited by the Iraq WMD disaster and his attendant disenchantment with and alienation from the White House.

So there I was, at the end of July 2004. Acting general counsel. Again.

Thus, at the time of the sudden, nearly simultaneous departures of Tenet, Muller, and Goldsmith, I was left with a festering situation where vari-

ous factors seemed to be conspiring to threaten the original legal and policy underpinnings of the EIT program. In his final few weeks, Scott Muller had gotten into a nasty dispute with OLC over whether it had earlier agreed to the proposition that the program did not violate the terms of Article 16 of the United Nations Convention Against Torture and Other Cruel, Inhuman or Degrading Treatment or Punishment.

Jack Goldsmith insisted that the OLC had never ruled on the question of whether or not the EITs violated the "substantive" terms of Article 16, meaning that they constituted "cruel, inhuman or degrading treatment" of the CIA detainees. The OLC contended that its conclusion was narrowly drawn on "jurisdictional" grounds: Since the EITs were being conducted outside the United States, the OLC concluded that Article 16 simply did not come into play. The OLC's view was there was no need to rule on the "substantive" question, since the "jurisdictional" grounds effectively took Article 16 out of the picture. Scott wasn't buying it—he was convinced that, months before, the OLC had agreed, albeit informally, that the EITs did not violate Article 16's "substantive" terms. To Scott, the OLC was now backsliding, running for cover in a changing, post–Abu Ghraib political environment.

For its part, the OLC, and the rest of the DOJ leadership, couldn't figure out what the big deal was. Basically, their position was: Hey, we are telling you CIA guys that Article 16 doesn't apply, that the EIT program is legal. We haven't changed our minds on that. What else do you need from us?

It was then, in one of my first acts back in the chair as chief legal advisor, that I decided we needed a new set of written legal opinions from the OLC. We were two years removed from the August 2002 Yoo-drafted memorandum to me on the EITs, and both he and his boss, Jay Bybee, were now long gone. The political climate was changing rapidly from the early post-9/11 months. We had to make sure we were still on solid legal ground for the sake of the Agency as an institution and, more important, for the dozens of rank-and-file Agency officers and contractors dutifully implementing the EIT program. They had to be assured, they deserved to have it confirmed, that under the law they were not engaging in torture. That what they were doing did not constitute "cruel, inhuman or degrading treatment." Those were powerful, portentous words. Our people weren't satisfied with getting by on some technical legal loophole

such as "foreign jurisdiction." If what we were doing—on its merits—was "torture," "cruel," "inhuman," or "degrading" by the OLC's 2004 legal standards, then we weren't going to do it any longer.

The Agency's posture in this regard did not endear us to the rest of the Bush national security team. A series of testy Principals Committee meetings in the White House Situation Room ensued that summer. Participants such as Condi Rice and Al Gonzales were impatient with John McLaughlin, the acting DCI after George Tenet's departure. I accompanied John to those meetings, and I was proud of the way he held his ground. A professorial, soft-spoken gentleman in every sense of the term, John had been at the CIA even longer than I, but never in a situation as tense and high-stakes as this one. His message was quietly delivered but insistent: Without a DOJ promise for a fresh set of OLC memos (especially on the "Article 16" issue), then count the CIA out of the EIT business.

The attorney general, John Ashcroft, resisted John's entreaties, which of course made him and me even more disconcerted. Condi Rice and Al Gonzales got ever more frustrated with us. Secretary of State Colin Powell, for his part, mostly just glowered. He had never hidden his unhappiness about having to attend any meetings on the EIT program, and by now he seemed totally fed up with the Agency in general, angry—understandably, to be sure—that the CIA's faulty assessments on the Iraq WMD issue had caused this proud and revered public servant to look like a fool in the wake of his high-profile speech at the UN the year before. (Around this time, the CIA analyst assigned to give Powell his daily intelligence update reported back that the normally courtly Powell was growing increasingly surly at these sessions. In the aftermath of the U.N. debacle, his attitude indicated he had trouble believing anything we were telling him.)

Finally, grudgingly, the Principals blinked first in the showdown. Ashcroft agreed that the OLC would prepare a new, updated set of legal memoranda on the EIT program. In the meantime, we agreed to continue administering EITs to new, deserving Al Qaeda candidates coming into CIA custody. We attached one condition: the OLC would have to provide us with advance written legal approval, on a case-by-case basis, for each of the techniques we proposed to employ on each new detainee entering the program. Everyone agreed to proceed on that basis.

And so the specific OLC approvals began coming to us in the summer of 2004. There were four of them, all classified top-secret and signed by Dan Levin, the new acting head of the OLC. Since I was now back as acting general counsel, they were all addressed to me. They were short and to the point, and each contained a boilerplate sentence promising that the OLC would "supply, at a later date, an opinion that explains the basis for this conclusion." Those longer, detailed OLC legal analyses did not begin arriving until almost a year later, in May 2005, and kept coming until July 2007. Again, they were all addressed to me.

In total, during the course of the EIT program from 2002 through 2007, there would be ten major OLC legal opinions issued to the CIA regarding the program. I was serving as acting GC on each occasion, so my name appears in bold print on top of each and every one. When the Obama administration decided to declassify and release them in April 2009, the media immediately dubbed them "The Torture Memos," a shorthand term that seems destined to live forever. Some in the blogosphere, in turn, took to referring to me as "The Torture Advocate."

Some guys have all the luck.

CHAPTER 13

Enter Porter Goss
(2005)

In early fall 2004, Porter Goss arrived at Langley as the new DCI. He had a unique set of credentials that made him seem tailor-made for the job. A longtime Republican congressman from Florida, Porter was fresh off a stint as chairman of the House Intelligence Committee. Moreover, as a young man he had joined the CIA in 1960 and served for the next decade as a clandestine service officer before having to resign because of illness. An independently wealthy conservative, he appeared to have all the right stuff to lead the Agency.

From a distance, he had appeared to be a courteous, low-key guy, but he had been surrounded at the HPSCI by a cadre of ambitious, pugnacious aides who had rubbed many senior career officials at the Agency the wrong way. He brought most of them with him to the Agency—contrary to the private advice he got from Acting Director John McLaughlin—and the word was soon being passed around the halls at Langley that the new director and his team (who quickly acquired the sobriquet "The Gosslings") were about to start a purge of all Agency executives who had been part of George Tenet's inner circle.

I assumed that included me, but even if the rumored mass purge did not come to pass, I had no expectation that I would stay in the number one chair in the OGC for very long. After all, Porter didn't know me, and I figured that surely either he or the White House had someone waiting in the wings to nominate for the general counsel position. A week or so after Porter's arrival, we had a brief courtesy visit in his office, which was pleasant but uneventful. Up close, he seemed to be as courtly and unassuming as the impression I had gotten from a dis-

217

tance, and he certainly didn't appear to fit the stereotype of the back-slapping, self-important politician. In fact, my impression was that he was a remarkably shy man. He told me at that first, short meeting that he hadn't given any thought to who the new general counsel might be, and I believed him.

Within a few weeks, most of George Tenet's closest associates on the seventh floor had departed from the scene. First to go was George's hand-picked deputy, McLaughlin, followed by Executive Director Buzzy Kron-gard, Deputy Director for Intelligence Jami Miscik, and the DCI chief of staff, John Moseman. I had developed great admiration for all of them over the previous years, but they were gone, and that was that. A couple of months later, Deputy Director for Operations Steve Kappes was sud-denly gone, too, and that was a far noisier parting. Steve, a revered career clandestine service officer, got into a fierce argument with Porter's newly installed chief of staff, Pat Murray, and abruptly resigned, a move that sent shock waves around the building and dealt Porter's image inside the CIA a blow from which he never fully recovered.

But as 2005 began, I was still standing as acting general counsel, and there was as yet no replacement on the horizon. So I just plowed forward and did my job. Foremost, that meant trying to keep the best handle I could on the EIT program, which was becoming more complex and con-troversial by the day.

To that end, I thought it was high time for me to pay a personal visit to the Agency's black site.

By 2005, the prisons had been up and running for almost three years, and I suppose I could have traveled to see them earlier than I did. But I didn't consider doing so a burning necessity—from the inception of the program, our lawyers in the CTC had been making regular trips to observe the facilities (the prisons would be periodically moved for secu-rity reasons), as well as the EITs as they were being applied to individual detainees. By all of their accounts, the black site, in each of its locations, was operating efficiently, pursuant to the detailed legal and policy guid-ance being constantly sent by CIA Headquarters.

Still, I decided I should see everything myself, not just to lay eyes on what was happening, but to meet with the interrogators, the guards, and everyone else on site to answer their questions and to offer them assurances that what they were doing was still fully endorsed by the nation's highest legal and policy-making officials.

I made trips to two different prisons during 2005. On both occasions, I was part of a small delegation headed by Kyle "Dusty" Foggo, a career CIA administrative support officer whom Porter Goss, to everyone's surprise, had plucked from the middle ranks to become executive director, the number three job in the Agency hierarchy. Dusty was a controversial, often divisive figure in the career workforce. He could be abrasive, sometimes vindictive, bullying, and crude, and in 2006 he caused himself (and the Agency) considerable grief and humiliation by being indicted for— and subsequently pleading guilty to—federal corruption charges. He fully deserved his ignominious fate—and the three-year prison sentence that came with it—but to me, Dusty was not without certain redeeming qualities. For all his bluster and foibles, I found Dusty to be bright in a "street smart" sort of way, and he clearly loved and was devoted to the Agency and everything it stood for. Plus, he never once got in my way and pretty much left me alone.

What follows here is a composite description of my eyewitness observations and impressions of the two black sites, which were located in two countries in two different parts of the world.

First, however, I should briefly note one difference between the two trips. For my first trip, to a hot and dusty locale, I had packed my usual casual attire, which consisted of a stack of Ralph Lauren polo shirts in a rainbow coalition of colors. I believe I had a pink number on when I came out of the local hotel and climbed into a waiting unmarked vehicle, manned by a couple of hulking armed CIA security escorts, to take me to the prison site. We were going to be driving through neighborhoods frequented by thugs and perhaps terrorist wannabes, so I was grateful to see them.

One of these burly, gun-toting guys took one glance at my pink shirt and suggested, with a tone of ill-concealed scorn, "Sir, why didn't you just put a bull's-eye on your back instead?" For the next trip, I stuck to earth tones.

Otherwise, the two visits fell into the same pattern. Upon our arrival in the country, Dusty Foggo and I, accompanied by the local CIA station chief, would pay a requisite courtesy call on the head of the host government's foreign intelligence service in his office. Over cups of tea and plates of mysterious-looking local pastries, we would swap awkward small talk with the head of the service while his two or three aides, otherwise silent, would nod or laugh on cue, based on what their boss was saying. The one specific topic that was off-limits was the fact that the host government had agreed to let us build and maintain a prison to hold Al Qaeda's most notorious operatives. Our host knew full well we were in the country to visit the prison, and we knew he knew that's why we had come. But neither side broached the subject, at least not in so many words. Over the tea and pastries, Dusty and I would dutifully convey the U.S. Government's thanks, and the CIA director's deep appreciation, for the host country's "courageous contribution" and "invaluable support" to the war against Al Qaeda. Our host would nod benignly.

In each of the two countries we visited, the atmosphere in these courtesy-call sessions seemed stilted and peculiar to me. There we all were, sitting and idly chatting, while media in the United States and around the world were in the midst of tossing around the names of all sorts of countries where CIA "black sites" were supposedly located. Yet there was nothing Dusty and I could offer in the way of explanation. And each time, our host neither said nor seemed to expect more. Then we would say our goodbyes and be on our way, off to visit our secret prison. Our hosts would stay behind. That was because no one from outside the CIA—not even from the local government—was allowed entry to the site.

The prisons I visited were hiding in plain sight, each housed in a squat, nondescript building that blended into the surroundings. The unmarked, unremarkable van carrying us would be whisked into an underground garage through an entrance tucked into the back of the building, where the steel gate magically opened just as our car approached it. Once inside, our waiting escorts took us through a number of locked security-coded doors and down some twisting hallways to the command center for an initial briefing by the Agency officers supervising the facility. Because there were no windows anywhere, it was hard to tell if we were now above ground level or still underground. The atmosphere was distinctly claustrophobic, and everything was very quiet.

The most striking feature in the command center was the bank of TV monitors mounted on the walls. And it was there, on the screens, that I first saw them, those guys whose fates had consumed so much of my time for the previous three years. They looked so . . . small, each in his individual cell, either sleeping, eating, or praying. So seemingly peaceful and harmless.

"Where are they?" I asked one of the guys assigned to watch the monitors 24/7.

"Down the hall," he replied laconically. "You came during quiet time."

I knew beforehand that we couldn't personally interact with the detainees; our psychologists and analysts stressed how important it was to minimize the number of people the detainees were exposed to, the fear being that master manipulators such as KSM and Zubaydah would seize on any new face as an excuse to bloviate, prevaricate, and otherwise try to one-up and divert their regular inquisitors. Still, having come all this way, I thought it was important for me to personally get some feel, some sense, of the conditions under which they were living. So arrangements were quickly made for KSM and a couple of the others to be separately shuttled to the facility's interview rooms so I could enter their surroundings and take a look.

So down Dusty and I went, escorted by the chief of the facility, through another set of hallways and through more locked doors, into the cell block. The first things I noticed were the overhead lights—bright but not blinding. "They are kept on twenty-four/seven," the chief explained. "Bright enough so we can see everything they're up to, but not so bright that they can't sleep. These guys don't seem to have any trouble sleeping."

And then I was struck by the music that was filling the cell block. It was the same music I had heard, but didn't take much notice of, when we first entered the command center. Only now it was louder, though not deafening. But it was the choice of music that I found most startling. Coming through the speakers on the ceiling were syrupy, familiar-sounding pop ballads warbled in English by a woman. "Who is that?" I wondered aloud.

"Anne Murray," the chief replied matter-of-factly, referring to the '70s-era Canadian soft-rock singer. "We keep the volume up loud enough just so the detainee can't hear some sound or voice that he's not supposed to."

"But why Anne Murray, of all people?" I asked. Was it some subtle psychological ploy?

"No particular reason," the chief shrugged. "I just happen to like her songs."

As I pondered the question of whether being involuntarily subjected to Anne Murray's musical offerings could be construed as cruel or inhumane treatment, I looked at the cells. They seemed large enough as far as cells go—maybe fifteen by twenty feet. Each had a stainless-steel toilet, a mattress, and a small table nailed to the floor, also in stainless steel. An individual shower stall was located nearby. Painted concrete floor and walls. Bars, not slabs, on the cell door, to ease the sense of claustrophobia. Everything looking and smelling clean, almost antiseptic. "All according to U.S. Bureau of Prisons standards," the chief noted. "Much better digs than what these characters had on the outside." I didn't know about that, but I was satisfied, looking at the surroundings with my own eyes, that these were hardly dungeons.

After a visit to a small room containing a makeshift prison library and another filled with medical supplies, Dusty and I returned to the command center to talk to the staff. This was taking place in 2005, remember. None of the most severe EITs, such as waterboarding, had been employed for some time. Most of the detainees had been in our custody for at least a year—for KSM, it had been two years; for Zubaydah, it had been three. They were all compliant, and as cooperative as they would ever be. I was struck by the almost paternalistic pride the staff had in some of these remorseless killers—they told us how KSM, for example, had become a lecturer of sorts, holding forth at length about all things Al Qaeda. I found the staff's attitude entirely understandable yet nonetheless weirdly disconcerting; it was as if I were seeing the Stockholm syndrome in reverse, with the captors forming a bond of sorts with the captives they were cooped up with in those windowless, locked-down facilities.

But I don't want to overstate things. The staff at these secret facilities were dedicated professionals, and they never lost sight of who these detainees were. At the same time, they were realists, and they understood, better than anyone else, that with each passing day these detainees were getting more stale. The raison d'être of the EIT program, after all, was to acquire information about Al Qaeda plots and capabilities and/or bin Laden's location. And people such as KSM and Zubaydah, cut off from the action and held incommunicado for years, no longer had much current information to provide on those things, even if they were now willing to provide it.

So that realization, more than anything else, is what drove the questions that were directed at me. We don't want any of these guys to die on us, the staffs at these secret prisons would tell me, sometimes in a group, sometimes in quiet, offline conversations. Do you people back in Washington have a plan about what to do with them? What's the endgame?

Unfortunately, I didn't know what to tell them, because as 2005 played out, the fact was that none of us at headquarters really knew. Not that we weren't trying.

Following Bush's reelection in November 2004, he reshuffled his senior national security team on the Principals Committee. Colin Powell and John Ashcroft left the administration, with Condi Rice and Al Gonzales moving over from the White House to replace them at State and Justice, respectively. Don Rumsfeld, however, remained in place at the DOD, and his presence, more than anything else, would serve to stymie the CIA's increasingly urgent entreaties to the Principals to adopt a strategy to take detainees such as KSM and the other 9/11 plotters out of our prisons. We wanted to be done with them and, four years after 9/11, we wanted them to face justice.

It was much easier said than done. Part of the problem was a matter of logistics. Shipping them off for custody by a third country was out of the question—some of these people had the blood of three thousand innocent Americans on their hands, and ceding control over them to a foreign government was unthinkable. If they were brought to the States and held in a federal prison somewhere, the DOJ warned that they would immediately "lawyer up" and start tying up the government in legal knots, with petitions for habeas corpus and the like. Besides, no politician on Capitol Hill would sit still for someone like KSM being held, much less tried, in his or her locality. Too much exposure, too much risk for a retaliatory Al Qaeda attack, on the congressman's home turf. No, the DOJ adamantly insisted, putting these guys on trial in the United States was a nonstarter, not even on a U.S. military base.

That left the Guantánamo Bay Naval Base in Cuba, where our detainees could be transferred and held somewhere in proximity to the detention facility built to house hundreds of Al Qaeda foot soldiers captured on the battlefield in the first months after 9/11. That way, they would face justice in the form of the U.S. military commission structure the Bush administration created in the wake of the attacks. If these newly created commissions were designed to be used for anyone, the theory went, it would be for KSM and his 9/11 cohorts.

Gitmo and the military commissions were a perfectly logical solution for our detainees, except for a couple of what would prove to be insurmountable obstacles. First, because of factors both within and outside the DOD's control, the military commissions' structure existed largely only on paper. Nobody detained at Gitmo had yet been brought to trial, and no trials were on the horizon. Condi Rice, the newly installed secretary of state, was pushing for putting a "big fish"—such as KSM—on trial first. The new attorney general, Al Gonzales, signaled he was willing to go along; his career DOJ subordinates were doubtless relieved they would be out of the crosshairs. The DOD and the military, for their part, pushed back: Unsure of the viability of their jerry-rigged, untested commission structure, they wanted to test-drive the thing by putting some of the lowest-lying fruit, some Al Qaeda spear-carriers, through the process first.

The real DOD resistance, however, was more basic, and it came from the top. Don Rumsfeld wanted no part of the CIA detainees. From the outset of the EIT program three years before, he had kept his distance, ducking Principals' meetings on the topic when he could, shuffling his papers and saying little at the meetings he couldn't avoid. And now, in 2005, he had the nightmarish legacy of Abu Ghraib continuing to bedevil him. The last thing he needed was to take on the CIA hot potatoes like "black sites" and "waterboarding." To be sure, I never heard Rumsfeld or his people ever come out and say that during this period. Still, his passive-aggressive approach to the issue, his subtle foot-dragging, was an unmistakable sign to us at the Agency. And it was effective. KSM and the others remained in the CIA secret prisons.

Around this time, a new figure entered the small circle of administration officials cleared into the EIT program. Harriet Miers was named White House counsel, filling the spot vacated by Al Gonzales when he became attorney general. Like Al, Harriet was a lawyer from Texas with long personal ties to President Bush. Her previous White House post was as cabinet secretary, where we had never crossed paths and where as best I could tell she had not been in the loop on intelligence matters.

Shortly after 9/11, Al Gonzales had asked me to begin coming to his office on the second floor of the White House West Wing on a weekly basis to discuss new and ongoing legal developments in the Agency's covert-action operations against Al Qaeda. My old friend David Addington, the highly influential and opinionated counsel/alter ego to Vice President Cheney, typically sat in on the meetings. When Harriet took over for Al, she continued the practice. Her first priority was to learn everything there was to know about the secret prisons and EIT program. So, after first wading through all the OLC memos that had been issued, Harriet spent most of her time in those early weekly meetings peppering me, in a polite and studious way, with questions about how exactly the black site was being run, how the detainees were being treated, and other nuts-and-bolts kinds of things. All the while, she would be taking notes with what I noticed was impeccable penmanship. It was a style markedly different from her predecessor, Al Gonzales, who had treated his weekly sessions with me as a sort of free-floating dialogue, often deferring to David Addington on where and how the conversation proceeded.

I soon came to learn that Harriet, notwithstanding her gentle, soft-spoken demeanor, had a steely and dogged resolve about particular aspects of the EIT program that mattered to her most. First and foremost, she focused on the physical condition of the detainees who had been subjected to EITs. By 2005 we had about twenty of them in our custody, and some had been there since 2002. As I have noted, one of the major factors driving the CIA's efforts to get the Bush administration to settle on an "endgame" strategy was a basic dread that sooner or later one or more of them would die in captivity. For me, at least, I can't say that it was motivated by any real sense of human compassion. Rather, I was worried that if and when they started keeling over—especially if it was someone linked directly to the 9/11 attacks—not only would they never face justice, the interrogation tactics the Agency had employed on them would inevitably be linked to their demise, no matter how attenuated or even specious those links were. In the political climate of 2005, I envisioned a topsy-turvy scenario where a dead terrorist would be elevated to victim status, and the CIA be reduced to the role of the accused.

I sensed that Harriet's immediate and continuing focus on the detainees' physical well-being was less self-centered than profound. For her, it seemed to be a matter of simple humanity. And so, in her own quietly persistent way, she single-handedly pressed the subject in Principals' meetings and in lower-level sessions she regularly convened with me and other senior administration lawyers from 2005 into 2006. She demanded to be kept apprised of any and all maladies each of the detainees was suffering, and what steps the Agency was taking to treat them. As it happened, none of them ever had any life-threatening emergencies or conditions during their time in Agency custody. The problems that would arise were ones anybody, anywhere might have—I recall cases of impacted molars, occasional gastric issues, things like that. The fact was, these characters were getting more and better medical attention than they had ever had in their lives. And yet Harriet didn't let up.

Her single-mindedness on the subject could be frustrating at times for us at the Agency, especially when reports would come from the prisons that some of the detainees were flat-out rejecting the medical treatment being offered. I remember one time when the head of the CTC section responsible for the prisons informed me that one of the detainees kept spitting out at the guards the pills prescribed for him to treat his high blood pressure. He asked me, in an exasperated tone, "What do you recommend we do to make him take his pills? Wash it down with a waterboard?" I resisted the temptation to recount the exchange to Harriet.

I do not mean to make light of any of this, of course, nor to in any way disparage Harriet for her behind-the-scenes crusade to ensure the physical well-being of a group of the most despicable creatures on the planet. On the contrary, I tell it here to demonstrate what a fundamentally principled, compassionate person she was. Today, Harriet is mostly remembered by the public for her abortive 2006 nomination to the Supreme Court, during which she was widely maligned and mocked for her supposed lack of intellectual firepower and professional legal credentials. While it is true that she didn't possess the sort of glittering résumé one normally associates with a Supreme Court justice, I can personally attest, based on my up-close experience, to her strength of character and sense of moral decency. None of which the public could see at the time, but which nonetheless, I would submit, are pretty impressive credentials in their own right.

Harriet was also at the center of an odd and unexpected crisis I got pulled into in the final hours of 2005. It started around eight o'clock on the morning of New Year's Eve, when the CIA operations center called me at home to relay an urgent message from David Shedd of the National Security Council staff. He and I had been friends for years. Rolling out of bed with a sigh, I hauled out my CIA-issued secure-line telephone from its "concealment" device, a piece of ordinary-looking furniture in which Agency technicians had carved a hidden compartment to hide the phone when it wasn't in use.

When I finally got through to David at the White House, I immediately sensed the tone of urgency in his voice even through the snap, crackle, and pop interference of the connection. I braced myself for some sort of political or operational catastrophe, likely having to do with our counterterrorist program. Instead, David began by asking, "You know who James Risen is, right?"

"Sure," I replied. Risen was a longtime investigative reporter for the *New York Times*, working the intelligence beat.

"Well," David said, "we just got word here that he's about to come out with a book that's going to blow the lid off a bunch of very sensitive intelligence operations, including at least one being run by the Agency."

And then David's voice got lower. "I can't tell you how, but we have gotten our hands on an advance copy of the final manuscript, and you need to get down here now to get it and then get it to the people at Langley who know about the operation. If it's as damaging as I think it is, we are going to have to see if we can stop it."

None of this was making any sense to me. I had heard nothing—the CIA had heard nothing—about an upcoming book by Risen. "Stop it?" I asked. "You mean, stop the operation?"

"No," David responded. "I mean stop the book."

Christ, I thought to myself. He's talking about prior restraint on publication. There goes my plan for a quiet, restful day at home with my wife, topped off with joining friends at a restaurant in Georgetown to ring in the new year.

Feeling supremely sorry for myself, I got dressed and drove down the empty streets to the Old Executive Office Building next to the White House to pick up the manuscript from David in his office. (He didn't trust the normal White House courier system to get it to Langley in a timely and discreet fashion.) Only, when I got there and saw it, it didn't look like some prepublication manuscript. It looked like a book, a finished book, with a dust jacket and all. It was titled *State of War*, published by Free Press, an imprint of Simon & Schuster.

"Jeez, David," I told him, "this looks like it's ready to come out. Any idea when the publication date is?"

"We're not sure. Maybe a couple of days, maybe a couple of weeks. The source who gave it to us doesn't know, either, but he doesn't want to get burned, so we don't want to do anything until we know the scope of the problem. But I think there's a big problem."

I skimmed the section of the book that David found the most troubling. Yup, it was definitely a problem.

I got on the phone to the CIA Command Center and had them track down all the people I thought needed to know about this besides me. I wasn't about to let myself be the only guy whose New Year's plans were going to be screwed up by this sudden mess. I then jumped in my car, clutching a copy of the book, and raced up the George Washington Parkway toward Langley.

Once back at headquarters, I had our chief of operations (a remarkably good sport about being dragged out of bed to come in) do a speed-read. He quickly confirmed that the details largely were all too distressingly accurate and damaging to CIA sources and methods. What to do now? I made a quick call to my boss, Director Porter Goss, at his Florida vacation home to tell him what was happening. Polite and unflappable as always, Porter asked me what I thought the next step would be. "I have no idea," I replied. I got on the phone again to Shedd, who told me to get back down to the White House, where he was convening an emergency meeting in the Situation Room.

Before hopping back into my car, I made a point to call the CIA Office of Public Affairs. "Do you have any insight into this? Has Risen ever called about any of it?" I asked. It has always been a long-standing custom for journalists working on national security stories that could involve classified information to contact Public Affairs in advance, partly as a matter of courtesy and partly to give the CIA a heads-up and an opportunity to make a case for the reporter to omit, or at least "fuzz up," some of the details most harmful to national security. Sometimes the journalist agrees, sometimes he or she doesn't, but the point is to give the Agency a chance. In my experience, virtually every serious journalist—whether friend or foe to the CIA and its mission—has operated on that basis. Risen, a seasoned reporter on intelligence matters, certainly knew the protocol, and he clearly had been working on this book for a long time.

The Public Affairs staff recalled that Risen had called in the recent past about some story he was working on for the *Times*, something that was no big deal. Then, right before hanging up, he casually mentioned he was working on a book "that will be coming out at some point."

And then it hit me, later than it should have. The classified, highly damaging information in the book we were focusing on had come up on the screen before. Almost three years earlier, the CIA had gotten word that the *New York Times* was preparing to publish an article laying out the same entire story. The article's author: James Risen. In an extraordinary step few administrations ever took during the course of my career, the Bush administration, in the person of National Security Advisor Condi Rice, summoned Risen and his boss at the *Times* to the White House to plead that the article not be published, spelling out in detail the grave national security interests at stake. To the surprise and relief of many of us at the Agency—this was the *New York Times*, after all, not exactly a toady for the Bush administration or the CIA—senior management at the *Times* ultimately agreed to spike the story. Risen, evidently, was not happy about the decision.

I know James Risen only by reputation. Inside the CIA, at least, he has had a reputation for being irresponsible and sneaky. This episode showed me that his reputation appeared to be richly deserved.

But on this frantic day there was no time to dwell on his professional ethics. Back in the Situation Room, David Shedd had assembled a small group of officials to review what we knew. I don't remember all the attendees (it was now the early afternoon of New Year's Eve, and the pickings of available senior people were slim), but I do recall that Harriet Miers was there, as always unobtrusive and quietly taking notes. I confirmed to the group that the stuff in that chapter was alarming and damaging. David had a few additional details about the timing of publication—as best anyone could tell, the books were printed in bulk and stacked somewhere in warehouses. After going around and around for a while, we arrived at a rueful consensus: game over as far as any realistic possibility to keep the book, and the classified information in it, from getting out.

It was getting dark as I walked back to my car around six o'clock for the drive home. I made a few calls on the way. One to the guys still on standby at headquarters, telling them they could go home. Another to Porter Goss, providing an update on where things stood. Finally, a call to my ever-patient and understanding wife, assuring her that we could still salvage the evening and make our dinner reservation. I knew that there would be a follow-up I would have to do—file a crimes report with the DOJ, start on a more detailed damage assessment on the harm caused by the revelations in the book—but that could wait for the first few days of 2006.

It was about four hours later, as Sharon and I were dining with friends at a crowded and noisy Georgetown restaurant, when my cell phone rang. It was from the White House, and I recognized the soft, Texas-twanged voice of Harriet Miers immediately.

"John, I am truly sorry to bother you again, but is the name Sumner Redstone familiar to you?"

"Sumner Redstone, Sumner Redstone," I stammered into the phone as I waded through the restaurant to get outside to escape the din.

"I am looking on the Internet," Harriet continued, "and it says that he is the chairman of Viacom, the parent company of Simon & Schuster." Oh, yes, I remembered, that Sumner Redstone, the legendary octogenarian corporate mogul.

"Well, I've been thinking that maybe you should give him a call. You know, explain to him the national security crisis we have here, and get him to order Simon & Schuster to pull back the books from the warehouses."

I was outside, dodging revelers teeming on M Street. I was hoping I wasn't hearing her correctly.

Harriet pressed on: "I suppose I or someone else in the White House could make the call, but I think it would have more impact if it came from the CIA, don't you? And we have to go to the very top. But you need to do it now," she said, her voice now more steely. "Here, I have the phone number. Do you have a pen handy?"

Numbly, I scrambled back into the restaurant and borrowed a pen, and a menu, from the startled hostess. I scribbled down the number, which Harriet apparently was reading off the Internet. It sounded like the main switchboard number for Viacom, if there was such a thing.

"Thank you so much," Harriet signed off cheerfully. "Happy New Year!" She said it without a trace of irony.

I stared at the phone in the cold, dark night, pondering my fate. It was almost ten on New Year's Eve, and I had just been ordered to make a cold call aimed at tracking down an iconic titan of business, a total stranger, then to invoke the Agency's name and mystique to somehow cajole him into ordering the summary suppression of a major book that one of his companies had already printed in God knows how many thousands of copies and scattered into God knows how many warehouses around the country.

The whole idea was so crazy, so preposterous, that I had to tell somebody. Having by now lost my appetite for a New Year's celebration, I quickly wrapped up the dinner and began to walk to our nearby Georgetown home with my wife. She could sense something was amiss with me since I had taken that phone call in the restaurant, so as we were walking I gave her an abbreviated version of what had happened and the pickle I was in. Sharon had joined the CIA in 1999, six years after we married, so she had the same top-secret security clearance I had. Still, I had previously been circumspect with her about some of the highly sensitive and hairy stuff I had been involved in since 9/11, such as the interrogation program. For one thing, I didn't want to worry her. Beyond that, there was that bedrock principle in the intelligence world called "need to know"; her holding a security clearance didn't necessarily mean that I could make her privy to all the secrets I knew. And she always understood and accepted that. I suppose Sharon didn't "need to know" that night what the Miers phone call was about, but trudging home as midnight approached, with my head spinning, I sure as hell needed to talk to somebody about it. And so I blurted out the whole surreal episode to her.

"Can't you talk to someone else at the White House, to make sure this is what they really want to do?" Sharon gently suggested. I hesitated—I liked and admired Harriet, and I was really torn about going around her. But this was too much: On the remote chance I could even hook up with Sumner Redstone in the final hours of New Year's Eve without being dismissed as a drunken crank or lunatic, the chances were beyond remote that he would ever agree to what I would be modestly proposing. What's more, if the word of any such call ever got out, it would spawn a huge, embarrassing sensation that would only draw more attention and customers to the book.

In desperation, trudging back to our house just before midnight, I somehow tracked down David Shedd's home phone number. Poor David. As I blurted my story out, he had every right to conclude that this was some sort of twisted, alcohol-fueled gag on my part. But he was patient and remarkably low-key. "Forget the whole thing," he said. "Apparently

there are copies already at bookstores. Just go to bed. I'll talk to Harriet."
He must have, because she never asked me about it again.

Thus officially ended 2005 for me.

A couple of days later I sent the requisite "crimes report" to the Justice Department on the unauthorized disclosure contained in the Risen book that had caused all the commotion. It coincided with the publication of the book, which went on to become a best seller. It would take almost four years, but in December 2010 the Obama Justice Department filed a ten-count indictment against a disgruntled former CIA undercover officer named Jeffrey Sterling, charging him with being the source of the leak to Risen. As this is written, the case has yet to go to trial because of extended procedural wrangling between the parties. Among other things, the prosecutors have subpoenaed Risen to testify at the trial about his sources. Risen has fought against testifying, claiming that the freedom-of-the-press guarantees in the Bill of Rights grant him a "reporter privilege."

CHAPTER 14

An Offer I Couldn't Refuse (2006)

The public controversy—and the behind-the-scenes machinations—surrounding the EIT program carried over into the new year of 2006. Media leaks about the program were now gushing, as newspapers, newsmagazines, and TV networks vied with each other on a daily basis to produce "exclusive" investigative pieces on the CIA "black sites" and what were now described as "brutal" or "torture" techniques the Agency was applying to its detainees. The word *waterboarding* was on its way to becoming firmly established in the national lexicon. It all made for sensational, headline-grabbing stuff. All of us involved in the program could only look on, silent and helpless, as collectively we were being publicly portrayed as untethered, sadistic goons. For its part, Congress offered no support or solace; still only a handful in Congress were privy to the underlying facts and demonstrable intelligence benefits the program was providing, and they weren't talking.

However, there was one curious episode during this general time frame where the CIA—in the person of yours truly—had to negotiate with a journalist to keep a key, extremely dicey element of our covert counterterrorist efforts from becoming public. Actually, it had nothing to do with the EIT program. Instead, it involved the Agency's innovative, complex initiative to uncover Al Qaeda's worldwide financial network. The program was hatched in the early days after 9/11 as a joint CIA/ Treasury Department effort to "follow the money" being generated by Al Qaeda. Like other post-9/11 CIA counterterrorist actions, it was unprecedented in its audacity and scope. In the years leading up to 9/11, the Agency had periodically floated something along its lines to policy makers in the Clinton and Bush administrations as one of the most effective ways to attack Al Qaeda at its roots, only to be summarily rebuffed each time. I remember being archly lectured by my counterparts at Treasury and State that the United States followed a strict policy, based on long-standing international conventions and understandings, not to engage whatsoever in practices that compromise the "sanctity" of worldwide financial networks. I vividly recall the use of the word *sanctity* because its quasi-religious connotation struck me as a peculiar status to accord a bunch of wheeling-and-dealing, ethically challenged fat-cat bankers.

Anyway, passenger jets being crashed into crowded buildings at the hub of the financial world served to dissipate erstwhile concerns about "sanctity," and post-9/11, the CIA was given the green light to begin a full-bore offensive against the Al Qaeda money machine. From the start, it proved enormously successful on a number of levels, not the least of which was that—unlike the EIT program—the details of this tightly held program remained secret. And secrecy was particularly essential for these operations—not only was there the risk of Al Qaeda being tipped off, but the sub-rosa, cooperative role played by foreign governments could also be exposed.

The sudden threat to the entire thing unraveling in public came in the unlikely person of Paul O'Neill, treasury secretary for the first two years of the Bush administration. I should emphasize at the outset that O'Neill bears absolutely no responsibility for the crisis, which was ignited when he was forced to resign his position at the end of 2002 after a relatively short, rocky tenure. Instead, the blame lies at the feet of the top levels of the Treasury bureaucracy, which made a decision to grant O'Neill's departing request for electronic copies of all documents—thousands and thousands of them—that had come to his personal attention during his time in office. His former subordinates obliged his request by transfer-ring everything onto DVDs and shipping them off to him shortly after he returned to private life. They did so without apparently bothering to review the stuff first—it wasn't scrubbed for any concerns about the pri-vacy of others, sensitive proprietary information . . . or highly classified intelligence matters. Writing about this years later, among all the flaps and screwups I observed in the government, I still consider what Trea-sury did to be unique in terms of its astonishing carelessness.

I cannot say for certain if O'Neill originally sought his records in order to write his memoirs, but in any case they played a key role in a best-selling book in 2004, *The Price of Loyalty: George W. Bush, the White House, and the Education of Paul O'Neill*, written with O'Neill's full cooperation by Ron Suskind, a well-known, experienced reporter with a Pulitzer Prize among his credentials. The book itself, while highly critical of various Bush administration policies, didn't raise a ripple at the Agency. What we didn't know then was that Suskind had his own copy of the O'Neill DVDs. And he was smart enough to recognize what he had— buried in the thousands of documents were accounts of National Security Council deliberations in which the top-secret CIA/Treasury joint operations against Al Qaeda were laid out in raw, comprehensive detail, with names, places, and dates. It was a journalist's ultimate wet dream, and Suskind clearly understood what had fallen into his lap.

To his credit, it was Suskind himself who first alerted the Bush administration that he was in possession of some extremely sensitive CIA operational information. Coincidentally or not, he was working on a new book, one in which he would catalogue the inner workings of the government's post-9/11 counterterrorist offensive against Al Qaeda. As I say, Suskind was a smart guy, and he did a smart thing, enlisting Wilmer-Hale, a blue-chip, politically connected D.C. law firm, to represent his interests. He wanted to make a deal. Much as I was tempted, given all the crises du jour I was juggling, to delegate the matter to someone else in the OGC, I decided I needed to handle the mess myself. For one thing, my boss was now Porter Goss, and Porter, not to put too fine a point on it, was contemptuous of most investigative journalists. His visceral reaction, when it came to reporters, was to treat them with malign neglect. But he was a realist, too, and he recognized Suskind had the Agency over a barrel. Suskind, after all, got access to the documents in question through O'Neill and only because Treasury had blithely set them loose without any strings attached. I told Porter that, under the circumstances, our leverage was limited. Legal action against a high-profile journalist like Suskind and/or against O'Neill, a Bush cabinet appointee turned harsh critic, would have been time-consuming and messy, with no guarantee that CIA information could be retrieved and protected.

"Make the best deal you can," Porter responded grudgingly, "but you need to do it yourself."

Thus began a series a negotiating sessions with the WilmerHale attorneys, led by Randy Moss, former head of the Justice Department's Office of Legal Counsel during the Clinton administration. I knew Randy well and trusted him completely to handle this delicate matter in a responsible, discreet way. I was accompanied to the sessions at the WilmerHale offices by the CTC's chief of financial operations, a brilliant, somewhat intense man who had masterminded the plans against Al Qaeda that were described in the O'Neill documents. As best I can recall, one or two Treasury representatives also attended. Suskind himself was nowhere to be seen.

We were making progress with Randy and his colleagues, albeit slowly. The discussions centered around how the government could get access to the massive volume of documents—the Agency, at least, still wasn't certain how many pertained to our operations and the precise level of detail they contained—and then figure out a way for the sensitive stuff to be redacted.

The talks were civil, with neither side issuing any threats or ultimatums. But they dragged on for a while, into early 2006, and Ron Suskind, waiting in the wings, apparently got impatient. One day, I got a call out of the blue in my office. It was from Suskind. We still hadn't met, but right off the bat, he put us on a first-name basis. "John," the staccato voice crackled on the other end of the line, "you and I can work this out ourselves. We need to get together, just the two of us."

I was startled, to say the least. I had always avoided reporters during my CIA career, and suddenly here was one on the phone with me, and he was going around his lawyers, to boot. I put Suskind off until I could contact Randy Moss to make sure he knew what was happening. I don't know if he did until I informed him, but Randy said he was fine with me meeting alone with his client. So was Porter, who seemed somewhere between baffled and appalled by the abrupt turn of events. So, with some trepidation, I called Suskind back and agreed to meet.

"Come to Bread and Chocolate on Connecticut Avenue at two o'clock tomorrow. Sit in the back of the place and I'll find you," he told me in urgent, furtive tones. Jeez, I thought to myself as I hung up the phone. It's like I was meeting some secret agent or something.

The next day, I arrived at Bread and Chocolate—a fancy coffee and pastry place—at the appointed time. It was dark and mostly empty, so I sat at a table in the back and waited. I ordered coffee, which came in a cup about the size of a rain barrel. A few minutes later, Suskind walked in quickly and sat down. Then he began talking. And kept talking, non-stop, for about an hour.

To establish his bona fides, he began by assuring me he wasn't interested in endangering national security and would do whatever I thought was necessary to ensure the security of the O'Neill files (as would O'Neill himself, he quickly added). The book he was writing would be "a positive story, a heroic story" about "Team Tenet." I had never heard the latter phrase before, and I was instinctively wary about any journalist claiming he was writing something "positive" about the CIA. But he was on a roll, so I just went with it, sipping my vat of coffee.

Eventually, Suskind got to his main pitch. He wanted the CIA's cooperation in the form of interviews with some of our people "in the trenches" of the counterterrorist war. Not Tenet himself or the people close to him—he cryptically alluded to being already in contact with some of them. Rather, he said he wanted to talk to people at the staff level, "the real heroes," as he put it. On and on he went, until I finally told him I had to go. I had barely gotten a word in, but he had exhausted me. "Let me get back to you," I said before finally escaping.

I reported all of it to Porter. For all of his fast-talking melodramatics, I found Suskind oddly likable. He had never linked his requests for interviews as a quid pro quo for giving us the O'Neill files. He didn't have to. I recommended to a clearly skeptical Porter that we make the deal. "Okay," Porter finally said, "but I wonder if he is being straight with us."

So I made the arrangements. Three of our preeminent Al Qaeda experts from the CTC separately met with Suskind, chaperoned by the CIA public affairs staff. It took a lot of reassurance on my part to get them to do it—CIA personnel, by nature and training, are spooked about talking to the media. Still, they gave Suskind some nuggets of insider stuff—war stories, really—about what the Agency was doing in its offensive against Al Qaeda. He seemed satisfied enough, at least for the time being. But he was a reporter, after all, and he soon wanted more. When he called me again, a few weeks before the book's scheduled publication date, Suskind's voice was tinged with even more urgency and furtiveness than I remembered, which I didn't think was possible.

Suskind had a simple (!) request: He wanted to interview the CIA source who had led us to Khalid Sheikh Mohammed in 2003. Once again, Suskind rattled off all of his reasons in a dizzying cascade of words. As I listened, it occurred to me that he knew more about the guy than I did. This time, however, I did manage to squeeze in a few sentences. "I'll check, Ron, but I think that's a bridge too far," I said, in what might have been the biggest understatement of my career. I never checked, and I never spoke to Suskind again.

In the end, Suskind did keep his end of the bargain. He let the government gain access to his O'Neill documents, and it took a squadron of people—from the CIA and other federal agencies—to wade through all of it. It was a laborious and time-consuming process, but it eventually happened.

Also, Suskind kept the most sensitive, damaging information about the CTC's financial operations against Al Qaeda out of his book, *The One Percent Doctrine*, which came out later in 2006. It was written the way Suskind talked: entertaining, breathless, rhetorically over the top. It became a best seller.

A coda to the story: Notwithstanding Suskind's omission of the most damaging details about the CTC's financial operations, *The One Percent Doctrine* was honeycombed with other classified information. I had no idea that Suskind had any of it, or where it came from. But Suskind had his job, and I had mine. Shortly after the book came out, the Agency filed a "crimes report" with the Justice Department about the unauthorized disclosures.

It wasn't personal. It was strictly business.

By the beginning of 2006, I was as tight with Porter Goss as I ever was with any CIA director, before or since. He was a little more than a year into the job by then, and I could never have predicted that our relationship would become so close. Surprisingly, for someone who was a veteran of many successful congressional campaigns, I found Porter to be preternaturally self-effacing and unassuming. Personalitywise, George Tenet was far better in the backslapping, flesh-pressing department, and George had never been elected to anything.

Inside the Agency's rank-and-file workforce, Porter's innate modesty and reticence were widely misinterpreted as remote imperiousness, but the truth was, he was a thoroughly decent human being without a pretentious or duplicitous bone in his body. Financially secure and holding a safe congressional seat, Porter had no desire or need in his twilight years to take over an institution awash in turmoil, but, as Bill Webster did two decades before, he took the job simply because he was a patriot and his president had asked him to do it.

Sometime near the end of 2005, Porter first raised with me the possibility of becoming general counsel, a position requiring presidential nomination and Senate confirmation. It was just a trial balloon on his part. Was it something I was interested in his pursuing with the White House, which would have the final say on the matter? "You know," he cautioned, "if your name is sent down to the Hill, it could get rough and ugly for you." He was alluding to the fact that by then my name was popping up in media accounts as one of the key players in the development and implementation of the EIT program.

I was not deterred, and I didn't play hard to get. "Sure," I responded immediately. "I would be honored to have the job." After all, I knew what the position entailed, having been the GC in everything but name for almost three of the preceding four years. Plus, there was the ego factor—for three decades, no career CIA attorney had held the top position on a permanent basis, and none had ever been confirmed by the Senate to the post. At the same time, apart from my own selfish motives, I thought my making it to the top could serve as a signal to the 120 or so OGC "lifers" in the office that, with enough hard work and patience, they could legitimately aspire to get there someday, too.

Finally, as for Porter's warning about a potentially bruising confirmation battle, I didn't pay that much heed. Surely, I figured, he was being overdramatic. I wasn't some untested political hack/dilettante being foisted on the Agency. What's more, it wasn't like I was being nominated for some cabinet position. I mean, who on the Hill or in the media would really care who the CIA's lawyer was?

"Okay," Porter said. "I'll pass your name to the White House. I don't know how the political people there will react, but it's going to take time for all of it to sort out. You'll have to be vetted and interviewed, if it even gets that far. So you need to be patient." No problem there. I had been around for thirty years, and this was a moment I never thought would come. I could wait for a while.

A couple of weeks later, my wife and I were in Marbella, Spain, in the middle of a long-scheduled vacation on the Costa del Sol. One morning, the hotel switchboard relayed a terse message in fractured English: "Your office says to call immediately." With a combination of fear and curiosity, I dialed the number from my personal cell phone. I had no CIA-issued secure cell phone with me, so I was contemplating how the hell I was going to be able to hear and say anything about what I assumed was some highly classified topic.

As it turned out, the topic wasn't classified, but it was stunning nonetheless. My office told me the White House had just called: My nomination was being finalized. There would be no interviews needed, but I had to fill out and sign some official White House forms. Now. The White House wanted a fax number to send them to me.

"Here?" I asked numbly. "Do they know I'm in this hotel in the middle of nowhere on the Spanish coast?" Yes, I was told, the White House knew that. I didn't know whether to be overjoyed or flummoxed by what I was being told to do.

I got the fax number from the hotel front desk and passed it along to my office. I didn't want to loiter indefinitely around the lobby, and besides, I told my wife we needed to go out somewhere to celebrate, or at least recover from, the unexpected news. When we returned to the hotel a couple of hours later, I went to the front desk and asked, as nonchalantly as I could, whether something had arrived for me. The young Spanish desk clerk, his eyes as big as saucers and his hands trembling, silently passed me a thick sheaf of papers. Right on top was the fax transmission sheet, with the name and image of the White House prominently displayed. Below that were numerous forms, largely blank except for two bold-faced typewritten references sprinkled throughout: my name, and the words *General Counsel, Central Intelligence Agency*.

Apparently the desk clerk could read English. I must say, the service at the hotel seemed to get a lot better after that.

Notwithstanding all the rush-rush in Marbella, my nomination was not officially announced by the White House and sent to the Senate until March 16, 2006. Inside the Agency, the news elicited lots of congratulatory notes from my co-workers. Outside the Agency, there was barely a ripple.

I didn't realize it at the time, but I had a lot more waiting to do. It would take the Senate Intelligence Committee fifteen months to schedule my confirmation hearing.

In the meantime, I didn't have the luxury to just sit on my hands. Outside events, and intensifying controversy, were driving the EIT program steadily downhill. The Agency was being rocked from top to bottom. And I continued to be in the middle of all of it.

Porter Goss deserved a better hand than he was dealt in 2006. He inherited the EIT program when he came to office in November 2004, and the wheels began coming off of it as soon as he arrived. He steadfastly believed in it, supported it unequivocally, but by the beginning of 2006 that was becoming a lonely position. The Bush administration was under siege—not just by the lingering, horrifying images of Abu Ghraib, but by its tone-deaf response to the Hurricane Katrina disaster and the growing disenchantment with the seemingly open-ended chaos in post-Saddam Iraq. The administration was counting on Porter to serve as the chief point man to save and maintain the beleaguered EIT program or, perhaps, to be the fall guy if it went down the tubes. It didn't help that Porter no longer had daily access to the president via the daily Oval Office intelligence briefings; his place had been taken by John Negroponte, director of the new, congressionally created Office of National Intelligence.

But Porter was both a gentleman and a good soldier, and he accepted his role and did the best he could to salvage the EIT program. He worked his network of friends and former colleagues in Congress—all but a handful of whom were still being kept in the dark about the program—but the deck was stacked against him. It wasn't just the Democrats, who, not surprisingly, were unanimously adamant in opposing a Bush-authorized program most of them knew nothing about. The most high-profile and influential opposition came from Senator John McCain, a Republican and, of course, a storied war hero and victim of prolonged torture by his North Vietnamese captors. McCain was characteristically blunt about what he was reading in the media reports about waterboarding, sleep deprivation, and the like: It sounded like torture.

Porter had been friends with McCain from their days together in Congress, and he got permission from the White House in late 2005 to lift its tight curtain of secrecy over the program so that he could give McCain a private, one-on-one briefing, walking him through all the techniques, how they were applied, the safeguards that were in place, the demonstrable results the EIT program had yielded, and so on. Basically, it would be intended to separate the actual facts from the hyperbole, the distortions that colored many of the media reports.

I remember when Porter came back from the briefing. A normally even-keeled, taciturn man, he was clearly shaken. "I got nowhere," he told me. "I don't think John even heard a thing I told him. He just sat there, stone-faced and looking straight ahead, like he didn't know me. No questions, no comments, no nothing. When I was done, he just said, 'It's all torture,' and got up and left." Porter paused and then this lifelong, rock-ribbed Republican quietly added, "It wasn't so much that he objects to what we're doing. I can accept that, and he has the right to feel that way more than anyone else. But it was like he was in another dimension."

The White House, in the person of National Security Advisor Steve Hadley, then decided to see if it could make any headway with McCain. It became my role to serve as the focal point with Hadley's staff, getting updates on his negotiations with McCain. The key language of a bill he was pushing—which came to be known as the McCain Amendment— barred the U.S. Government from committing "cruel, inhuman or degrading treatment or punishment" on its detainees. I passed a series of suggested "fixes" to Hadley's staff, like an exception for "lawfully autho- rized activities" or immunity for officers operating "in good faith pur- suant to presidential direction." McCain rejected all of them. When that happened, I realized that now the Agency was in an even deeper hole— gone was any possibility down the line to assert that the broad language of the bill was not intended to encompass the EIT program. There was now a record that removed any doubt that that's exactly what McCain intended, and it was also clear that he wanted Agency employees, even if they were just following orders, kept personally in the crosshairs. Above all, I couldn't get McCain's terse verdict to Porter—"It's all torture"—out of my head.

Hadley ultimately did manage to wring a small concession from McCain, who agreed to insert vague language into his bill that essentially would have allowed anyone involved in the EIT program to use "good faith" reliance on legal advice as a "defense" in any ensuing proceeding. It gave me little or no comfort; it still left CIA officers involved in the pro- gram perilously exposed. Any future investigation—presumably not by the Bush Justice Department, but who knew about a succeeding admin- istration?—could take months or even years, even if no charges were ultimately filed. It would be a harrowing ordeal, with potentially dozens of middle- and even low-level CIA officers having to hire and pay for their own lawyers, all because they had just been doing what the highest levels of the government had assured them for years was authorized and lawful. Maybe as a practical matter an actual criminal investigation was a long shot, but to me, with the EIT program becoming more politically toxic by the day, it was a scenario that seemed all too plausible.

Nonetheless, the Bush White House declared victory, and even had the president pose for a picture shaking hands with McCain to memorialize the agreement. The McCain Amendment became law in late 2005. Hadley evidently assured Bush that the EIT program had survived intact. But no one asked me, and I was anything but assured. I was deeply worried that our people—still administering EITs to newer-arriving detainees, including the guy who succeeded KSM as Al Qaeda's operational commander—would someday, somehow, be left hung out to dry. So I decided to take a step that would prove even more fateful than I realized at the time: I recommended to Porter that he formally notify the White House that the Agency was suspending the EIT program—immediately and across the board—pending receipt of new, written, authoritative legal guidance from the Justice Department about the scope and impact of the McCain Amendment.

Before approaching Porter, I went over and over in my mind the potential implications. I knew that the CIA's sudden suspension of the EIT program would cause ripples inside the Bush administration, but I couldn't gauge how big the ripples would be. I briefly considered, but decided against, first broaching my deep concerns about the impact of the McCain Amendment with my counterparts at Justice and the White House. I figured what I would get back would be assurances not to worry, which I knew wouldn't assuage my worries, which were more inchoate and gut-level. Besides, the people being put in the legal crosshairs were those in the Agency—my clients, the career rank-and-file employees—not those political appointees at Justice or the White House who would be long gone if and when the shit hit the fan.

I will confess to also thinking about how what I was about to do might affect my own career. Porter had just recommended me to the White House for the GC position. My prospects looked good, but the White

House had not yet formally submitted my nomination to Congress. My fingerprints were going to be all over any decision to suspend the program. The Bush people, including those holding my future in their hands, were not going to be pleased with me.

But in the final analysis, I decided there was no other way. I went to talk to Porter.

"Are you sure about this?" Porter asked me. He fully grasped that what I was proposing would mean giving the detainees an indefinite reprieve while simultaneously pissing all over the Bush-McCain kum-baya moment. I felt grubby about putting him on the spot.

"This is a whole new ball game for us. I just think our people could be in serious jeopardy. Maybe not tomorrow. Maybe not next year. But someday," I replied.

That was all Porter needed to hear. "Draft a memo to go from me to Steve Hadley and [Director of National Intelligence] John Negroponte," he instructed. "Lay out all the reasons why I have decided to suspend the program."

The memo left the CIA on the last day of 2005. The same day, head-quarters ordered interrogators at our secret prisons to halt the use of any EITs. This edict included Al Qaeda's operations commander, a hard-ened character named Abu Faraj al-Libbi. Prior to his capture several months before, he had unparalleled personal access to bin Laden and to Al Qaeda's operational plans. Finally, his interrogators thought, he might be about to talk.

Back in Washington, Porter's memo had a separate sort of impact: It effectively doomed him. Hadley was furious when he saw it. He had negotiated doggedly with McCain on the language and thought he had a deal that would preserve the EIT program. No sooner than Hadley had assured Bush that the program could continue, the CIA director sends him a missive written by me pulling the plug on it. Hadley felt Porter had blindsided him with the commander in chief.

I remember Porter telling me at the time, "Hadley's not happy about the memo," but Porter didn't make a big deal about it, so I assumed the unhap-piness would go away over time. Apparently, it didn't. Six months later, in June 2006, Porter was summoned to the Oval Office and fired as CIA direc-tor. Now it was Porter's turn to feel blindsided. He hadn't seen it coming.

A few days later, after the shock had worn off and he had time to reflect, I met privately with Porter in his office, packing boxes all around us. "It was the memo," he quietly told me. "That's what did me in." He didn't say whether he had been told that or if he had simply arrived at that conclusion himself. But he said it without any rancor toward anyone, including the guy sitting across from him who had urged that he send it in the first place. What I had done was to write the professional death warrant of a man I had come to admire enormously and who had been so kind and generous to me. I felt terrible about it. I still do.

There was an ironic, poignant coda to the Goss tenure. On June 29, 2006, just about the time Porter was being unceremoniously kicked to the curb, the Supreme Court issued a long-awaited ruling that effectively put the EIT program, as it then existed, out of business even more definitively than the McCain Amendment did. The case was *Hamdan v. Rumsfeld*, and it involved a former bin Laden bodyguard and driver being held in U.S. military custody at Guantánamo Bay. The Court, among other things, held that Common Article 3 of the Geneva Conventions governed "the conflict with Al Qaeda." While the McCain Amendment had no explicit criminal application, the Court's application of Common Article 3 brought the treatment of U.S. Government detainees—including those in CIA prisons—directly into the ambit of the congressional war crimes statutes. In other words, hundreds of my Agency clients who had been involved in the EIT program (and me personally) were on notice that we could be potential war criminals.

It was a whole new ball game indeed.

General Mike Hayden arrived as CIA director in September 2006. Mike was career air force and came to the Agency with more credentials in the field of intelligence than any CIA director I served under, before or since. His two previous positions had been as head of the National Security Agency and number two man at the newly created Office of the Director of National Intelligence (ODNI). He was eager to take on the CIA job as the swan song to his long and distinguished government career, which I found encouraging if somewhat puzzling. He had a spotless record of public service, and here he was happily wading into the quicksand of the EIT program, something that was now threatening the careers and reputations of anyone associated with it.

Why did he do it? Three reasons, I think. First, he was a soldier and lifelong patriot, and when his commanding officer—in this case, his president—asked him to take on an assignment, he was going to salute. Second, he loved (and perhaps needed) new challenges, and God knows, taking the reins at the CIA in 2006 offered all manner of new challenges. The third reason became clear to me only when I had watched him up close in the job for a while: Mike Hayden loved being a spymaster, by which I mean he reveled in conceiving and running covert operations involving real people and back-alley intrigue. His years at the NSA and the ODNI involved him deeply in intelligence matters, to be sure, but by his own account it had been all "techie, wonky stuff." And the CIA was, well, the CIA. Mike Hayden had been a working-class kid from Pittsburgh who drove cabs to put himself through college. With the possible exception of George Tenet, I never saw anyone more palpably enthralled about the very notion of being CIA director.

At the same time, Mike was no dewy-eyed romantic vicariously living out his own Ian Fleming fantasy. He knew the EIT program was on life support, and he wasn't about to embrace it, to try to save it, unless the professional in him concluded it was worth the effort. So on his first day on the job, he dived in—reading all the thousands of intelligence reports, grilling everyone in the building, down to the most junior operators and analysts, who had anything to do with the program. Was it well run? Was it effective? Was it indispensable? And perhaps most important for this straight-arrow, devout Catholic: Was it morally justifiable? After a few weeks, Mike Hayden was satisfied on all counts. He determined that the program was worth fighting for. He identified himself with it, it became his for better or worse, and he never looked back.

And then Mike's canny political instincts kicked in. The major problem with the program, he concluded, was that it was shrouded in too much mystery. It had been in existence for four years, and for all that time the Bush administration had steadfastly refused to say a single thing publicly about it. It also had insisted on keeping knowledge of the program—including details about the techniques and the intelligence information derived from it—confined to only a handful of members of Congress. Inevitably, the result was a corrosive mix of suspicion and misunderstanding that was slowly enveloping the program. For what it was worth, I told him his approach was exactly what the beleaguered Agency workforce wanted and needed.

Mike made one more cold-eyed, practical decision: The program had to be modified, slimmed down, if it was going to survive. I took the lead on that one. On the one hand, I had to determine which of the original EITs still could safely be deemed "legal" in the aftermath of the McCain Amendment and the *Hamdan* decision. On the other, I had to look to the CTC managers of the program for their professional assessment, based on their experience, of which of the existing techniques were "must haves" in order for the program to remain viable and productive. It was a complex, delicate balancing act. I knew, and the CTC recognized, that waterboarding was pretty much out the window. And then a bizarre sort of horse-trading began, with others in the administration weighing in. Secretary of State Rice sent her emissaries—my old friend John Bellinger and her old friend the brilliant but brittle Philip Zelikow—over to my office to insist that nudity be halted; Rice's singular aversion to men being interrogated while naked remained as implacable as ever. The CTC held out strongly to maintain sleep deprivation as an option, convinced it was the one technique that had broken KSM.

Back and forth I scurried, between our people, the White House, Rice's coterie, and the Justice Department. Finally, after a few weeks, a truncated list of six techniques made the final cut: dietary manipulation (read "Ensure"), sleep deprivation, plus the so-called "attention getting" techniques, facial hold, attention grasp, abdominal grasp, open-fingered abdominal slap, and open-fingered facial slap. I remember only one significant last-minute dispute, and it was over the "walling" technique. The CTC wanted to keep it, and Rice's people wanted it out. Their respective reasons now escape me, but Rice eventually prevailed. Still, the CTC considered the tools that remained—grasps, slaps, and no sleep—sufficient for them to do their jobs. We had come a long way from waterboarding and bugs in a box.

Meanwhile, Mike Hayden quietly set out to drive the process inside the administration to "open" the program up. In September 2006, his efforts bore fruit. President Bush gave a standing-room-only speech in the East Room acknowledging and defending the existence of the CIA prison system (albeit nothing about the EITs). Bush also announced the imminent arrival at Gitmo of the remaining fourteen detainees in the prisons, including KSM and his cohorts with 9/11 blood on their hands, thus accomplishing the "endgame" we in the CIA had been insistently pushing inside the administration for the previous two years. At the DOD, Donald Rumsfeld's long-standing resistance seemed to have vanished; perhaps he was just worn down, or perhaps he sensed that his days at the DOD were numbered (he would resign, or be pushed out, as secretary two months later).

A couple of days before the Bush speech, I accompanied Mike Hayden to a Principals' meeting in the Roosevelt Room in the White House. It was chaired by Bush, which was the first time I ever saw the president personally participate in any meeting in which the EIT program was being discussed. But the thing I found most memorable were the images of two absent officials, beamed in on screens erected on either side of the large polished conference table. On one was Secretary Rumsfeld, on the other was Vice President Cheney. Rumsfeld seemed resigned, almost indifferent, to the plan as it was being laid out. Cheney seemed to listen intently but had his typically stoic look—until, that is, Bush asked for one final vote. All the Principals went along with the new version of the EIT program and for the meticulously planned East Room rollout, except for the vice president. He voted "No" in a loud voice. He said he was against all of it—Cheney wanted to maintain the secrecy of everything, not change a thing about the EIT program. Not for the first time, I felt a certain admiration for the man: He wasn't about to back off on his beliefs for anything or anybody. For an instant, the room was silent as everyone there, including the president, stared at Cheney's image on the screen. No one's mind was changed, of course, but it was a hell of a scene to behold.

Last but not least, that same month, Mike Hayden got agreement from the White House to brief the EIT program—both the old one and the new one—to the full membership of the House and Senate intelligence committees. Better (at least a little better) late than never.

Mercifully, those eventful, frenetic first couple of months of Mike Hayden's directorship gave me little time to fret about my own future. My nomination for general counsel, championed by the departed Porter Goss, had gone nowhere since the White House sent it to the Senate Intelligence Committee the previous March. Its chairman, the Kansas Republican Pat Roberts, demonstrated zero interest in it or in me, for that matter (to this day, I have never met the man). Perhaps it was because I wasn't a politically connected Republican. Perhaps it was because Roberts was becoming wary about the whole "waterboarding," "secret prisons" imbroglio, to which my name was now linked in media reports, and Roberts just didn't want to be bothered by a messy confirmation hearing (this was Porter Goss's theory). In any case, my nomination was languishing with the Intelligence Committee.

Although we didn't know each other well when Mike became director, I never really worried that he would seek to have his own person replace me as nominee. For one thing, that wasn't his style—he brought only one longtime aide with him when he came to Langley, and his pattern in previous high-level jobs was to retain whatever legal advisor he inherited from his predecessor. Moreover, I knew that I had continuing backing from senior members of the Bush administration legal brain trust, people such as Al Gonzales, Harriet Miers, and David Addington. Especially David, my young subordinate at the CIA in the early '80s and now a strong-willed, influential White House figure in his position as counsel to Vice President Cheney. David was a man of fierce principles and fierce loyalties. He never forgot people he distrusted or people he respected, and, owing to our long association, I was firmly in the latter category. Although David never told me so, I have no doubt that the White House would never have approved my nomination in the first place had it not been for his strong endorsement.

Ironically, my nomination began to move on the Hill only because of the November 2006 midterm elections, when congressional Republicans (owing in large part to growing public disillusionment with the Bush administration) suffered a huge shellacking, losing their majorities in the House and Senate. The new chairman of the Senate Intelligence Committee was Jay Rockefeller, a Democrat from West Virginia. Shortly after he assumed the chairmanship in January 2007, Rockefeller wrote a letter to Mike Hayden, saying one of the committee's priorities would be to take up my long-stalled nomination and schedule my confirmation hearing. Naïvely, I was elated. I didn't focus on the fact that Rockefeller and his fellow Democrats on the committee were now highly vocal opponents of the Bush administration's counterterrorism initiatives—especially the Agency's enhanced interrogation program, which was garnering more and more attention and controversy in the media even though it officially remained classified at the top-secret level.

For the next few months, I assiduously plowed through a slew of written "questions for the record" the committee staff sent out to me to answer in advance of the promised confirmation hearing. At least, that's what I thought I was preparing for. In hindsight, what the committee was preparing for was a show trial. I probably should have seen it coming. A few sympathetic committee staffers were quietly passing warnings to their friends in the OGC. My chief of staff, Melody Rosenberry, told me about one call she got. "I don't know why John is going through with this thing," the staffer told her. "They are going to absolutely slaughter him."

CHAPTER 15

Out of the Shadows
and Into the Spotlight
(2007)

On the afternoon of June 19, 2007, I settled into the witness chair at my confirmation hearing.

It was an improbable and surreal scene. The cavernous room in the Dirksen Senate Office Building was aglow with television lights and ringed by C-SPAN cameras. About half a dozen photographers (although they seemed like a thousand to me) scurried about, crouching and snapping away as I entered the room from the rear, gingerly making my way through clots of people milling around in the spectator section.

I had known this day was coming for more than a year, and I had spent hours trying to visualize this entry scene, attempting to prepare myself—rehearse, really—for how I would look, act, and feel when I first walked onto this very public stage. But now that the moment had finally arrived, I found myself feeling oddly detached—as if I were an observer to an only-in-D.C. political/media event swirling around someone I had perhaps heard of but never met. It was only when I sat down at the witness table, when I turned around and saw my family sitting behind me, looking proud but pensive, when I felt the lights and TV cameras aiming at me, when the photographers scampered in front of me and hunkered down five feet from my nose, that it really hit me: Jeez, this is all about me.

Actually, it was far more complicated than that. One issue would dominate this hearing: my central role in the creation and implementation of the CIA's counterterrorist detention and interrogation program. That was the only reason for the cameras, the photographers, the reporters, the dozens of spectators I didn't recognize.

By this time I had served nearly thirty-two years—more than half of my life—as an attorney at the CIA. But, like virtually everyone else's in the spy world, my work was secret, and I was largely unknown. My nomination changed all that. And it wasn't because the CIA general counsel position was so attention-grabbing in itself—sure, the job is significant and prestigious in its own way, but never before had it been a position with lightning-rod controversy attached. The nominations of my two immediate predecessors had sailed through the Senate without a hitch or a blip on the political/media radar screen.

When my nomination happened to come along, it made for a perfect political storm: Few if any Bush nominations were then pending on the Hill, and my fingerprints had been all over the CIA's post-9/11 detention and interrogation practices since their inception. And so I became a foil, a symbol, and, ultimately, a casualty of the noisy national war of words over how the U.S. Government should legally and morally conduct the war on terror.

Notwithstanding all of my years of experience at the CIA, it is clear to me only now that I was still a naïf on that day as I entered the hearing: It really wasn't about me at all.

It's not that I didn't expect to be questioned aggressively. Most of the classified written questions the Senate Intelligence Committee sent to me in advance of the hearing were about the detention and interrogation practices and my role in their creation. Moreover, in the weeks leading up to the hearing, various articles in the media speculated that Democrats on the committee would seize the occasion to rail against the wisdom, legality, and morality of these practices. On the morning of the hearing, a *New York Times* piece previewing the session quoted Buzzy Krongard, the former CIA executive director, as predicting that I would be used as a "piñata" by some of the senators. Clearly, this would be no cakewalk, and I knew it.

But I didn't anticipate a public flogging, either. For one thing, the hearing was being divided into two back-to-back segments, the first open to the public, followed by a "closed" session to allow discussion of classified matters. At the committee's direction, I drafted separate opening statements for both, but because the Agency's post-9/11 counterterrorist activities were encased in the highest secrecy, my focus was on gearing up for the closed session. That would be the longer and more contentious session, I figured, and the open session would be likely sparsely attended by the senators and largely bland and perfunctory in nature.

I did allow myself to think that the open session would afford an opportunity to offer to the committee—and whoever in the public cared—my perspective on the essential role that the rule of law plays in the intelligence world and the unparalleled responsibilities, risks, and rewards for an attorney operating in that world. Nothing dramatic or explosive, I thought, but it could present a rare opportunity to contribute to Congress's and the public's understanding of the Agency while perhaps debunking some of the enduring misconceptions and myths about the big, bad, lawless "rogue elephant" CIA.

Finally, purely as a matter of my own self-interest, I hoped that I could use the open session to demonstrate that it was an enormous plus to have someone in the top CIA legal job in the post-9/11 era who was already steeped in the spy business. No previous incoming general counsel ever had those sorts of credentials, I reasoned, and so my decades of experience would surely count for something.

Those were my expectations and hopes on the day of my hearing. They proved to be unfounded.

The canary in the coal mine came in the unlikely form of Kit Bond, the burly Missouri Republican vice chair of the Intelligence Committee. Minutes before the hearing began, he bounded into the holding room in the Dirksen Building where I was waiting to be summoned, expectant but not (I thought) overly anxious about what awaited me. As he greeted me with a vigorous handshake, Bond grinned and asked, "Are you ready for a buzz saw?" It was not exactly a confidence-building icebreaker.

In fact, despite my being nominated by the president of his own party, Bond had never bothered to meet me before that day, having rebuffed my request for the traditional courtesy call a nominee makes to the members of the committee considering the nomination.

This encounter with Bond underscored a cold reality about my situation: Republicans on the Intelligence Committee—with the notable exception of John Warner—had no particular stake or even interest in my being confirmed. While by definition I was a "political" appointee, I had no Republican pedigree or connections. Indeed, during the lengthy White House vetting process, no one in the Bush administration had ever asked me about my party affiliation. Not once. (For the record, I am a registered Independent who grew up in Massachusetts, and since 1972 I have resided in the District of Columbia. Hardly Republican bastions.) Here again, I was hopelessly naïve: I figured the fact that I was a career public servant at the CIA, not some partisan dilettante/hack parachuting into the most necessarily apolitical of all federal agencies, would garner me some trust and credibility with both sides of the committee. In the end, it got me nothing.

The only senator in my corner, to my initial surprise but everlasting gratitude, was John Warner, the patrician Republican from Virginia who was approaching the end of a distinguished public career. We had known each other only slightly before then, but alone among his colleagues he stepped forward to offer me advice and support. Warner loved the CIA and over the years consistently demonstrated his affection and respect for the Agency workforce, so I suspect he was instinctively drawn to a CIA "lifer" like me. It had to be that, because while I had worked for over three decades in his state, I have never lived there. So, besides our lack of personal ties, I wasn't even a constituent.

"Our backgrounds are a lot alike," Warner told me at one of our private meetings leading up to the hearing. This from a man who in his twenties had been a decorated naval officer during World War II and then went on to become a federal prosecutor, a secretary of the navy, and ultimately an immensely popular and respected member of the Senate for almost thirty years. And who had once been married to Elizabeth Taylor, for crying out loud.

I was deeply touched and flattered that he thought we had anything in common, but the comparison was laughable, and I almost did laugh when he made it to me. Nonetheless, looking back now, when John Warner passed word to the Agency that he would be "honored" to introduce me at the hearing, it was the high point, and my proudest memory, of my confirmation process.

With Warner seated next to me at the witness table, I did my best to look relaxed as I waited for the Intelligence Committee chairman, Jay Rockefeller, to gavel the hearing to order. And then, one by one, the members filed in and took their places: Dianne Feinstein, Ron Wyden, Russ Feingold, Sheldon Whitehouse, and Carl Levin. Counting Rockefeller, the six senators had two things in common: they were all Democrats, and they were all harsh critics of the Bush administration's counterterrorist policies and practices.

On the Republican side of the dais was Bond, presumably in attendance only because protocol demanded his presence as the committee vice chair. Aside from Warner, no other Republican bothered to show up. (The official record of the hearing lists the Maine senator Olympia Snowe as having attended; the truth is she came in midway through the hearing, walked over to her assigned seat, flipped her nameplate over, tossed me a desultory glance, and then turned and walked out. A fifteen-second appearance.)

Surveying the scene in front of me, I thought to myself: Uh-oh. Next to me, Warner murmured, "Good gracious," before gamely trying to buck me up. "Nice turnout," he whispered, nodding toward the murderers' row of Democrats arrayed before me.

Of the Democrats on the committee, only Sheldon Whitehouse and Carl Levin had granted my request for a courtesy call in the weeks prior to the hearing. ("Dianne Feinstein is not courteous," her staffer curtly responded to a CIA congressional liaison officer who had conveyed my request for a brief get-together.) I had a pleasant and unremarkable chat with Whitehouse, a relatively new member of the committee. Although he did express some unhappiness about the Bush administration's refusal to turn over to him documents related to the National Security Agency's post-9/11 terrorist surveillance program (about which I knew very little), we largely talked about his home state of Rhode Island, where I had gone to college, and where we had some mutual friends. He was cordial enough but gave no hint about his views on my nomination.

The Carl Levin "courtesy call" was an entirely different experience. With his rotund, rumpled appearance and prodigious comb-over, Levin always reminded me physically of the character actor Jack Weston, except that Levin is much smarter and harder-working, and more aggressive, than any of the characters Mr. Weston ever played in the movies. Levin lumbered into our meeting in the Intelligence Committee's secured offices a few days before the hearing, toting a thick stack of files that he had amassed in his capacity as chairman of the Senate Armed Services Committee (SASC), with jurisdiction over the Department of Defense. The SASC was in the midst of a long-running investigation of the DOD's terrorist detention facility at Guantánamo Bay, and Levin had hired a passel of former prosecutors who for months had been peppering the DOD with volleys of extensive document demands.

Nothing wrong with that, of course, but Levin's SASC investigators were also insistently pushing for information on the CIA's detention and interrogation practices. The problem was that the CIA's activities by design were separate and distinct from anything the DOD was doing; the high-ranking Al Qaeda operatives the Agency had been holding for years in CIA-run facilities overseas had only recently been transferred to Gitmo, and the Agency had never conducted any enhanced interrogation techniques there. Like all covert-action programs, the top-secret CIA activities were, by law, carried out under the aegis of the Intelligence Committee—of which Levin was a member—not the SASC. By mid-2007, the CIA had given the Intelligence Committee all the details of the program (save for the locations of the secret prisons), and it was the Agency's position—with which I fully agreed—that those details were simply none of the SASC's jurisdictional business. Accordingly, we had been politely but firmly rebuffing the SASC investigators.

So Levin was a frustrated and impatient man when he arrived, accompanied by the same stone-faced SASC staffer we had been stiffing for months. And Levin showed it, dispensing with any introductory pleasantries and immediately launching into a gruff cross-examination, shoving in front of me DOD documents alluding to the CIA that I had never seen before. I was caught off-guard, though in retrospect I should not have been.

I did my best under the circumstances, even attempting a couple of lame and utterly useless stabs at levity—"Don't you want to save some of your good stuff for the hearing, Senator?" I wanly asked him at one point. Levin just grunted and plowed forward. He was not nasty, and he never threatened to delay or oppose my nomination. But by any measure this "courtesy call" went very badly because I was not prepared for it. I should have seen it coming, so I blame myself, not Levin.

And, hell, at least the guy took the time to meet with me.

• • •

In the immediate aftermath of the hearing, I actually thought I had survived it and done okay. The next day's *Washington Post* described my demeanor as "affable and calm," which gave me a modicum of encouragement. The article also noted that, with the exception of Dianne Feinstein, none of the senators in attendance expressed any outright opposition to my nomination.

For its part, the *New York Times* weighed in with a basically neutral assessment of how the hearing went, but it did comment (as did the *Post*) on the brevity of many of my answers. This was true, since I was often pressed for information about the CIA's counterterrorist authorizations and actions that I simply couldn't get into in front of the TV cameras. On those occasions, I dutifully—and repeatedly—pledged to the senators that I would fully respond in the closed session to immediately follow the open hearing. At the outset of the hearing, both Rockefeller and Bond had encouraged me to adopt this posture whenever I felt it necessary to do so. An eminently fair and understandable approach, I thought at the time.

But now, years later, after looking at the C-SPAN videotape of my hearing and reflecting on how the events of the day unfolded, it seems so painfully obvious that my fate was sealed before I ever sat down at the witness table.

I will not rehash here all of the back-and-forth that took place in the course of the nearly two-hour open session. To his credit, Kit Bond used his time to pose questions that allowed me to showcase my experience and perspective derived from being a lawyer in the national security arena for so many years. Otherwise, however, the hearing basically consisted of a tag team of half a dozen Democrats swinging away at the Bush administration's post-9/11 counterterrorist policies, with me playing the role—sure enough—of piñata.

Some of the biggest "sound bites" in the hearing came when I was being pressed to answer questions that, because they involved classified information, I simply couldn't meaningfully address or put into their proper context with the TV cameras staring at me. Today, the CIA's post-9/11 detention and interrogation program is long since over and done with; the "secret prisons" have been emptied and closed, and the "torture memos" were declassified and released almost verbatim to the public early in the Obama administration. Virtually all aspects of the program can now be discussed and debated in the open. But in June 2007, the program was ongoing, and all of it was still highly classified.

So it's both painful and poignant to see myself now on videotape. I was heeding the admonition of Rockefeller and Bond, but it still looked bad. Sitting there helplessly, repeatedly confronted with pointed questions requiring me to parse instantly in my head how much I could say in public, I would hesitate, stammer, deflect, and retreat into pleas to the committee that I be allowed to respond in the closed session. I appeared to the entire world to be something that I am not—evasive, disingenuous, and unsure of myself.

On National Public Radio the next day, Mary Louise Kelly reported:

> John Rizzo has more than three decades' experience as a CIA lawyer and it seems he's learned a thing or two over the years about how to dodge questions on activities the CIA would prefer to keep quiet. Yesterday's hearing marked the senators' first chance to question Rizzo publicly on matters such as extraordinary renditions and detainee interrogations, but Rizzo's answers were not exactly expansive.

To illustrate, the Kelly piece on NPR included a snippet of an exchange I had with my new best friend, Carl Levin.

> LEVIN: *Have detainees been rendered by us—including the CIA—to countries that use torture?*
> ME (hesitatingly): *That's an important question. I would—the only way I could give it a proper answer would be in the classified session.*
> LEVIN: *I'm not asking which countries, I'm just asking you whether we have ever rendered detainees to countries that use torture.*
> ME: *Well, again, if you don't mind, Senator, it's difficult to give a yes or no answer to that in open session. I would just greatly prefer to give it the attention it deserves in closed session.*

That ended the exchange, but Levin was not quite through with me yet. He later returned to the hearing, triumphantly brandishing a piece of paper that he inserted into the hearing record, which he described as "a statement of the president in December 2005 that we do not render to countries that torture—a statement made in public—in contrast to Mr. Rizzo's statement that he could not answer that question in public."

Sitting there witnessing this little scene by Levin, I had no idea what he was talking about, and I didn't get to see this "gotcha" document until days later. Turns out it was a December 6, 2005, White House press release of a transcript of an Oval Office meeting that day between President Bush and the head of the World Health Organization. And there it was in the transcript released by the White House press office. Mr. Bush, responding to a reporter's question about whether he had "any plans to change the policy of renditioning [sic]," declared, "We do not render to countries that torture. That has been our policy, and that policy will be the same."

The problem with that, and the problem I had been trying to address in Levin's question, is that what the president said was false. It's not that he deliberately lied—I am sure that he did not. Still, his answer wasn't true. It wasn't true when he gave it that day, it never became true, and it hadn't been true for years, going back through administrations of both parties.

Before explaining why, I should provide a thumbnail, somewhat oversimplified description of what a "rendition" is. Essentially, it occurs when an individual is transported involuntarily from one country—where the individual is found—to another country where he (every CIA rendition I can remember involved a man) is facing criminal charges or is wanted for questioning in connection with an investigation. Sometimes he is taken back to his home country, and sometimes he is taken to a third country.

In any case, a rendition is conducted outside normal judicial processes such as extradition, where papers are openly filed by the country requesting the transfer. Historically, the United States—and other countries—resort to rendition only when a) the government of the country where the individual is located is unwilling or unable for political reasons to openly cooperate with, or even acknowledge, the transfer, or b) there is no applicable extradition treaty in place between the country where the guy is and the country that wants him. Thus, it is a practice that has been employed through the years in extraordinary circumstances. (By the way, *extraordinary rendition* is another term that has become a seemingly permanent part of the post-9/11 lexicon, but I had never heard of it previously, and to me it just amounts to a pejorative redundancy.)

Renditions were carried out long before 9/11 ever happened. Remember the daring and fabled operation by Israeli commandos in 1960 to snatch Adolf Eichmann out of his hiding place in South America to stand trial in Israel for his Nazi war crimes? That was a rendition. Mir Aimal Kansi, who randomly murdered three CIA employees outside the front gate of Agency headquarters in 1993, was later rendered to the United States from Pakistan to face homicide charges; he was eventually convicted and executed in Virginia. A year later, the notorious international terrorist "Carlos the Jackal" was rendered from Sudan to stand trial in France—an action, notably, that was later upheld by the European Court of Human Rights.

Rendition is such a generally recognized, accepted practice that in January 2009 the incoming Obama administration, even as it was publicly repudiating the Bush administration's detention and interrogation policies, carefully preserved its authority to conduct renditions. Indeed, two days after taking office, in the same executive order abolishing enhanced interrogation techniques and ordering the closure of the Guantánamo detention facility in a year's time, President Obama endorsed the use of rendition. Except that his staff couldn't bring itself to actually put the word into the order, apparently so as to avoid the perceived stigma it acquired during the Bush years. Instead of "renditions," the term chosen by the Obama people was "short-term transfers."

It does sound much more pleasant.

Which brings me back to Levin's question at the hearing: "Have detainees been rendered by us—including the CIA—to countries that use torture?" The short answer—the one I declined to give in a public setting—is "Yes."

To be sure, with Levin peering balefully down at me from the dais, I was briefly tempted, in the three seconds or so I had to ponder my response, to just say "No" and leave it at that. Certainly, if Levin instead had asked something along the lines of "Have detainees been rendered by us—including the CIA—with the intent, or with the knowledge, that they will be tortured?" then I would have immediately and unequivocally answered "No." But, unfortunately, that wasn't his question.

At the same time, in the moment and on the spot, I couldn't simply say "Yes," either, even though that was the accurate one-word answer. My refusal to say "Yes" was not done out of fear about how that answer would play publicly (although it is easy to visualize what the next day's headlines would have been: "Top CIA Lawyer, Contradicting Bush, Acknowledges U.S. Link to Foreign Torture Practices"). I held back because while a "Yes" would have been the short, simple answer, the truth here is not that short or simple. And certainly not conducive to being told in the public political theater in which I found myself.

Here is an expurgated version of what I wanted to explain to Levin in the closed session. Post-9/11, most of the renditions the CIA conducted—and they were in the low double figures, not the crazy numbers of hundreds or even thousands some clueless pundits and human rights activists have alleged—involved transporting known, active terrorists to or between countries in the Middle East. Although these countries are close allies with the United States in combating Al Qaeda, most cannot be accurately categorized as Jeffersonian democracies. They are, and have always been, authoritarian regimes that have never hesitated to jail and, yes, brutalize those they consider enemies of the state. But since our First Amendment guarantees of free speech and assembly have not to date been embraced universally by political strongmen in that ever-turbulent part of the world, many of those rounded up are more likely political dissidents, not dangerous threats.

It may not be morally edifying, and it shouldn't be surprising, but that's the reality about the governments the United States must work with closely in the post-9/11 era. And when the CIA grabs a terrorist who is facing charges in one of those countries, or is a native of the country, that's the most logical place for him to be rendered—and turned over to the custody of the host government. Even if that government has a track record of human rights abuses.

But is this the CIA turning a cynical, cold-blooded blind eye, or worse yet, "outsourcing torture" (another lurid canard coined after 9/11)? No.

And it's not just because that would be illegal, although it would be, and as the CIA's lawyer that naturally would be at the top of my personal list of reasons not to do it. But pesky legalities aside, people at the CIA just don't operate that way. They want no part of torture—it has never been countenanced, much less facilitated. Not once in my Agency career, before or after 9/11, has the CIA ever considered torture an acceptable or even unavoidable by-product of carrying out the mission.

Besides, there's no percentage in it. If history and experience have taught Agency careerists anything, it's that no secret stays secret forever. Especially "bad" secrets—ones that show CIA officers hiding something, covering something up, or maybe just looking the other way when something bad is about to happen. "Bad" secrets have had an increasingly short shelf life during the course of my time at the Agency, a time that has coincided with a sixfold increase in the number of CIA lawyers, the exponential growth of congressional oversight, a more aggressive and independent office of CIA inspector general, and the inexorable rise in the number of leaks to the media. And when those kinds of secrets come to light, as they always do, there's hell to pay for the institution and for the people involved.

That's why, as much out of self-protection as anything else, the Agency for some time has had in place rules that apply when it renders someone into the hands of a foreign government with a history of human rights abuses. Our local chief makes it clear to his or her counterpart—usually the head of the country's intelligence or security service—that there is to be no abuse of the guy. None, no matter what. No winks and nods, and the assurances our chief gets on that score must be credible. And, in most cases, there are ways of checking: It may be that the CIA has a "unilateral" penetration of the service that privately reports back about how the prisoner is being treated; or, if prudence warrants, our local chief will insist on personal monitoring and visits.

Is this a fail-safe system? Of course not. But in my experience it has been largely effective, and that's because the system has teeth. If the Agency discovers that the foreign government has done something that violates the prisoner's human rights, our local chief confronts his counterpart. (When the incriminating information has come from a "unilateral," the confrontation has to be scripted and choreographed more carefully to protect our source's identity, but it is done.) The first time, there is a stern warning to knock it off. If necessary, the warning is underscored by a senior CIA or White House official to the political leadership of the foreign country. If it happens again, the sanctions become tangible: the suspension of funds, equipment, or training or, if the abuse is persistent, the cutoff of the entire CIA relationship.

For these foreign services, who in most cases are utterly dependent on the CIA's largesse and cachet, risking the relationship has proven to be a price simply too high to pay. Not so for the Agency; I know of at least four occasions, pre- and post-9/11, when the Agency took action to either suspend, or end outright, its relationship with a foreign service that had violated its commitments regarding human rights issues. So it is not an empty threat, and our counterparts know it.

The fundamental point here is that the people rendered by the CIA into a foreign government's custody tend to be treated with kid gloves, relatively speaking, not the iron fist the government may normally employ with its own prisoners. Indeed, based on my experience and observation, the far greater risk is that the individuals the Agency has rendered post-9/11 will be prematurely set free to cause mayhem again.

The Bush and Obama administrations faced a similar conundrum in figuring out what to do with the dozens of Yemeni nationals still, at this writing, being held at the Guantánamo Bay detention facility that the Obama administration has been so desperate to empty and close. These are people who can't be prosecuted in U.S. military tribunals or civilian courts because of a paucity of usable evidence but who nonetheless are still too dangerous to simply let go. Remanding them to the custody of the Yemeni government has always been the most obvious and preferred option—until it became evident what happened to a previous batch of Yemenis held at Gitmo that the Bush administration in its last year sent home, based on a pledge by the Yemeni government to hold them or, at a minimum, keep close tabs on their activities. Instead, most were held only briefly and then set scot-free to return to the battlefield against the United States in Afghanistan and elsewhere. So the remaining Yemenis in Gitmo have languished, with the Obama administration understandably frozen by fear of the potential nightmare scenario playing out—the next catastrophic attack on the homeland being carried out by someone it once had under wraps but stood by and let walk out the door.

In the post-9/11 world, that's the truly scary thing about a rendition: not that the guy will be sent to a country that will torture him, but that he'll be sent to a country that lets him run amok.

All of this was rattling around in my head in the seconds after Levin asked, "Have detainees been rendered by us—including the CIA—to countries that use torture?" A "No" response would have been literally false, and a "Yes" response would have been grossly misleading. Perhaps it was the lawyer in me, but in that instant, I made the decision to demur on answering. Best to leave something this sensitive and complex to the closed session, I concluded. Levin deserved a full answer, chapter and verse, with names and examples. And I would be able to give it to him there. Or so I thought.

Next after Levin in the Democrats' batting order was Ron Wyden from Oregon. Having blown off my request for a prehearing courtesy call, this would be the first time he ever spoke to me.

Wyden quickly went on the offensive. Following a line of questioning begun by Rockefeller and Levin, he began by hammering away at me on the August 1, 2002, unclassified legal analysis, authored by John Yoo, which a new set of Bush appointees at the OLC had withdrawn and publicly repudiated by late 2004 because of its clearly gratuitous, over-the-top rhetoric regarding the legal threshold for torture: "equivalent in intensity to the pain accompanying serious physical injury such as organ failure, impairment of bodily function, or even death." (When the Obama administration in 2009 publicly released all the Bush-era OLC memos on interrogation, this memo came to be known as "Bybee I." Its classified analogue was "Bybee II." They were named after the man who signed both memos, Jay Bybee, head of the OLC in 2002. For ease of reference, that's how I'll refer to them here.)

Bybee II—the top-secret memo addressed to me, which specifically described each of the EITs and the careful, regulated manner in which we proposed to carry them out—contained none of Bybee I's incendiary language. And Bybee II had been reviewed and endorsed intact by the new Bush OLC team in 2004. All of which was known to Wyden and his colleagues, since all members of the Intelligence Committee had been given access to Bybee II months before my hearing (it first had been provided to the committee leadership back in 2004).

But Bybee II—like the EIT program itself—was still highly classified as I sat there in the open hearing. I couldn't talk about it. And so I struggled, and Wyden pounced.

WYDEN: *Just so we're clear on this Bybee Amendment [sic], because I know*
a number of colleagues have asked about it, the key part of that

> *memo is the question of inflicting physical pain and it not being torture unless the pain is equivalent to organ failure and the related circumstances. Do you think you should have objected at that time?*
>
> ME: *I honestly—I can't say I should have objected at the time. I read the opinion at the time. As I say, I want to emphasize that there was a companion opinion issued to us that did not contain that sort of language and that we really relied on. But no, I can't honestly sit here today and say I should have objected.*
>
> WYDEN: *I think that's unfortunate, because it seems to me that language, on a very straightforward reading, is over the line. And that's what I think all of us wanted to hear, is that you wish you had objected.*

In the years since, I have frequently thought about this exchange with Wyden, since he would repeatedly later cite it publicly as the primary reason he decided to take the lead role in blocking my nomination. Could I have answered it in a better way? Perhaps. Could I have answered it in a different way, to say that I should have objected to Bybee I? No.

Suppose I had acknowledged to Wyden, in front of the TV cameras, "Yes, Senator, in retrospect I should have objected to Bybee One because of that language in it that you quoted." In the first place, it would have done me no good. Wyden was a foe who could not be appeased. Almost certainly, he would have jumped all over me: "So, only now are you telling us this, five years later? Why didn't you object when it would have made a difference? You stood by quietly and let stand an opinion on the torture statute, of all things, that you thought was seriously flawed? Is this one of those 'confirmation conversions' we sometimes get up here?" All of which would have been obvious, logical questions.

But there was another, far more important reason I couldn't say what Wyden piously claimed he wished I would have said: It would have meant publicly throwing the Agency—and the hundreds of CIA officers at all levels who had been involved in the still-ongoing interrogation program—to the wolves.

For years, I had been assuring all of these people—my colleagues, clients, and friends—that the program from the beginning had the authoritative, written imprimatur of the Justice Department. To be sure, the key legal document for us had been Bybee II, the top-secret memo to me that

Justice never backed away from. Not Bybee I, which was addressed to the White House and consisted of a lengthy, dense, aggressively argued analysis that set a baseline for torture ("organ failure . . . or even death") that the EITs, in the way they were to be administered, never came close to approaching.

And yet Bybee I and Bybee II—memos issued on the same day by the same man—were inextricably linked. After all, they were both prompted by my request for definitive, written Justice Department guidance. I couldn't distance myself from one without potentially eroding the legitimacy of the other. And I simply couldn't do that. I couldn't do it to the people who had trusted and depended on my word that the EITs were legal, who would never have participated in a program—no matter how critical to preventing another 9/11—that constituted torture, one of the most repellent words in the English language.

For me to start backpedaling in front of the committee simply to curry favor for a better job title would have been worse than feckless—it would have been a craven betrayal. It was—and is—unthinkable.

As the open session mercifully wound down, I found myself increasingly eager to get off that public stage and into the closed session. To answer Levin. To answer Dianne Feinstein, the California Democrat who also had pressed me on sensitive details about CIA counterterrorist activities that I similarly said had to be deferred until we could all get behind closed doors. To answer Wyden.

Especially Wyden. In addition to his barbs about my not disavowing Bybee I, Wyden pushed hard in the open session about CIA operations in Iraq and about the CIA's authority to capture, detain, and interrogate U.S. citizens abroad suspected of involvement in terrorist activities. With everyone watching, he wagged his finger at me and vowed to get deeply into these issues at the closed session. In fact, Wyden voiced these intentions in the last few minutes of the open hearing, so his words were ringing in my ears as I left for the committee's secure hearing room in the Hart Senate Office Building. It was just yards away, and the closed session would begin in only a few minutes. I was looking forward to my opportunity, away from the TV cameras and reporters and the spectators, to answer the serious questions and charges from Levin, Feinstein, and Wyden then.

Except that I never got the chance. When Chairman Rockefeller gaveled the closed-door session to order, Carl Levin was nowhere to be seen. Neither was Dianne Feinstein. And neither was Ron Wyden.

None of them showed up for the duration of the hearing. Rockefeller mentioned something about an ice cream social at the White House that was due to begin shortly. And then, after a few random questions from the members who were present, it was over. The closed session lasted forty minutes. It was one third as long as the open hearing.

The next I heard from the committee was six weeks later, when Ron Wyden gave a speech on the Senate floor in which he declared me "unqualified" to be the CIA's general counsel.

CHAPTER 16

A Failed Nomination, and the End of a Program (2007–2008)

On June 20, the morning after my confirmation hearing, I was thrust back into the real-life world of the EIT program. Secretary of State Rice wanted a personal briefing on the newly refined, slimmed-down set of techniques, and she wanted to get it directly from the original architects of the program, two outside psychologists the Agency had hired under contract more than five years earlier. I worked to set up the briefing with my longtime friend John Bellinger, whom Rice had brought with her from the NSC in 2005 to serve as State's legal advisor. The fact that it took place the day after my hearing was a coincidental bit of timing; the date had been set weeks before in order to accommodate Rice's busy work and travel schedule. Actually, I welcomed the opportunity to attend the briefing—it kept me from dwelling on my performance at the hearing and the coverage it was getting in the media.

We arrived at Rice's office that morning at the appointed time and were quickly escorted into a cozy, antiques-laden sitting room normally reserved for private meetings with high-ranking foreign visitors. She immediately disarmed me with some good-natured teasing about my "newfound media stardom," citing an NPR report about my hearing that she had listened to while getting ready for work. It was the most personal thing she had ever said to me, and I was surprised and flattered by the warmth of her gesture. It was a side of Rice I had not seen before. She then directed us to a set of plush wing chairs arrayed around a small coffee table, and the briefing began.

The two EIT architects, perhaps intimidated by the surroundings and Rice's presence, started their presentation in a low-key, diffident manner. They talked about their backgrounds, the genesis of the original techniques they came up with, the safeguards built into the program, the way the program had evolved and been refined over the years, and so on. It was probably nothing Rice hadn't already heard about at a dozen Principals' meetings, but she patiently sat and listened, occasionally interjecting about how she had always been impressed by the professional and effective way the CIA was conducting the program. It was a much more cordial and relaxed atmosphere than I had expected. After a while, the EIT architects loosened up a bit.

Maybe loosened up a bit too much. When the time came for them to describe the newly slimmed-down EIT program going forward, which did not include waterboarding and some of the other, harsher original techniques, my guys decided to do a more, um, visual demonstration. Suddenly, one of them jumped up from his chair, about three feet from where Rice was sitting, and began "acting out" on himself what he was describing. Looming directly over Rice, he would grasp his face, then slap his face, then grasp his stomach, offering color commentary all the while. John Bellinger, with a look of alarm, shot me a glance that said: Did you tell these characters to put on this self-flagellation act in front of the secretary of state? I pretended not to notice his look. I had carefully gone through their presentation with them in advance, but now they were winging it.

Avoiding John's disapproving stare, I turned back just in time to see my guy demonstrate the sleep-deprivation technique, which, unfortunately, didn't involve him pretending to sleep. Instead, he attempted to show how the detainee would be kept awake, which entailed keeping the detainee standing by elevating his arms in chains anchored to the ceiling. And there he was, almost touching Rice's bare knees, poised over her in a scarecrow-like stance. She was gazing up at him with an expression of bemused equanimity.

Thankfully, that ended the visual demonstrations, and I quickly wrapped the meeting up, stammering something about how busy the secretary must be and how grateful we were for her time. Right to the end, Rice was unruffled and courteous. Nonetheless, as we left, I remember thinking: Thank God we didn't keep nudity as one of the EITs.

A Failed Nomination, and the End of a Program (2007–2008)

On the way out, I ran into John Negroponte, who was in the reception area of Rice's office waiting to see her. He had recently left his post as director of national intelligence to become Rice's senior deputy at State. John had a copy of that morning's *New York Times* in his hands, and he greeted me by pointing to a lengthy article describing my confirmation hearing the day before. "It sounds like it went all right for you," he said. I laughed and responded, "It was a bloodbath."

I meant the comment to be facetious. The truth was, I, too, thought that on balance the hearing had gone all right. I would prove to be very wrong about that.

At first, the reviews I got from my CIA colleagues and the White House were encouraging. Harriet Miers, David Addington, and Al Gonzales had watched the hearing on C-SPAN and told me I'd held my own with the Intelligence Committee. I did not hear from the president, nor did I expect to. The fact was that he scarcely knew me personally; all of our interactions before and after he nominated me consisted of brief encounters at the end of several large group meetings at the White House. In our early encounters, he addressed me as "counsel"; later, the salutation evolved into "chief," accompanied by a comradely poke on the arm (which I thought was progress). I didn't care—I was deeply grateful to Bush for having nominated me in the first place. I wasn't yearning for us to be on a first-name basis.

By July, however, the Agency began to get informal soundings from committee staffers that my nomination was in trouble. The word was that no Democrat was likely to vote in my favor, partly because of a perception that I wasn't sufficiently forthcoming in my answers during the "open" session of the hearing and partly because I refused to repudiate the legal reasoning behind the OLC's memos. The unified opposition of the committee Democrats was disheartening, but not entirely surprising. After all, the EIT program—for which I had become the public poster boy—was a highly controversial Bush administration initiative, and I could understand and accept that opposition as being based on both political and moral grounds.

What I didn't expect was hostility from Kit Bond, the Republican vice chairman of the Intelligence Committee. Not because of the EIT program—Bond supported that wholeheartedly. Bond's big problem with

271

the Agency was his conviction that senior management never held its personnel "accountable" for lapses or malfeasance in their conduct of intelligence activities that went awry. How did that apply to me? One of my most highly experienced and conscientious lawyers was involved in the early stages of a rendition of a terrorist suspect that took place a couple of years after 9/11. In early 2007, after a four-year investigation, the CIA inspector general had issued a report that strongly criticized the performance of a number of CIA officers, including the lawyer. In a footnote, the IG helpfully noted that I promoted the lawyer a year or two after the rendition, years before the completion of the IG report concluding that the lawyer was at fault. The lawyer was disciplined as a result of the report, but to Bond that was beside the point. He was furious that I had promoted the lawyer years before, back when anyone's culpability, including the lawyer's, was not even close to being determined. Bond was implacable. He passed the word that he wasn't going to support me, and most of his Republican colleagues on the committee—with my lack of Republican credentials glaringly apparent—likely were going to shrug indifferently and follow his lead.

So there it was, if I had been willing to see it. I was not just going to lose a committee vote, when or if that took place. I was going to be crushed, humiliated.

I was dead, but I wasn't psychologically ready to accept my fate. Not even when Ron Wyden announced in August that he was putting an indefinite "hold" on my nomination, something I first learned by reading an interview Wyden gave to the *New Yorker*. He claimed to be acting on behalf of "hardworking, well-intentioned CIA officers." As if I hadn't been, for the previous three decades.

My stubborn, foolish myopia continued into September 2007. Mike Hayden, displaying loyalty far beyond the call of duty, worked the phones with individual members of the Intelligence Committee. He got nowhere. The committee, evidently concluding correctly that I wasn't responding to a subtle nudge, decided to publicly apply a two-by-four to my head via a piece that appeared in the September 13 *Washington Post*. The headline was nothing if not direct: "Senate Intelligence Panel Seeks CIA Nominee's Withdrawal." Sourced to "[t]wo U.S. officials familiar with the committee's decision," it cited a "private" call the committee had made to Mike Hayden the day before. As I say, not exactly subtle.

A Failed Nomination, and the End of a Program (2007–2008)

Up to that point, the White House had been keeping a studied distance as my nomination was circling the drain. But the *Post* piece did serve to get the attention of one White House official: the president. Mike Hayden returned from an Oval Office meeting with Bush on the morning the piece appeared. He came to my office to deliver a message from the commander in chief: You're my nominee. Hang in there. To be sure, it was an indirect message, and one I doubt the people around him enthusiastically endorsed. But it was enough to sustain me. At least for a couple of weeks.

The committee scheduled the vote on my nomination for Tuesday, September 25. Maybe as a compassionate warning, or maybe as a blunt threat, as the day approached, the committee staffers on both the Democrat and Republican sides were now sending the same insistent message to Langley: If this nomination goes to a vote, Rizzo will get three or four votes, tops. It will be a wipeout, not just a rejection. He can't stay in his job if that happens. Is that how he wants his career to end?

And still—still—I resisted. Mike Hayden and the White House were not telling me to throw in the towel. It was my decision, I was told. On Friday, September 21, I convened my entire staff—about 180 people— and told them I was going to insist on a vote. To my embarrassment, I choked up a bit.

I didn't sleep much that weekend. I kept turning things over and over in my mind. I talked with my wife, Sharon. She knew and loved me enough to know to give me some space; she said she would support whatever I decided. I talked to my son, James, now a grown man of twenty-nine. His life had spanned virtually my entire CIA career. Although James had previously confided to me that he thought my situation was hopeless, he now told me basically the same thing that Sharon had.

When I returned to work on Monday, one day before the committee vote, everyone largely left me alone to my thoughts. Mike Hayden was out of the country, so his deputy, Steve Kappes, was holding down the fort. The Bush White House had persuaded him to return to the CIA as Mike Hayden's deputy, three years after his abrupt retirement following a clash with Porter Goss and his staff. Steve was a universally admired career CIA operative, and he and I had been good friends for years. A ramrod-straight former marine, he truly lived by the credo of duty, honor, country. I checked in with him in the morning to see if he had heard anything new about my nomination. He said he hadn't, except for the fact that John Warner had told someone in the White House over the weekend that my situation was "very difficult."

Ah yes, I thought, John Warner. In my self-absorbed state over the previous couple of weeks, I had forgotten that Warner had a stake in my fate as well. He had been my only advocate on the Senate Intelligence Committee, generously offering to introduce me at my confirmation hearing and continuing to offer his stalwart support even as my prospects were plummeting. If my confirmation was going to be rejected by his colleagues by a lopsided vote, that was bound to be a source of personal embarrassment to him. He would never tell me that, of course; he was far too gentlemanly to lay that sort of guilt trip on me. But the thought haunted me for the rest of the day. It contributed to my dawning, if overdue, recognition of reality: My nomination was doomed. Dragging it out to the inevitable end would only hurt me, the Agency, and people who were too loyal and kind to shake me by the lapels and tell me otherwise. People such as Mike Hayden and John Warner.

I should have pulled the plug that Monday, on the eve of the committee vote. But, against all logic and out of pure obstinacy, I decided to sleep on the whole thing one last night.

The next morning, I was driving to work with Sharon at the moment I came to my final, final decision. I hadn't said anything to her the night before about the nomination, and she had steered clear of the subject. We were close to headquarters when, out of the blue, she softly said: "For what it's worth, I think you should withdraw now, before it's too late. Why put yourself through the pain of a vote when you know how it's going to come out?" That settled it for me. One of the things that had been nagging at me all along, that was holding me back, was how I was going to break the news to my family that, in essence, I was giving up. With a tremendous sense of relief, I told her that that was the same conclusion I had come to.

Once I got to the office, I didn't have a moment to spare. The committee was scheduled to vote around lunchtime. The first person I talked to was Melody Rosenberry, my unflappable, loyal, and discreet chief of staff. I told her to draft a letter from me to the president asking him to withdraw the nomination. Something simple and dignified, I told her, with no recriminations directed against anyone. I then walked down the hall to tell Steve Kappes so that he could pass the word to Mike Hayden overseas. Steve said he understood and was truly sorry, and I believed him. I knew he wouldn't try to talk me out of it, and I knew that Mike Hayden wouldn't either. Steve called National Security Advisor Steve Hadley with the news, and Hadley, businesslike as always, simply said, "Okay. You and Mike manage it." Steve then passed the word to our head of congressional affairs so that he could give the committee staff a heads up. "The White House has two hours to formally notify the chairman," Jay Rockefeller's staffer tersely responded when he got the message. "Otherwise, there will be a vote."

By the time I got back to the office, Melody had a draft withdrawal letter waiting for me. It was perfect in both language and tone. I signed it without changing a word, and off it went to the White House. I didn't want to get ahead of the White House, but the clock was ticking and it was essential to me that my staff learn about my decision from me, before it leaked out from somewhere else. I sat down at my computer and tapped out a long e-mail to the entire office. Under the subject heading "My Decision," I laid all my reasons out, and I tried to be as candid and complete as I could about the realities of my situation. I must say, it was one hell of an e-mail message.

As the noon deadline approached, I decided I needed to reach out to one more person. I placed a call to John Warner's office, and he called back almost immediately. For the first time that day, my emotions got the better of me. I thanked him profusely for everything he had done for me, and then I asked for one last favor. "I would like to stay on here at the Agency," I choked out. "I hope the committee won't try to prevent that." Warner gently replied, "Don't you worry. That won't happen, and if anyone down here tries it, you just let me know."

The formal letter from the White House withdrawing the nomination arrived at the committee just about the time it was going into a meeting to cast its vote. The committee then took the nomination off its agenda. It was over.

The news hit the papers the next morning. I thought the second paragraph of Mark Mazzetti's piece in the *New York Times* summed up the saga pretty well: "The nomination of the 32-year Agency veteran to become general counsel is the most prominent casualty of the partisan fight over the spy agency's program of detaining and questioning top terrorism suspects since the September 11 attacks."

• • •

I returned to my job the next day. Same office, same duties, same title (acting general counsel) as I'd had for the previous three years. As time went on, it became clear that John Warner was right: The Senate Intelligence Committee was not only done pursuing me, it seemed to have lost all interest in me one way or another. Nobody appeared to care that I was still the chief CIA legal officer in everything but formal title. Not even when my name and face unexpectedly burst back into the news a few months later, when the *New York Times* broke the explosive story of the CIA's 2005 destruction of videotapes depicting the waterboarding of terrorists held in the Agency's secret prisons. In all the ensuing Sturm und Drang, there was not a peep from anyone on the committee about me still holding down the top legal job at the Agency. It was weird in a way, as if my entire confirmation debacle had never happened, as if it had all been just a bad dream. I guess the committee, having exacted its public pound of flesh, simply decided to move on.

Nothing much changed about my standing at the Agency and the White House, either. Mike Hayden assured me I would be his lawyer as long as he was CIA director, and that he wasn't going anywhere. The White House also passed the word—I am certain because of David Addington's influence—that the administration would not put forward another nominee for the position for the balance of its time in office (although given its lame-duck status and the public flogging I had gone through, I wonder if the administration could have found any sane lawyer willing to take the job).

By March 2008, my name had largely faded from public attention. The refined, slimmed-down EIT program had been under way for more than a year, with Congress having passed the Military Commissions Act of 2006, which, among other things, served to minimize the risks that CIA personnel carrying out the new program could face criminal prosecution in the future for their actions. In the meantime, the OLC produced a fresh series of long opinions—all addressed to me—confirming that the six EITs that comprised the new program were lawful. These were the memos that I had insisted the OLC prepare in the wake of the passage of the McCain Amendment and the Supreme Court's *Hamdan* decision. The new program, in short, now appeared to be on solid legal footing.

Nonetheless, as 2008 wore on, it seemed apparent, at least to me, that a new sort of endgame was playing out, which was the demise of the

EIT program altogether. The two presidential nominees, Barack Obama and John McCain, were both on record as being strongly against any U.S. government policy to maintain a system of secret CIA prisons where detainees could be subject to aggressive interrogation of any sort. The program was still alive, but it had all seemed so anticlimactic ever since the Agency had transferred to Gitmo all the key figures in the 9/11 plot, on the eve of Bush's East Room speech on September 6, 2006.

Looking back now, 2008 thus seems almost uneventful, at least in comparison with the stress, uncertainty, and turmoil I constantly had to cope with in the previous six post-9/11 years. I remained busy, of course, and life for a CIA lawyer is never mundane. I took considerable gratification, for instance, in serving as Mike Hayden's point man in fostering an unprecedented relationship between the CIA and the International Committee of the Red Cross (ICRC). It was an odd-couple pairing, to say the least, that began in late 2006, with the State Department's John Bellinger playing matchmaker. The ICRC approached us quietly, tentatively, to explore the possibility of establishing a dialogue about the location and fate of the Al Qaeda operatives that the Agency either was holding in its prisons or had captured and transferred to third countries. The truth was, there was no way we were going to provide that sort of sensitive national security information, and I don't think the ICRC ever had any illusions that we would.

But I also think the ICRC leadership was pleasantly shocked that we even agreed to meet with them at all (as was the Bush-Cheney White House, except their shock couldn't be described as "pleasant") and the ICRC was eager to maintain a dialogue, even if no concrete results were forthcoming. Mike Hayden deserves the primary credit for keeping the dialogue going in the face of skepticism even from inside our building—the CTC in particular seemed baffled as to why we were talking to anyone from the ICRC—but I was a major proponent as well for establishing a line of communication between the two organizations. From the start, I served as the go-between, and the more I interacted with the ICRC representatives, the more I was impressed by their professionalism, their discretion, and, above all, their nonjudgmental posture toward the CIA and the actions it felt were necessary to take in the post-9/11 world. Not to mention their nonjudgmental posture toward me and my role in those actions, which by 2007 were all too well documented in the media.

Eventually, a remarkable relationship of respect and trust developed between two organizations with wildly disparate missions. Today, long after the demise of CIA prisons and the EIT program, I understand that the relationship between the CIA and the ICRC may be continuing. If that's so, I am happy and more than a little proud of the role I played in its creation.

On Election Day 2008, I voted for Barack Obama. For the first time in three decades, I was casting a vote in a presidential election that I was confident could have no conceivable impact on my professional life at the Agency. I fully assumed that no matter who won, I would be told to step aside from my job shortly after Inauguration Day on January 20, 2009. Which was fine with me. I recognized and accepted that, politically speaking, I was radioactive because of all I had been involved in, and become notorious for, in the years after 9/11. Besides, after more than three decades at the Agency, I was ready to retire, with no complaint or regret.

For one last time in my CIA career, I would be proven wrong again.

CHAPTER 17

The Arrival of Obama, and a Long Goodbye (2009)

Soon after his 2008 election, Barack Obama named Greg Craig to head up his transition team on national security issues. Greg was a high-profile D.C. lawyer with strong ties to the Democratic foreign-policy establishment, and we had been friendly acquaintances for quite some time. With his energetic charm, ruddy complexion, and thick thatch of hair, he acted and looked like a fifth Kennedy brother (and, in fact, was close to the Kennedy family). Shortly after Obama tapped him, Greg asked me to serve as his point man with the Agency in setting up transition briefings for the president-elect and his incoming national security team.

Obama, like all Democratic and Republican presidential nominees before him, had been offered the opportunity to receive intelligence briefings from CIA representatives during the fall campaign. He quickly accepted the offer (while John McCain, notably, did not). Intelligence briefings of nominees are limited to "analytical issues" such as the current situation in the Middle East, Russia, and so on. Information about CIA covert operations ("the sexy stuff," as the incoming president-elect George W. Bush put it pithily at the time) is reserved for the victorious candidate after the election but before the inauguration. So that's what Obama was now going to get for the first time.

Greg Craig and I worked out the timing for the briefings. As I recall, there were two of them, one in Chicago and one in Washington. I did not attend those; Mike Hayden and Director of National Intelligence Mike McConnell headed a very small delegation from the intelligence side.

Greg and Mike Hayden told me after both Obama briefings that, substantively, they had gone well. Obama, among other things, got his first detailed look into the EIT program. I was told that he was deeply attentive, but entirely noncommittal.

The next step was for Greg and me to set up a series of longer covert-action briefings at CIA Headquarters for a slightly larger circle of Obama advisors. Ultimately, there were two sessions, held in December and early January, that each lasted for several hours. As it turned out, I knew a few of the Obama representatives who showed up: Besides Greg, there was my friend and ex-Agency general counsel Jeff Smith, my friend and former longtime CIA colleague John Brennan, and (for the second session) the former Oklahoma senator and Intelligence Committee chairman David Boren. The meetings took place in the CIA director's conference room, and Mike Hayden kicked off both sessions from our side of the table, with me sitting next to him. The first topic right out of the chute was, not surprisingly, the EIT program. Mike Hayden told Greg at the outset that he would be happy to skip the subject if the new administration had already decided to end the program. Greg assured him the administration had an open mind on the subject. Notwithstanding my respect and fondness for Greg, I didn't believe that for a second. The EIT briefing proceeded, with Hayden taking the lead and the CTC chief and me occasionally chiming in. Greg and his colleagues took it all in, staring impassively at us.

I did notice that they perked up considerably when the talk turned to lethal CIA operations against Al Qaeda. They asked lots of questions, but what struck me most was their enthusiasm. The new president, they assured us, was going to pursue a vigorous, aggressive fight against Al Qaeda. For the first time, the thought occurred to me: These guys are trying to send us a message that Obama is no academic dilettante. That he is going to be a tough, action-oriented guy. That he is going to take no prisoners, figuratively or literally.

In retrospect, Mike Hayden never had a realistic chance of being kept on as CIA director, despite his wishes and hopes to the contrary. It all came down to his role in the EIT program and, to a lesser extent, his previous role, as NSA director, of architect of the Bush administration's controversial terrorist electronic surveillance program launched in the early days after 9/11. In many ways, his fate was as unfair as it was predictable. Here was a lifelong military officer with an impeccable record of service and integrity. Mike didn't help create the EIT program (as I did, for instance), he inherited it at the height of its contentiousness and proceeded to coolly analyze it, scale it back to reflect the prevailing political realities, and bring Congress more fully into the loop. But by saving the program, he inevitably came to "own" it. During the campaign, Obama was withering in his criticism of the EIT program, calling it "torture." There was no way he was going to ask Mike Hayden to stay on as his CIA director. I thought it was uncharacteristically naïve of Mike to apparently hope otherwise.

That said, Mike Hayden had spent his entire adult life serving his country, and the way the incoming Obama administration treated him, whether out of thoughtlessness or callousness, was shabby. At first, they let this proud man twist in the wind, as the transition team floated the names of possible replacements to Capitol Hill and to the media. Then Obama himself reached out to Steve Kappes, Mike's deputy and a non-presidential appointee, to ask him to remain in his post, while Mike waited and waited, hearing nothing one way or the other. Mike finally had to force the issue with the incoming White House staff to officially learn his fate via a brief phone call from the new president.

Finally, when Obama's surprise pick for the new CIA director, Leon Panetta, was preparing for his confirmation hearing, Mike made only one request. On behalf of the career Agency workforce, he implored his successor not to use the word *torture* to describe the EIT program during the hearing. Criticize the program, say it is being scrapped, but avoid that word, Mike pleaded. He told Panetta it would be a gratuitous, crushing insult to the hundreds of Agency employees who had worked on the program for years in good faith. Once you're on the job, he counseled Panetta, look at the program in depth, how it was actually conducted, the safeguards that were in place, the results it yielded, and then make a judgment. But not now, not yet.

Mike Hayden would be ignored one last time. One of the first things out of Panetta's mouth at his Senate confirmation hearing, in front of the TV cameras, was about the EIT program. It was torture, Panetta unhesitatingly said. Back at Langley, I was one of the probably hundreds of CIA employees who were watching. Just like that, he had publicly branded us as war criminals.

I won't last five minutes when this guy gets here, I thought.

• • •

I had never met Leon Panetta, had never been in the same room with him during his long career in high-level government jobs, beginning with his years in Congress in the '70s and '80s up through his service as Bill Clinton's White House chief of staff in the mid-'90s. As best I could tell, he had never exhibited any interest, much less involvement, in intelligence matters in all that time. If he had been one of the ten new CIA directors I had previously served under, I suppose his apparent lack of credentials and enthusiasm for the job would have concerned me more. But I knew I was a goner, so the fact was, it didn't matter all that much to me. For the sake of my colleagues, I hoped he would turn out to be okay, but that was about it.

Meanwhile, I was doing my best to pass the word that I wasn't going to be a bother. Even before Panetta came on the scene, I had told Greg Craig, now counsel to the new president, that I was ready to step aside and retire, without complaint or recrimination, at any time. I said the same thing to Jeremy Bash, Panetta's incoming chief of staff, when he inquired about my plans. I knew Jeremy from his previous job as counsel to the House Intelligence Committee, and I trusted him to convey that message to his boss and to pass back Panetta's answer. I didn't want to force Panetta to personally tell me to step aside; as we were strangers to each other, it would have been awkward for both of us. Jeremy agreed and asked me to stand by.

Panetta was confirmed by the Senate in mid-February 2009. A few days after he arrived at Langley, my special assistant, Donna Fischel, got a message from Panetta's staff that he was coming down the hall to see me. Before I had a chance to process what this unexpected visit meant, he came bounding into my office, accompanied by Jeremy. He plopped down on the couch, asked for coffee, and then just began to schmooze. It was our first conversation ever, but after about two minutes the realization hit me that Leon Panetta was the most instantly likable CIA director I had ever met. It had nothing to do with what he was saying, which was so unremarkable that I can't remember a single thing he told me, other than a chuckling, offhand remark that I didn't "look like a Rizzo," meaning that my fair skin and blue eyes didn't reflect my Italian name. For his part, he looked every bit as Italian as his name, but it was more the way he came across—sunny, earthy, without a shred of formality or phoniness—

that reminded me of my late father and all of his brothers who had been the products, like Panetta, of a first-generation Italian American family.

After about fifteen minutes, Panetta popped up from the couch and said, "Well, I gotta go. See you around." And then, just like that, he was gone. I sat alone for a minute, trying to figure out what had just happened and what it meant. What I decided was that it meant I would be around for a while longer than I'd expected.

I saw Panetta daily for one reason or another over the next couple of weeks, and I thought we were hitting it off quite well. He loved to laugh and joke, as did I, and we were forming an easy, bantering relationship. A lot of it probably had to do with the fact that we both understood the situation—that the White House was looking for my replacement (Panetta himself didn't have anyone in mind) but that in the meantime he and I could comfortably work together.

Thus, everything seemed fine between the new CIA director and me. That is, until early March, when I nearly blew the whole thing.

For several years, a federal court in Manhattan had been wrestling with a lawsuit under the Freedom of Information Act filed by the American Civil Liberties Union (ACLU) against the Bush administration, seeking the declassification of massive amounts of documents regarding the administration's policies and practices with respect to detainees captured during the post-9/11 era. Among many other things, the ACLU was seeking the declassification of all Justice Department legal opinions on the CIA's EIT program. In other words, the ACLU was pressing for the public release of all the OLC's "torture memos." On behalf of the government, career Justice Department litigators in New York and Washington were fighting against the release of the OLC memos on the grounds that their exposure would jeopardize intelligence sources and methods. The presiding judge, Alvin Hellerstein, had been handling the gargantuan, long-running case with a dogged but evenhanded toughness, ruling for the government in some areas, for the ACLU in others.

When the Obama administration took office, the career DOJ lawyers on the case were relatively optimistic that the judge would ultimately rule that the substantive portions of the OLC memos—those identifying and describing the EITs—should remain classified. The new Obama legal brain trust, however, quickly concluded otherwise.

I found this out via a phone call from Greg Craig in early March. "We've been looking at the ACLU case," Greg told me in his usual friendly conversational tone, "and the view here is that the government is going to lose on the issue of protecting the OLC memos. Therefore, I want to let you know that we are going to inform the judge that the government is going to declassify the memos in their entirety."

I was flabbergasted. I had never heard the career DOJ lawyers handling the case express such a view. I thought—everyone who had been following the case for years thought—that there was a compelling, winning argument for keeping the details of the EIT program secret. Not because they were illegal or shameful, which none of us ever believed, and which Judge Hellerstein would have seen through and never countenanced anyway.

By March 2009, the EIT program was dead and buried—Obama had accomplished that with considerable fanfare through an executive order he issued three days after taking office. In the same order, Obama explicitly rescinded all the previous OLC memos on the EIT program, a move that was startling and troubling to me, but something that in retrospect should not have been entirely unexpected. But all of that was beside the point. It had always been a fundamental, inviolate tenet in the intelligence business that just because a covert program was over didn't mean that everything about it had to be made public. To do so would threaten to expose the details and the means of how the program was carried out, where it took place, and, most critically, the foreign governments or individuals who cooperated in the program on the condition, and on the CIA's promise, that key details of the program would remain secret. Otherwise, the covenant of trust that must exist between an intelligence organization and its foreign cooperating sources would be breached, perhaps irreparably. Those critical, if inchoate, considerations existed in spades when it came to the EIT program, even if it was defunct (at least until some future president, responding to another catastrophic attack, might decide to try to replicate it in some form).

Greg Craig is an honorable, forthright guy. He quickly made it clear to me that the decision to declassify the OLC memos was based on policy, not solely legal, considerations. He also made it clear that he, along with the new attorney general, Eric Holder, supported the decision. Still trying to wrap my head around it all, I asked him, "So when will it be announced that they are going to be declassified?" "In three days," Greg replied. Holy shit, I thought.

I didn't know what to do, other than to tell somebody in our building. Panetta had just departed for his first overseas trip, and Greg hadn't said anything to indicate that Panetta knew about the decision. I rushed down to Steve Kappes's office to tell him the news. Steve was just as taken aback as I had been, but in his typically calm and Marine-bred fashion he crisply said he would try to reach Panetta to let him know. And then we discussed who else in the CIA family needed to be told right away. We decided to hold off for the time being on telling the troops who had worked so long, so selflessly, and so thanklessly on the program. It would be devastating news to them, we knew, but we needed more time—at least a day or two—to figure out a way to do it, to try to assuage the shock. We decided we owed a quiet heads-up to the three previous CIA directors—George Tenet, Porter Goss, and Mike Hayden—who had presided over the creation and development of the EIT program. It was a matter of simple respect and professional courtesy. We didn't think these dedicated, distinguished men ought to learn about it only by seeing the news on TV or in the newspapers. I volunteered to call each of them individually; they had all played such a central role in my life and career post-9/11, and I wanted them to hear it from me directly.

I went back to my office and placed the calls. All the former directors were incredulous at the news. It was the reaction I expected, and I explained as much about the reasoning behind the decision as I could. I didn't ask, and didn't expect, them to do anything about it. That was a major miscalculation on my part.

Tenet and Hayden separately began working the phones furiously, reaching out to people they knew in the Obama White House, apparently protesting against the decision in vehement terms. The word quickly got back to Greg Craig, and I soon got another call from him. This time his usually friendly voice had an edge to it. "I intended what I told you to be kept in confidence. I didn't expect you to unleash a lobbying campaign." I profusely apologized, saying I had nothing to do with encouraging George's or Mike's actions, all the while silently kicking myself for not anticipating what they had done. Greg laughed and seemed mollified. Sort of.

Leon Panetta then called in from his plane overseas somewhere. The

White House had gotten to him before Kappes could. Evidently the first he heard about the White House decision to declassify the OLC memos was when someone in the White House told him, minutes before, that I had recruited his predecessors to push back against the decision. The tone in his voice was not that of the cheerful, easygoing man I was just beginning to know. Once again, I stammered out an apology and tried to explain the sudden, unexpected chain of events that had started hours before. Panetta didn't sound nearly as mollified as Craig. "In the future," he curtly told me over our lousy phone connection, "when you learn about something like this from the White House, I expect you to first let your current boss know before telling your former bosses." With that, he hung up.

Ouch. Staring at the phone, I wondered to myself if I should move up the timing for my departure once again. Like, to within days.

The ruckus I had inadvertently set off did cause the White House to put on hold its decision to declassify and release the OLC memos. After reaming me out, Panetta apparently contacted Rahm Emanuel, his former protégé in the Clinton White House who was now Obama's chief of staff, and persuaded him not to take any action until Panetta could return home and be brought up to speed on what was going on. By the time he arrived back at Langley a few days later, Panetta's understandable anger toward me seemed to have dissipated. When I saw him again, I apologized. Panetta responded by shrugging. "These things happen," he said. "Just don't let them happen again." By then, Steve Kappes, ever the stand-up guy, had told Panetta that he and I had jointly made the decision to alert the former CIA directors about the White House decision. Panetta had tremendous respect for Steve, so I suspect that that more than anything else defused Panetta's ire toward me.

In any event, I was coming to understand that Leon Panetta was a man inclined to look forward, rather than dwell on and stew about the past. What he wanted to know was exactly why public release of the OLC memos would be so harmful to the Agency's morale and mission. I realized that I was not the right choice to make that case. For one thing, my name was prominently displayed at the top of all the potentially inflammatory OLC memos, so it could look like I had a personal, parochial motive to keep them under wraps. Moreover, I was only the Agency's lawyer, after all, and it was the CIA's operational cadre that had the most at stake, that had the most to lose in terms of foreign relationships damaged, of trust betrayed. Panetta needed to hear it from those guys, not just me.

Kappes, the quintessential symbol of the traditions and values of CIA operational personnel, became their chief advocate with Panetta. He brought in people from the working ranks of the CTC to meet with Panetta, to supplement and buttress the case he made. There were a number of such meetings that March. I sat in on most of them, and I kept watching Panetta as he listened attentively, connecting with these career spies on a personal level. Partly because he was a politician but mostly just because of the guy he was, it was clear that he could read and relate to working-level people. That came across to the people he was talking to as well. He didn't bullshit them, and they didn't bullshit him.

It took a week or so for him to make his decision. "Fuck it," he told a few of us one day. "I am going to fight at the White House against release of the memos." (He had a fondness and facility for dropping the "f-bomb" into everyday conversation to an extent unmatched in CIA directors I had known, with the possible exception of George Tenet.)

And fight he did, forcefully and insistently in several meetings on the subject held in the Situation Room during the next couple of weeks. I know because I accompanied him to a couple of them. He took the case personally to Obama as well, whom Panetta reported was agonizing over the decision. His top advisors were split—Panetta and Rahm Emanuel on one side, Greg Craig, Eric Holder, and the new DNI, Denny Blair, on the other. (Releasing the memos would be "a one-day story," Denny confidently predicted at one of the meetings.) As for the potential effect on Agency morale, Denny casually assured Panetta, "Let me worry about that." It was at that moment, I believe, that Panetta began to dislike Denny.

Around and around the debate went. I was surprised at the extent to which the new president was personally involved in the process. On the one hand, as someone so vested in the outcome, I was gratified by the obvious attention Obama was paying to the CIA's sensibilities and equities. On the other hand, as just an ordinary citizen, I kept thinking that with all the problems he had on his plate, not least among them the crappy economy, maybe he shouldn't be chewing up a lot of his time on an internecine squabble over a bunch of legal memos. I voiced that sentiment to Panetta sometime in that period, and he said he agreed: "Yup,

[National Security Advisor] Jim Jones should break the logjam and just make the call, but Jones can't, or won't, do it."

Ultimately, Panetta and the Agency did not prevail. In mid-April, word came from the White House that Obama had decided to publicly release the OLC memos. I had long-standing plans to start a short vacation to Scottsdale, Arizona, with my wife, and I was actually grateful to get out of town when the memos came out. I knew they would precipitate a classic Beltway shit storm, with my name plastered, one last time, all over the media. In doing so, I missed out on my first (and only) opportunity to meet the new president. Graciously, he had invited a few of us from the Agency to the White House so he could personally explain his decision. My deputy, James Archibald, attended in my place. It was just as well. I have no idea what I would have said to him.

Even though Panetta had lost the debate on the memos, he won something perhaps even more important and enduring: the gratitude and respect of the CIA workforce. By and large, the Agency remains a closed, silent place to the outside world, but inside the building and in the CIA's secret offices around the world, news always travels fast and far. Before long, word of Panetta's dogged, seemingly quixotic efforts to go to the mat with the White House spread throughout those cloistered environs. It was a fight, we all recognized, that he could have easily and logically avoided; after all, he had no connection whatsoever to the disbanded EIT program and was already on the record as having publicly decried it as "torture," just like Obama had done. Yet he jumped into the fray, ferociously and to the end.

At the time, a few cynical outside pundits speculated that Panetta was only going through the motions, giving lip service to the CIA "old boy network." That is bunk. I was there by his side at the time, and I never once doubted his motives or his sincerity. Neither did anyone in the CIA clandestine service, a population collectively endowed with a well-honed bullshit detector. From that point forward, Leon Panetta was not just a "made" man, so to speak, but the beloved capo in the eyes of the far-flung Agency family.

In the years since my retirement, I have been asked on occasion what attributes I think a CIA director has to have to be successful. There are three, I believe: 1) access to and clout with the president; 2) credibility and influence with Congress; and 3) respect and trust from the work-force. Most of the eleven directors I worked under had one of those attributes. A few had two. Leon Panetta, in my opinion, is the only one who had all three.

The formerly top-secret OLC memos hit the streets on April 16, 2009. There were four of them in all: the August 1, 2002, "Bybee II" memo listing and approving the original set of EITs, plus three memos authored in 2005 by Steve Bradbury, one of Bybee's successors as head of the OLC. All of them, as I indicated earlier in this book, described the EITs in graphic and, yes, chilling detail, just as I had intended when I requested the OLC's views all those years ago. And, as the addressee, my name was right there in bold print, for all the world to see, at the top of each of the memos. The media, of course, had a field day with them. For the next couple of weeks, they were excerpted, analyzed, and widely (if not unanimously) attacked in all the major newspapers and cable networks. In all of this eye-glazing marination of every word of the memos, the conspicuous presence of my name on all of them drew predictable attention.

On April 19, the *Washington Post* published an article headlined "Justice Department Memos' Careful Legalese Obscured Harsh Reality." It had a box with photos of Jay Bybee, John Yoo, Steve Bradbury, and me ("the legal minds behind the [EIT] program," the caption read) and a summary of what each of us was doing now. I was the only one listed as still holding the same job—acting CIA general counsel—as the ones we had in 2002 and 2005, when the memos were prepared. On April 29, National Public Radio ran a piece titled "In Torture Memo Furor, Rizzo's Name Is at the Top," duly noting that I was "still in charge . . . of well over 100 CIA lawyers." Even my old antagonist Senator Ron Wyden popped up again out of nowhere, telling Rachel Maddow on MSNBC on April 28 about how "bizarre, even by Washington, D.C., standards" it was that I was still the top legal advisor at the Agency.

Just what I needed, in the waning weeks of my career. (Panetta's pithy counsel was to ignore the shots: "Fuck 'em," he told me.) By then, at least, I could see the light at the end of the tunnel. A very smart and seasoned Washington lawyer named Stephen Preston had been identified as my replacement, and his name was wending its way through the confirmation process. By June, my name once again had largely drifted out of the press. There was only one small, final insult to endure: I was told that during Preston's courtesy call on Senator Dianne Feinstein, she told him she hoped my continuing presence wouldn't "poison" his tenure. This from a woman who had never deigned to have a conversation with me during her seven years on the Intelligence Committee.

None of this should leave the impression that the last few months of my career were depressing. In fact, I felt a deep sense of satisfaction and relief. Preston, I knew, would do well in his stewardship of the Office of General Counsel. Panetta was a continuing joy to be around; I like to think that we became friends in the relatively short time I worked for him. I was proud of the 120 or so lawyers who made up the CIA's legal team; over three decades, I had played a role in hiring and mentoring the careers of virtually all of them. One of my old bosses in the OGC, Stan Sporkin, once told me that in the final analysis, the only true legacy the head of a legal office has is the quality of the young lawyers he brings on board and leaves behind when he departs. I never forgot that, and I believe I did pretty well in adhering to Stan's dictum.

In terms of my own career, I had gotten far more out of my thirty-four-year roller-coaster ride than I ever could have hoped for. There was no doubt in my mind about that. There was also no doubt in my mind that it was time for the ride to end.

The Senate confirmed Stephen Preston as CIA general counsel in early July 2009. Stephen asked me to remain on board for a transition period, and we settled on a Labor Day date for my departure from the OGC. He told me he wished I would stay longer, and I think he was sincere about that. I will confess to having occasional twinges of "separation anxiety" at that time about how I was going to adjust to being outside the secret world I had been happily dwelling in for so long. Being privy to secrets, after all, is something that's alluring, seductive, exciting, special. I worried that it might also be addictive, and here I was about to go cold turkey.

But they were twinges, that's all. The inescapable reality was that I needed to walk away. I had been an architect, who had turned into a public symbol, of a hugely controversial Bush-era program that the new president had not just ended, but had repudiated in the harshest possible terms. I had no business trying to hang around in the Obama administration. It would be an unfair burden to Panetta and Preston. The Agency needed a clean break from the past, and I represented the past. I didn't want to have to be pushed out, as I had seen happen all too frequently to aging Agency veterans over the years who couldn't accept that their time was over. It was always such a painful and embarrassing thing to watch. Besides, I was now over sixty, and I had spent literally more than half of my life at the CIA. It was never my goal to close out my career by keeling over in the halls of Langley. Enough was enough.

I moved out of the GC's office to make room for Preston. I moved to a small adjacent office, and I tried to be as helpful to the new guy in his acclimation process as I could. (Lord knows, I had plenty of experience doing that.) Mostly, though, I tried to stay out of the way. In the late morning of my last day in the office, the quiet Friday before the long Labor Day weekend, I wrote my final e-mail to the staff. I knew that many of them had already departed for the weekend and wouldn't see it until after I was gone. That was the way I wanted it.

It was a farewell message captioned "Checkout Time at the Hotel OGC." Determined that it not be syrupy or maudlin, I ended the e-mail by quoting the '50s-era comedian and satirist Mort Sahl, someone most of the lawyers were likely too young to have ever heard of. Identifying him as a "noted philosopher," I lifted a quote from the title of one of Sahl's old comedy albums. "The future," I wrote in my departing words, "lies ahead."

I then turned off my computer and left the building. The fact was, I had no plans, no idea really, about what lay ahead for me in the future. Except that after the CIA, I was never going to seek another full-time job again.

Why did I feel that way? I can't really explain it, except to say that maybe it was for the same reason DiMaggio never remarried after Monroe.

Postscript

August 30, 2012, marked yet another milestone in the tangled and turbulent decade-long history of the Agency's post-9/11 detention and interrogation program. On that day, on the cusp of the Labor Day weekend, the Justice Department released a brief written statement from Attorney General Eric Holder that at long last eliminated the possibility that, after years of investigations and rancorous public debate, any CIA officers would be criminally charged for abuse of prisoners in the aftermath of the 9/11 terrorist attacks. Out of the more than one hundred cases Holder's DOJ team had been investigating—actually, reinvestigating—over the previous three years, it had all come down to the deaths of two detainees allegedly at CIA hands, one in Afghanistan, and the other in Iraq in 2003. The terse Holder statement announced that "because the admissible evidence would not be sufficient to obtain and sustain a conviction beyond a reasonable doubt," the Justice Department was not going to prosecute anyone for the two deaths.

And, on that oddly quiet and anticlimactic note, it all finally ended. No one from the CIA faced the specter of prison for abusing a detainee.

I was sitting alone at home, with my Agency career ever more distant in the rearview mirror of my life, when I saw the announcement on one of the cable networks. My reaction was a sense of relief combined with a lingering degree of bitter frustration that a result so predictable was nonetheless so long in coming.

The final two cases examined in the Holder probe—the details remain mostly classified—were long known to many of us in the CIA; indeed, it was the Agency itself that reported the two deaths to Justice shortly after each occurred. So there was no institutional effort to cover anything up. It was nonetheless apparent from the outset that a handful of CIA officers involved in each case made serious errors in judgment for which they were investigated and disciplined at the time; whether their conduct rose to the level of criminality was less clear, which is why the DOJ was brought into the loop. Holder's decision not to prosecute did not come until a decade later.

Neither of the detainees involved, however, had anything to do with the enhanced interrogation program. The death in Afghanistan was in another CIA facility. That is no excuse, of course. But at the same time, I and other senior Agency officials also deserve our share of criticism—in our single-minded focus on establishing rules for and closely monitoring the treatment of the likes of Zubaydah and KSM, we didn't devote sufficient attention and resources in those frantic early years to other, less significant detainees captured on the battlefield and held elsewhere. In the wake of the death in Afghanistan, we tried our utmost to do better in this regard, and I think we did.

As for the 2003 death in Iraq, not only was the detainee not part of the EIT program, he wasn't even in CIA custody. Instead, he was captured and held by the U.S. military in its own facility, the soon-to-be-infamous Abu Ghraib prison. The military gave CIA officers access to question the prisoner, after which things evidently got out of control. There was no question that he was physically abused and that he died as a result. Not as clear was who—CIA or military—delivered the fatal blows, but in the ensuing CIA IG investigation, the Agency guys obfuscated and perhaps did things to obstruct the investigation. Again, the CIA disciplined the officers involved and referred the matter to Justice in early 2004 to sort out their potential criminal liability. An ugly case all around, made even more painful by the fact that it is the only link—attenuated as it is—to the separate and widespread abuse of prisoners by U.S. military guards that would give the name Abu Ghraib its permanent stain in the public consciousness.

The announcement came as a relief, of course, finally closing the book on a couple of the most sordid chapters in the CIA's performance in the post-9/11 era. But why did it take Justice so long to decide not to prosecute? The answer to that question is the reason I—and I believe many of my colleagues still at the Agency—were frustrated by the denouement. In 2006, a group of seasoned career prosecutors at Justice—not some Bush administration lackeys—decided, after an exhaustive investigation of the two cases along with dozens of other incidents of possible detainee abuse, that the available evidence didn't support proceeding with any prosecutions. At the time, all of us at the CIA thought, absent some new evidence in these old cases somehow surfacing, that that settled things.

It was not an unreasonable assumption—when the DOJ announces it is closing an investigation, it almost always stays closed. Especially when it comes to criminal cases in the national security arena, everybody involved is entitled to have a final decision to rely upon. In my experience, any criminal investigation into CIA activities or personnel turns the Agency topsy-turvy—CIA personnel and resources have to be diverted to support the Justice investigation, and dozens of Agency employees (not just the alleged miscreants) are subjected to intensive questioning, with all the attendant uncertainty and anxiety. So finality is critical: the DOJ ultimately gives the Agency a firm and definitive answer in any given case—prosecution or no prosecution—and we deal with it. So the life, and the mission, of the intelligence community can move on. That's always been the pact between the Agency and the Justice Department, no matter what attorney general, Republican or Democrat, has been in charge. Until, that is, the arrival of Eric Holder.

In August 2009, still in his first few months in office, Holder blindsided everyone at the Agency—especially me—by publicly announcing that Justice was going to reopen all of the old detainee abuse cases. Just like that, with no explanation about what was so flawed, or what was missing, in the career prosecutors' decision only three years earlier not to prosecute. New or overlooked evidence? New or overlooked witnesses? Evidently not, according to the Holder aides I talked to. In fact, one of them privately told me, Holder hadn't bothered to read the career prosecutors' reports on why they had recommended against prosecution. I was at a loss to understand why Holder was taking such an extraordinary step, reopening cases that had only gotten older, staler, in the ensuing years. It made absolutely no sense. It was also, I thought, a profoundly unfair thing to do to the Agency's drained and beleaguered workforce. Only a few months earlier, when President Obama took the extraordinary step of declassifying the Bush-era "torture memos," he nonetheless pledged that his new administration henceforth would "look forward, not backward" and not rehash all the controversies of the past. Holder's out-of-the-blue decision gave the lie to that.

By this time, I was nearly out the door at the Agency, but what I was subsequently told by my erstwhile colleagues was all too depressingly predictable. Once again, dozens of rank-and-file employees faced grillings by gimlet-eyed prosecutors and FBI agents on what they might have said or done in the course of events that took place years before. Bewildered employees who had only been on the periphery of these long-ago events felt compelled to hire private lawyers. Untold amounts of CIA funds and manpower—not to mention focus and morale—were chewed up in the process. In 2011, Holder announced that Justice was dropping its inquiry into all the cases save for two, for which there now would be full-blown investigations. Yet more Agency resources had to be called upon, more Agency personnel diverted and disrupted from their regular duties.

Finally, mercifully, the end came with the curt written statement released in Holder's name on August 30, 2012, throwing in the towel. While it didn't offer much in the way of explanation, the statement did cryptically allude to problems with "statute of limitations and jurisdictional provisions." Sitting at home, reading those words, I could only ruefully smile. They sounded almost exactly like the legalistic code words the career Justice Department prosecutors had given me, in 2006, for deciding not to pursue prosecution of the very same cases. Basically, it is Justice saying: Look, these were incidents that took place a long time ago, in isolated, war-torn locales, where we have no body to examine and no reliable evidence or available eyewitnesses. Evidently, it took Holder and his staff until 2012 to reach the same conclusion their predecessors had come to six long years earlier. The only things that had changed were that the cases had gotten even older, and that probably millions of additional taxpayer dollars had been blown on a corrosive and feckless exercise.

I was struck by one other brief phrase in the Holder statement. It said the decision not to prosecute "was not intended to, and does not resolve, broader questions regarding the propriety of the examined conduct." The conduct Holder was referring to was that of the Agency, not his own.

Lessons Learned
and a Look Forward

In January 1976, I arrived at the CIA as a naïve, unworldly twenty-eight-year-old guy. I came aboard based solely on a hunch and a huge leap of faith. In the ensuing thirty-four years, I met people, traveled to places, and dealt with issues that were at once wonderfully unimaginable and endlessly fascinating. I managed to climb farther up the ladder than any career CIA lawyer had ascended before. And I wound up becoming an unlikely and controversial public figure in the late stages of my career, which spanned the entire modern history of the Agency. So it's a fair question to ask: What conclusions have I drawn, what lessons did I learn, from all that time, all those experiences, at the CIA?

First, let me address the momentous, fateful years since the attacks of September 11, 2001. To me, the most ironic lesson to be drawn by the post-9/11 era is this: It is far less legally risky, and in many quarters considered far more morally justifiable, to stalk and kill a dangerous terrorist than it is to capture and aggressively interrogate one. That at least is the de facto consensus that emerged over the first post-9/11 decade among influential segments of the U.S. Congress, the media, and the human rights community. How else to explain all the noisy outrage and long, splashy investigative articles about CIA secret prisons and interrogation techniques, while all the while Al Qaeda operatives were getting blown to bits, in plain sight, by U.S. drone aircraft without generating a ripple of criticism anywhere in Congress, the media, or from any international human rights organization? To these entities, killing didn't appear to be that big a deal, up through the time I retired at the end of 2009.

By contrast, for many of us at the CIA, being directed by the presi-

dent of the United States to target people for death—even Al Qaeda terrorists—was always a big deal. Late in his administration, Bill Clinton
had issued some ambiguously worded and highly caveated MONs to the
Agency about killing bin Laden and any of his cohorts who might be
unlucky enough to be around him at the time. With bin Laden nowhere
to be found, the Agency never came close to putting him in its crosshairs.
That moment would not come until the night of May 2, 2011, in that
walled compound in Abbottabad, Pakistan.

I still find it so odd, so perverse, that the same groups that were
stridently attacking the EIT program as not just lawless but morally
repugnant—the (mostly) Democrats in Congress, the ACLU, Amnesty
International, even the United Nations—until recently couldn't seem
to muster a scintilla of concern, much less outrage, about a U.S. program of summary, targeted killings—even ones that occasionally caused
the deaths of innocent bystanders—that was being simultaneously conducted with results that all the world could see.

From the earliest days after 9/11, the Agency's priority was to capture Al
Qaeda leaders, not kill them. Except when it came to bin Laden, whenever
the location of an important Al Qaeda operative came on the screen, the
preferred option was to try to take him into custody if at all possible. In
March 2002, when Abu Zubaydah was located in a house in Faisalabad,
the Agency ordered its Pakistani colleagues to take him alive. Zubaydah,
however, declined to go quietly and was seriously wounded in the ensuing
gunfight. Rather than let him die, the CIA moved heaven and earth to get
him the medical care that saved his life. Subsequently, he was subjected to
extensive waterboarding, as was Khalid Sheik Mohammad a year later. Both
men, of course, would go on to become the two most prominent and productive subjects of the Agency's enhanced interrogation program.

That the CIA so instinctively and insistently hewed to this approach
shouldn't be surprising. First and foremost, it is an intelligence-collection organization, and collection of intelligence from human beings is in
its institutional DNA. Always has been. You can't collect intelligence—
whether about an upcoming catastrophic attack on the homeland or anything else—from a dead man. It's as simple as that. Accordingly, during
my time in the post-9/11 years, killing terrorists was the final option.
And certainly not the only option.

Now, flash forward to today. Times have changed indeed. As this is written, bin Laden has been dead and buried for two years; the EIT program has been dead and buried for four years, as have the CIA secret prisons. Thus, by all appearances, the Agency is out of the detention and interrogation business. So what continues to be the fulcrum of the Obama administration's offensive against Al Qaeda? According to a nonstop stream of media accounts over the past four years (which is all I have to go on by now), it's killing people, a lot of people, via a relentless and escalating barrage of drone attacks. Apparently even a U.S. citizen or two along the way. I don't doubt that virtually all of them were bad guys who richly deserved their fate. Yet it also seems evident that the U.S. Government's efforts to capture and interrogate Al Qaeda operatives overseas have effectively ground to a halt. Again, according to media reports, the Obama administration's scorecard in this regard at this writing: one terrorist detained.

So the question ultimately becomes: Was the Obama administration's enthusiastic embrace of a robust, aggressive policy to kill terrorists directly connected to, even compelled by, its decision to repudiate a robust, aggressive policy of capturing and interrogating them? Obama aides (notably, my old friend and colleague John Brennan) have adamantly denied it. With due respect to John, I don't believe you need to be a sage CIA analyst to connect the dots on this one.

Which leads to the question of what the CIA's assigned antiterrorism role will be in the future. I can't imagine the Agency ever again coming close to running detention facilities or engaging in any sort of even mildly coercive interrogation practices. Given the seemingly enduring controversy over the legacy of "waterboarding" and "black sites"—the widespread popularity and vitriol generated by the 2012 film *Zero Dark Thirty* is but one example of this phenomenon—I can't see any president ever reopening that can of worms again. What's more, no CIA director in his or her right mind would ever let the organization go down that path again. To do so would be beyond folly. I don't think even another catastrophic 9/11-like attack will change that.

Aggressive all-out intelligence collection against terrorists and terrorist threats? Absolutely. Intelligence collection, as I noted earlier, has always been the lifeblood of the Agency. There has always been a consensus that it is not only an appropriate but a vital CIA mission. Plus, there has seldom been any political risk or downside to spying, save for those relatively few cases where the CIA has been caught red-handed bugging some foreign government installation or trying to recruit a foreign government official. In any case, the worst fall-out result is a compromised operation, the attendant political embarrassment, and maybe some snarky media stories. It is a rare case indeed for someone to get killed carrying out, or being the target of, a CIA intelligence-collection operation.

Which brings me to what the future holds for the CIA to conduct covert actions aimed at terrorists. It has been only in the last year or so that segments of Congress, the media, and the human rights community have begun criticizing the U.S. Government's lethal drone operations, a practice that dates back more than a decade. This delayed reaction is attributable to two factors, I believe. First, the Obama administration has upped the ante, dramatically expanding the numbers of drone strikes, the permissible targets, and the number of foreign locations in the bull's-eye. The second factor, which admittedly reflects a certain cynicism on my part, is that there is no longer any EIT program for the critics to kick around. Human rights and civil liberties groups, notably the ACLU, have needed a new national security bogeyman to attack, so belatedly, after being studiously quiet about it for years, the drone program is now on their (ahem) target list.

Whatever. I believe that the drone program is here to stay, not just under Obama but whoever his successors may be. In the counterterrorist arena, for sure, but someday soon drone attacks are likely to be aimed at hostile foreign governments deemed to pose an imminent threat to unleash weapons of mass destruction against the West, our allies, or even their own people. The technology has gotten so good and is bound to get better. Drone attacks are antiseptic, stealthy, and—after the recent long-running adventures in Afghanistan and Iraq—a far more preferable option for any presidential administration than "boots on the ground" and flag-draped coffins arriving at Dover Air Force Base. When those drone strikes happen, count on whatever administration that carries them out to trot out its lawyers to duly rationalize its lethal actions as being totally in accordance with international law.

Thus, I would respectfully predict that future presidents will not only continue to be in the business of killing, but will double down on it. And that the CIA will salute the commander in chief and be in the middle of it, without hesitation or resistance.

I mean, anything is less risky than building "black sites" again.

. . .

Finally, let me offer some "big picture" observations about the CIA—the lessons I drew from my experience there and what I think the future will bring for the organization.

Foremost, I learned over time that the Agency is a remarkably resilient organization. My career was pockmarked by episodes of crisis and controversy at the CIA. Actually, it was bookmarked with them—I arrived in the mid-'70s in the wake (and because) of the Church Committee revelations, and I retired three decades later dogged by the tumult of the defunct enhanced interrogation program. Along the way, there were the Casey crusades in Central America in the '80s, the Iran-contra scandal later that decade, the Ames spy case in the early '90s, the "dirty asset" flap a couple of years after that, and, of course, the 9/11 attacks and the Iraq WMD fiasco shortly after the turn of the new millennium.

Each time, doomsayers in Congress and the media decried the performance, the integrity, and even the raison d'être of the institution itself. And each time, the Agency has weathered the storm and bounced back. Why? Two primary reasons, I think.

First, every one of the seven presidents I served came to turn to and depend on the CIA. Granted, for Carter and Clinton, it took a while, but like the others, they came around. Presidents learn that the Agency is a unique asset—it can move quickly, without the normal fiscal or operational constraints of other agencies, and it can do what it does in secret. It has no other client, no other master, than the occupant of the Oval Office. The CIA, in short, is a president's personal pop stand. It does what—and only what—he (or she) tells it to do, including covert action. Especially covert action. None of them is going to give that up, and so the Agency survives, no matter what.

Second, the CIA abides because of the people who work there. Most, like I did, spend much of their professional lives there. You never get impervious to the recurring crises and controversies that buffet the place, but after a time you come to learn that each will pass. The organization will take its lumps, learn some lessons, and move on. And so will you.

Take the CIA Office of General Counsel. The majority of the lawyers there have joined the office in the post-9/11 era, like the rest of the current CIA workforce. They are young enough not to have been exposed to its run-up but old enough to be seared by memories of the horror. I

301

hired a bunch of them myself, and dozens more have arrived since I left. (Another lesson I have learned over the years: the CIA will always have lawyers, lots of them, and they will be woven into the fabric of everything the Agency does.) If experience is any guide, many of them will stay there for decades, like I did. They will see their share of controversies and crises, and maybe get sucked into them, like I did. But they will learn, and they will persevere, like I did. Because they love the organization and what it stands for, like I did.

And perhaps, if they are lucky—like I was—a few will someday, when they are much older, have the opportunity to put their experiences down in writing, to give their young colleagues and their fellow citizens on the outside a sense of what it was all like, what it was all about, and why it was all worth it.

Which, now that all is said and done, are the reasons I decided to write this book.

Acknowledgments

I wrote every word of this book myself, and the large majority of it is dependent on my memory. In part, that was a matter of choice—I believe I have a good facility for recalling interesting and meaningful events and conversations I took part in during my long career. In equal part, however, relying on my memory was a matter of necessity. Pursuant to Executive Order 13292, only former presidential appointees are permitted to have access to classified government documents from their period of service in order to conduct historical research. If the Senate in 2007 had confirmed President Bush's nomination of me to be the CIA's general counsel, I would have been eligible to request such access to my classified CIA files to aid me in writing this book. Alas, my nomination cratered, so in putting this book together I had to turn to other means to assist me in refreshing or confirming my recollections of specific episodes down through the years.

In this regard, I greatly benefited from the willingness of a number of my former CIA colleagues—some now retired, others still working at the Agency—to answer my questions, swap memories with me, and steer me in the right direction. For various reasons, they all requested to remain anonymous, but they know who they are, and I want them to also know how grateful I am to them.

I also found that my own recollections of certain events, especially ones that happened years ago like Iran-contra and the Ames espionage case, were jogged and frequently buttressed by reading hundreds of contemporaneous media accounts and a dozen or so books written by both CIA insiders and outside journalists describing the events in question. It had been a very long time since I had done this nitty-gritty sort of research, which is why I am deeply indebted to the Hoover Institution at

ACKNOWLEDGMENTS

Stanford University, which in early 2010 extended to me an appointment as Visiting Scholar to support the production of this memoir. Hoover's role was indispensable to me throughout this process, and its help extended from research assistance to administrative and technical support, including generously giving me an office in its Washington, D.C., facility. In the D.C. office, I was given invaluable and ever-patient support over a three-year period by Sharon Ragland, Christie Parell, Amy Palguta, Tyler Hernandez, Michelle Ring, and Kara McKee. I also want to thank Peter Berkowitz, an intelligence scholar from the Hoover Policy Group, for helping make my Hoover appointment happen. Finally, I want to express my deep appreciation to Hoover president John Raisian and vice president David Brady for green-lighting the appointment, as well as my close friend Jack Goldsmith for starting the entire process. My association with the Hoover Institution has been an honor and a pleasure.

I owe a particular debt of gratitude to Bob Asahina, my collaborator on this book. Bob was involved from the very beginning, and I can state authoritatively that a major reason why any publishers were interested in a neophyte, noncelebrity author like me was that Bob's name was attached to the project. Bob has a sterling reputation and track record in the publishing industry, both as a collaborator and editor. His expertise in shaping and refining the sweeping narrative arc of my thirty-four-year CIA career—what areas to emphasize, which ones would be of less interest to the reader—was unerring. Bob had no prior exposure in his career to the unique and sometimes bizarre world of spies, but his outsider's perspective, easygoing demeanor, and keen editorial eye were godsends to me. Bob not only was my invaluable collaborator, but has become a trusted and lasting friend.

Bob Asahina was originally brought to my attention by Jay Mandel and Eric Lupfer, my literary agents at William Morris Endeavor in New York City. That is only one of the many reasons why I am so grateful to them. Jay and Eric took me on as a client in early 2010 when my memoir was nothing more than my own inchoate idea (or fantasy). I knew nothing about the world of literary agents, other than having a general sense that it was a very tough one for a first-time, non-household-name aspiring author to break into. Nonetheless, after one short phone conversation and before I had written a word, they took me under WME's protective, prestigious wing and have been nothing but wise and encouraging in shepherding me through the long and winding manuscript production and marketing process. I still don't understand exactly what Jay and Eric originally saw in me, but I can't thank them enough. In addition, I am very grateful to Erin Conroy in WME's Los Angeles office, who somehow has managed to interest a major television studio in my story based solely on my bare-bones book proposal. Erin, shrewd yet infectiously optimistic and cheerful, thus successfully paved my even more unlikely path to at least the entry gates of Hollywood. Amazing.

I also had the supremely good fortune of having Scribner as my publisher. When I was first mulling the idea of writing a memoir, I talked to several journalist friends who were published authors to get their take on the pros and cons of embarking on such an endeavor. They all separately offered the same rueful piece of advice: even if a major publisher agrees to back your book (a decidedly iffy proposition at the time), don't expect to get much hands-on attention from whoever is assigned as your editor. Today's publishing industry is shrunken and strapped, they told me, and an individual editor in any given publishing house typically has to juggle dozens of manuscripts simultaneously. None of these editors, I was warned, would have the time or inclination to guide some rookie author like me through the editing process. It was the sort of unvarnished, candid advice I was looking for, but in my case, at least, it proved to be wildly off the mark. My editor at Scribner, Paul Whitlatch, could not have been more caring, patient, and attentive at every step along the way. He carefully and skillfully pored over every word of the manuscript, steadfastly championed my cause with his Scribner colleagues, and always made time for me either in person or by phone. A younger man than my own son, Paul's savvy and sophisticated eye belies his years. I have been so lucky to have him on my side.

Like every former CIA officer turned author, I was required to submit my manuscript in advance to the Agency's Publications Review Board (PRB) to ensure that it did not reveal any currently classified information. Based on my many years at CIA observing the process from the other side, I can attest to the difficult and at times thankless task the PRB has to perform. The PRB required me to make a number of deletions to my original manuscript. I disagreed with a few, but I understood the rationale for most of them and, of course, ultimately accepted them all.

ACKNOWLEDGMENTS

Overall, the PRB was eminently fair with me and did its work in a conscientious and timely manner. For that, I thank PRB chairman Richard Puhl and his dedicated, and doubtless overworked, staff.

No list of acknowledgments would be complete without a salute to all of the people at CIA I met and worked with down through the years. It is not an exaggeration to say that there were thousands of them, spanning three generations. It was my privilege and joy to know them; a more consistently excellent, courageous, and selfless workforce does not exist anywhere. In particular, I was proud to be associated for so long with my colleagues in the CIA Office of General Counsel. The ones I worked with during my early years have largely departed now, but most of those who are there today are people I hired and was honored to lead during the turbulent post-9/11 decade. I have cited a few in this book, and I wish I had the space to acknowledge by name all of the other exemplary attorneys, paralegals, and support staff who were so extraordinarily dedicated to me and, far more important, to our country. I do, however, want to give a special, heartfelt thanks to James Archibald, Fred Manget, Valerie Patterson, Nancy Fortenberry, Melody Rosenberry, Donna Fischel, Petra Lewis, and Bruce Hunt. These folks spent time at my side, watching my back, during the last decade of my career spent in the OGC front office when the CIA—not to mention yours truly—was facing unprecedented crisis and controversy. I am indebted to them so much from both a professional and personal standpoint, and I will never forget them.

I have reserved my deepest expression of thanks for last. Some may note that I have not devoted a lot of space in this book to talking about my family. There are a couple of reasons for that. This memoir is first and foremost a chronicle of my CIA career, and I presume that's what any reader is going to be interested in, rather than be burdened with having to slog through pages of details about my personal life before and while I was at the Agency. Second, I reckon that my personal life is, well, personal; I can't imagine why anyone other than me and those closest to me would have the slightest interest in knowing more about it.

That said, my family means everything to me, and I love and owe them much more than anything else in my life. I have been blessed since the day I was born. My late parents, Arthur and Frances, were utterly devoted to me and my sisters, Nancy and Maria. They gave us everything we needed to succeed in life as we were growing up, but their greatest gift was their unstinting love and loyalty. My sisters and I all achieved considerable success in our respective professional fields, though my career was marked by public controversy and some harsh outside criticism near its end. By the time I suddenly popped up in the public firing line post-9/11, my parents had been deceased for years. They had been avid news junkies their entire lives. I asked Maria a few years back how she thought they would have reacted to seeing and reading about their baby boy becoming such a divisive public figure. "They'd be thrilled and proud," she replied without hesitation. I hope so.

My son, James, is my only offspring. He's in his midthirties. He was born the year after I joined the CIA (I vividly remember changing his Pampers one night on a bench outside the headquarters front doors), so the arc of his life has virtually paralleled the arc of my Agency career. Much as I love the Agency, it is nothing—absolutely nothing—compared to the love I have for him. If this book does nothing else than to serve to give James a better sense of what his old man was up to at work all those years as he was growing up, then I will be a very satisfied guy.

Last, there is my beloved Sharon, my wife for the past two decades and the mother of my terrific stepdaughter Stephanie Breed. I have noted elsewhere in this book that applying to Brown University and later to the CIA were two of the best decisions I ever made in my life. But my best decision of all, hands down, was marrying Sharon. She has been my loyal and loving life partner ever since. Sharon is beautiful, smart, funny, and simply a joy to be with. I am an enormously lucky man to have her.

Index

INDEX

INDEX

INDEX

INDEX

INDEX

INDEX

Tenet, George, 7, 12, 145, 167, 169, 175, 182, 183, 217, 218, 237, 246
  Al Qaeda MON desired by, 173
  Al Qaeda targeted by, 166
  on Ames's treason, 156–57
  at CTC Updates, 177
  cursing by, 157, 287
  EITs and, 186, 187–89, 193, 197–98, 199, 285
  kept on by GW Bush, 167–68
  made CIA director, 155
  on 9/11, 172
  personality of, 155–56, 157–58, 168, 238
  Plame leak and, 207
  at Powell's U.N. speech, 206
  on Principals Committee, 196, 197–98
  and proposed snatch of bin Laden, 162, 165
  resignation of, 213, 215
terrorism, 100, 159, 160, 161, 165
  at CIA headquarters, 138–39
  see also September 11, 2001, terrorist attacks
Thiessen, Marc, 209
Thomas, Evan, 35
Tierney, John, 26, 27
torture, 184, 233
  Panetta on EITs and, 281
  renditions and, 260–63
  see also enhanced interrogation techniques
"torture memos," 4, 216, 257–58
  release of, 283–88, 289, 295
"torture tape" case, 1–29, 276
  author's testimony on, 2–9
  congressional testimony on, 2, 8–9
  decision to make tape, 4–5
  destruction of tapes in, 5–7, 12, 14–16, 18
  IG report on, 9–10, 12
  9/11 Commission on, 10–11
  publicity of, 22–23
Townsend, Fran, 177
Treasury Department, U.S., 32, 38, 45, 129, 159

Al Qaeda money tracked by, 233–34, 235
Turner, Stansfield, 52, 62, 68, 69, 77

United Nations, 298
  General Assembly of, 205–6
  Security Council, 173–74
United Nations Convention Against Torture and Other Cruel, Inhuman or Degrading Treatment or Punishment, 214
unmanned aerial vehicles (UAVs), 178

Vanity Fair, 208
Veil (Woodward), 81, 118–20
Very Best Men, The (Thomas), 35
Viacom, 230
Vietnam, 49
Vietnam War, 31, 36–37, 44

walling, 184, 247
wall standing, 185
Wall Street Journal, 194
Walsh, Lawrence, 115–16, 124, 133
Ward, Terry, 147
Warner, John (CIA general counsel), 40, 41, 48
Warner, John (U.S. senator), 253, 254, 255, 274, 275, 276
Warren Commission, 32
Washington Post, 52, 80, 257, 272–73, 289
waterboarding, 21, 193, 194, 198, 224, 233, 249
  of Khalid Sheikh Mohammed, 194–95, 196, 197–98, 209, 298
  legacy of, 299
  Pelosi's knowledge of, 201
  Rizzo's initial opposition to, 186
  of Zubaydah, 1, 4, 5, 6, 8, 9, 185, 196, 197–98, 200, 209, 298
Watergate scandal, 31, 60, 130
weapons of mass destruction, 205–6, 213, 215
Webster, William, 130–31, 132, 133, 134–35, 189, 239
Weiner, Tim, 150–51

INDEX